Grammar Sense

Sense

4

Advanced Grammar and Writing

SERIES DIRECTOR & AUTHOR
Susan Kesner Bland
with Alice Savage and Patricia Mayer

OXFORD
UNIVERSITY PRESS

OXFORD
UNIVERSITY PRESS

198 Madison Avenue
New York, NY 10016 USA

Great Clarendon Street, Oxford OX2 6DP UK

Oxford University Press is a department of the University of
Oxford. It furthers the University's objective of excellence in
research, scholarship, and education by publishing worldwide in

Oxford New York

Auckland Cape Town Dar es Salaam Hong Kong Karachi
Kuala Lumpur Madrid Melbourne Mexico City Nairobi
New Delhi Shanghai Taipei Toronto

With offices in

Argentina Austria Brazil Chile Czech Republic France Greece
Guatemala Hungary Italy Japan Poland Portugal Singapore
South Korea Switzerland Thailand Turkey Ukraine Vietnam

OXFORD and OXFORD ENGLISH are registered trademarks of
Oxford University Press.

© Oxford University Press 2008

Library of Congress Cataloging-in-Publication Data

Bland, Susan Kesner.
    Grammar Sense 4 / Susan Kesner Bland.
        p. cm.
    Includes index.
    ISBN: 978-0-19-449017-7
        1. English language—textbooks for foreign speakers.
1. English language—Grammar—Problems, exercises, etc.
I. Title: Grammar Sense four. II. Title.
    PE1128 .B588 2008
    428.2'4—dc21   2002192661

Editorial Director: Sally Yagan
Publishing Manager: Kenna Bourke
Associate Editor: Scott Allan Wallick
Senior Designer: Michael Steinhofer
Art Editor: Robin Fadool
Production Manager: Shanta Persaud
Production Controller: Soniya Kulkarni
Indexer: Leonard Neufeld

ISBN: 978 0 19 449017 7

Printed in China

10 9 8 7 6 5

This book is printed on paper from certified and well-managed sources.

*The publisher would like to thank the following for their permission
to reproduce photographs:*

Nils Juul-Hansen: **p. 2**; Images & Stories: Mehmet Gulbiz,
p. 34; Topfoto/The Image Works: Charles Walker, **p. 52**;
Topfoto/The Image Works: Roger-Viollet, **p. 74**; Mauritius
/SuperStock: Martin Wendler, **p. 90**; Jupiter Unlimited: **p. 132**;
Topfoto/The Image Works: **p. 170**; Arco Images/Alamy: **p. 190**;
Masterfile: **p. 212**; Jupiter Images: Peter Samuels, **p. 262**;
Purestock/SuperStock: **p. 292**.

*The publisher would like to thank the following for their permission to
adapt and reproduce copyright material:*

pp. 2-3. Adapted from *Newsweek*, May 9, 2005 © 2005 Newsweek,
Inc. All rights reserved. Reprinted by permission.; **pp. 16-17**.
"Ripening at the Center of the World" by Donald Batchelder. This
article first appeared in the 1974 Edition of the *Parents League
Review*. © 1974 Parents League of New York (212) 737-7385, www.
parentsleague.org. Reprinted by permission; **pp. 34-35**. Adapted
from "The Secret Treasures of Zeugma", © Gedeon Programmes,
by permission of Terranoa, Paris; **pp. 74-75**. Adapted from
Essentials of Understanding Psychology (5th Edition) by Robert S.
Feldman. © 2003 McGraw-Hill. Reprinted by permission; **pp.
132-133**. Adapted from Gallup Poll: Almost All E-mail Users Say
Internet, E-mail Have Made Lives Better, July 23 2001. © 2001
Gallup Organization. Reprinted by permission; **p. 138**. Adapted
from "The Internet and Education: Findings of the Pew Internet &
American Life Project" by Lenhart, Simon, and Graciano. © 2001
Pew Internet & American Life Project. Reprinted by permission;
pp. 150-151. Based on the report, *Overwork in America*, from
the Families and Work Institute; conducted 2004; **pp. 190-191**.
Adapted from "Why Don't We Just Kiss and Make Up"
by Lee Dugatkin, *New Scientist*, May 7, 2005. © 2005 Reed Business
Information. Reprinted by permission.

Acknowledgements

Adding a fourth book to the *Grammar Sense* series has once again given me the opportunity to work with a superb team of talented and creative individuals.

In particular, I am grateful to Kenna Bourke for her amazing ability to simplify, for her calmness and efficiency, and most of all for her focus and vision. Likewise, a special debt of gratitude goes to Alice Savage and Patricia Mayer for seamlessly integrating their expertise in writing pedagogy with grammar teaching, and for really understanding how to use grammar as a writing tool; to Andrew Gitzy and James Morgan for their extraordinary creativity and talent in bringing everything together; and to Janet Aitchison for her support and encouragement. I would also like to thank Diane Piniaris, Daria Ruzicka, Shira Seaman, Kim Sanabria, Angelo Pitillo, Ellen Rosen, Danielle Steider, Wendy Crockett, and Dorothy Lindsay for their contributions and hard work in the early stages of this project.

This book is dedicated to the memory of my parents, Sam and Bess Kesner, and to the three most important people in my life, Bob, Jenny, and Scott.

Susan Kesner Bland,
Series Director

The Series Director and Publisher would like to acknowledge the following individuals for their invaluable input during the development of this series:

Marcia Adato, Delaware Technical and Community College, DE; **Harriet Allison**, Atlanta College of Art, GA; **Donette Artenie**, Georgetown University, DC; **Alex Baez**, Southwest Texas State University, TX; **Nathalie Bailey**, Lehman College, CUNY, NY; **Jamie Beaton**, Boston University, MA; **Michael Berman**, Montgomery College, MD; **Linda Best**, Kean University, NJ; **Angela Blackwell**, San Francisco State University, CA; **Vera Bradford**, IBEU, Rio de Janerio, Brazil; **Glenda Bro**, Mount San Antonio Community College, CA; **J**ennifer Burton**, University of California, San Francisco, CA; **Shannonine Caruana**, Kean University, NJ; **Sharon Cavusgil**, Georgia State University, GA; **Robin Rosen Chang**, Kean University, NJ; **Wendy Crockett**, University of California, Riverside, CA; **Magali Duignan**, Augusta State University, GA; **Anne Ediger**, Hunter College, CUNY, NY; **Carol Gavin**, Burlington County College, NJ; **Joyce Grabowski**, Flushing High School, NY; **Ruth Griffith**, Kean University, NJ; **Marcella Farina**, University of Central Florida, FL; **Virginia Heringer**, Pasadena City College, CA; **Rocia Hernandez**, Mexico City, Mexico; **Nancy Hertfield-Pipkin**, University of California, San Diego, CA; **Kieran Hilu**, Virginia Tech, VA; **Rosemary Hiruma**, California State University, Long Beach, CA; **Peter Hoffman**, LaGuardia Community College, NY; **Michelle Johnstone**, Mexico City, Mexico; **Kate de Jong**, University of California, San Diego, CA; **Eileen Kelly**, Holyoke Community College, MA; **Pamela Kennedy**, Holyoke Community College, MA; **Jean McConochie**, Pace University, NY; **Karen McRobie**, Golden Gate University, CA; **Elizabeth Neblett**, Union County College, NJ; **Adrianne Ochoa**, Georgia State University, GA; **Carol Olavessen**, University of Memphis, TN; **Patricia Palermo**, Kean University, NJ; **Dian Perkins**, Wheeling High School, IL; **Fausto Rocha de Marcos Rebelo**, Recife, Brazil; **Kent Richmond**, California State University, Long Beach, CA; **Ellen Rosen**, Fullerton College, CA; **Judy Ross**, Howard Community College, MD; **Mildred Rugger**, Southwest Texas State University, TX; **Shira Seaman**, Hunter College, CUNY, NY; **Dawn Schmidt**, California State University, San Marcos, CA; **Katharine Sherak**, San Francisco State University, CA; **Lois Spitzer**, University of Nebraska-Lincoln, NE; **Maxine Steinhaus**, New York University, NY; **Laura Stering**, University of California, San Francisco, CA; **Jody Stern**, University of California, San Diego, CA; **Nancy Storer**, University of Denver, CO; **Annie Stumpfhauser**, Morelios, Mexico; **Frank Tang**, New York University, NY; **Claude Taylor**, Baruch College, NY; **Marshall Thomas**, California State University, Long Beach, CA; **Anthea Tillyer**, Hunter College, CUNY, NY; **Margery Toll**, California State University, Fresno, CA; **Connie Tucker**, Citrus College, CA; **Julie Un**, Massasoit Community College, MA; **Susan Walker**, SUNY New Paltz, NY; **Cheryl Wecksler**, California State University, San Marcos, CA; **Teresa Wise**, Georgia State University, GA; **Anthony Zak**, ELTC, Manado, Indonesia.

Contents

Introduction

Grammar Sense: A Discourse-Based Approach

Grammar Sense is a comprehensive four-level grammar series based on the authentic use of English grammar in discourse. The grammar is systematically organized, explained, and practiced in a communicative, learner-centered environment, making it easily teachable and learnable.

Many people ask, why learn grammar? The answer is simple: meaningful communication depends on our ability to connect form and meaning appropriately. In order to do so, we must consider such factors as intention, attitude, and social relationships, in addition to the contexts of time and place. All of these factors make up a discourse setting. For example, we use the present continuous not only to describe an activity in progress (*He's working.*), but also to complain (*He's always working.*), to describe a planned event in the future (*He's working tomorrow.*), and to describe temporary or unusual behavior (*He's being lazy at work.*). It is only through examination of the discourse setting that the different meanings and uses of the present continuous can be distinguished from one another. A discourse-based approach provides students with the tools for making sense of the grammar of natural language by systematically explaining *who, what, where, when, why,* and *how* for each grammatical form.

Systematically Organized Syllabus

Learning grammar is a developmental process that occurs gradually. In *Grammar Sense* the careful sequencing, systematic repetition, recycling, review, and expansion promote grammatical awareness and fluency.

Level 1 (basic level) focuses on building an elementary understanding of form, meaning, and use as students develop basic oral language skills in short conversations and discussions. Level 1 also targets the grammar skills involved in writing short paragraphs, using basic cohesive devices such as conjunctions and pronouns.

At **Level 2 (intermediate level)** the focus turns to expanding the basic understanding of form, meaning, and use in longer and more varied discourse settings and with more complex grammatical structures and academic themes. Level 2 emphasizes grammar skills beyond the sentence level, as students begin to initiate and sustain conversations and discussions, and progress toward longer types of writing.

At **Level 3 (high intermediate level)** the focus moves to spoken and written grammar in academic discourse settings, often in contexts that are conceptually more challenging and abstract. Level 3 emphasizes consistent and appropriate language use, especially of those aspects of grammar needed in extended conversations and discussions, and in longer academic and personal writing.

Finally, at **Level 4 (advanced level)** the focus shifts to written grammar for the purpose of academic writing. There is increased emphasis on meaning and use and on self-editing skills, on the assumption that advanced level students have mastered much of the basic structure of the language, but still need help in transferring this knowledge to more effective, concise, and grammatically correct academic writing.

Grammar Sense Student Books 1, 2, and 3

Introduction of Form Before Meaning and Use

In *Grammar Sense* Student Books 1–3, form is introduced and practiced in a separate section before meaning and use. This ensures that students understand what the form looks like and sounds like at the sentence level, before engaging in more challenging and open-ended activities that concentrate on meaning and use.

Focus on Natural Language Use

Grammar Sense uses authentic reading texts and examples that are based on or quoted verbatim from actual English language sources to provide a true picture of natural language use. To avoid unnatural language, the themes of the introductory reading texts are only subtly touched upon throughout a chapter. The focus thus remains on typical examples of the most common meanings and uses.

Exposure to authentic language helps students bridge the gap between the classroom and the outside world by encouraging awareness of the "grammar" all around them in daily life: in magazines, newspapers, package instructions, television shows, signs, and so on. Becoming language-aware is an important step in the language learning process: Students generalize from the examples they find and apply their understanding to their independent language use in daily living, at work, or as they further their education.

Special Sections to Extend Grammatical Knowledge

Understanding grammar as a system entails understanding how different parts of the language support and interact with the target structure. *Grammar Sense* features special sections at strategic points throughout the text to highlight relevant lexical and discourse issues.

- **Beyond the Sentence** sections focus on the structure as it is used in extended discourse to help improve students' writing skills. These sections highlight such issues as how grammatical forms are used to avoid redundancy, and how to change or maintain focus.

- **Informally Speaking** sections highlight the differences between written and spoken language. This understanding is crucial for achieving second language fluency. Reduced forms, omissions, and pronunciation changes are explained in order to improve aural comprehension.

- **Vocabulary Notes** provide succinct presentations of words and phrases that are commonly used with the target structure, such as time expressions associated with the simple past, or the use of *say, tell,* and *ask* in reported speech.

- **Pronunciation Notes** show students how to pronounce selected forms of the target language, such as the regular simple past ending *-ed.*

Student-Centered Presentation and Practice

Student-centered presentation and practice allow learners at all levels to discover the grammar in pairs, groups, and individually, in both the Form and in the Meaning and Use sections of each chapter. Numerous inductive activities encourage students to use their problem-solving abilities to gain the skills, experience, and confidence to use English outside of class and to continue learning on their own.

Grammar Sense Student Book 4

Form Combined With Meaning and Use

It is often the case that advanced-level students have a good grasp of form yet continue to struggle with appropriate use of the grammatical structure in question. *Grammar Sense* Student Book 4 acknowledges this by placing much greater emphasis on meaning and use than it does on form, and by shifting form practice to the development of self-editing skills. Form is reviewed in every chapter, and appendices containing form charts and verb paradigms are supplied for any student in need of a refresher, but the focus of each chapter centers on applying knowledge of form, meaning, and use to practical, meaningful communication, both spoken and written.

Special Sections to Extend Grammatical Knowledge

- **Vocabulary Notes** provide succinct presentations of words and phrases that are commonly used with the target structure, such as time expressions associated with future forms, or adverbs used with or in place of modals.

- **Usage Notes** raise students' level to advanced by concentrating on structure-specific additional information, and giving students a greater awareness of the scope of the structure, such as a special class of verbs that can be either transitive or intransitive depending on the meaning of the sentence, or the use of the past perfect and past perfect continuous for flashback scenes in narrative writing.

Writing For Academic Purposes

- **Editing Charts** train students in avoiding common errors in their writing. These errors are systematically reviewed, and are followed by editing practice to help students develop an instinctive awareness of the common mistakes they tend to make.

- **Beyond the Sentence** sections have been greatly expanded to provide students with models of typical uses of target structures in extended written discourse. This provides the learner with a scaffolded approach to academic writing: first they see the grammar in action; next they try out certain features for themselves in follow-up practice; then they put it all together in their own compositions.

- **Writing Tips** answer the question: why learn this particular grammatical structure? Before tackling an extended writing assignment, students are given an explanation of the practical application of the target structure to academic writing, for example, how the passive is often used to describe results or processes involving things rather than people.

- **Writing Checklists** give students an opportunity to reflect on their ability to use the grammatical structures they have studied in their own academic writing. They also encourage self-editing by prompting students to check their work.

- **Beyond the Classroom** offers yet more writing practice in the form of topics for essays.

FLEXIBILITY TO SUIT ANY CLASSROOM SITUATION

Grammar Sense offers teachers great flexibility with hundreds of intellectually engaging exercises to choose from. Teachers may choose to skip chapters or sections within chapters, or teach them in a different order, depending on student needs and time constraints. Each Student Book is self-contained so teachers may choose to use only one book, or the full series, if they wish.

Components at Each Level

- The **Student Book** is intended for classroom use and offers concise charts, level-appropriate explanations, and thorough four-skills practice exercises. Each Student Book is also a useful reference resource with extensive Appendices, a helpful Glossary of Grammar Terms, and a detailed Index.

- The **Audio CDs** feature listening exercises that provide practice discriminating form, understanding meaning and use, and interpreting non-standard forms.

- The **Workbook** has a wealth of additional exercises to supplement those in the Student Book. It is ideal for homework, independent practice, or review. The Answer Key, on easily removable perforated pages, is provided at the back of the book.

- The **Teacher's Book** has many practical ideas and techniques for presenting the Form and Meaning and Use charts. It also includes troubleshooting advice, cultural notes, and suggestions for additional activities. The Answer Key for the Student Book and the complete Tapescript are provided.

- The **ExamView**® **Assessment CD-ROM** allows you to create fully-customized tests and provides the option to add your own test items. It offers thousands of different evaluation exercises correlated to each level of *Grammar Sense*.

- **TOEFL**®**-Style Tests** and Answer Keys, along with advice on conducting the test and interpreting the results, are available for teachers to download from the Internet. (See www.oup.com/elt/teacher/grammarsense)

Tour of a Student Book Chapter

Each chapter in *Grammar Sense* 4 follows this format:

The **Grammar in Discourse** section introduces the target structure in its natural context via a high-interest authentic reading text.

> • *Authentic reading texts show how language is really used.*

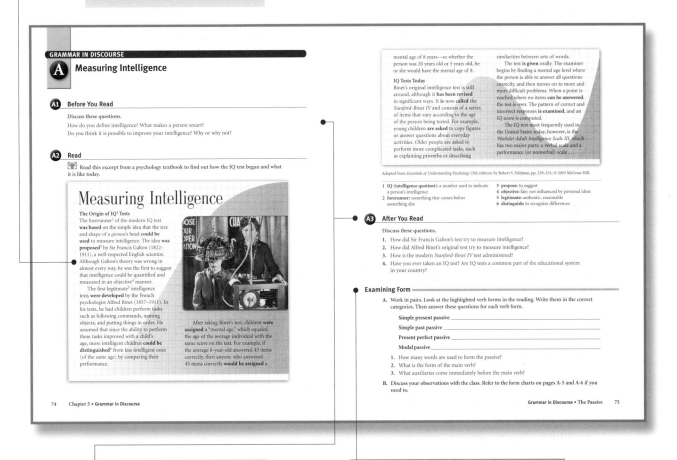

> • *Structured reading tasks help students read and understand the text.*

> • *Inductive **Examining Form** exercises remind students how to form the target structure.*

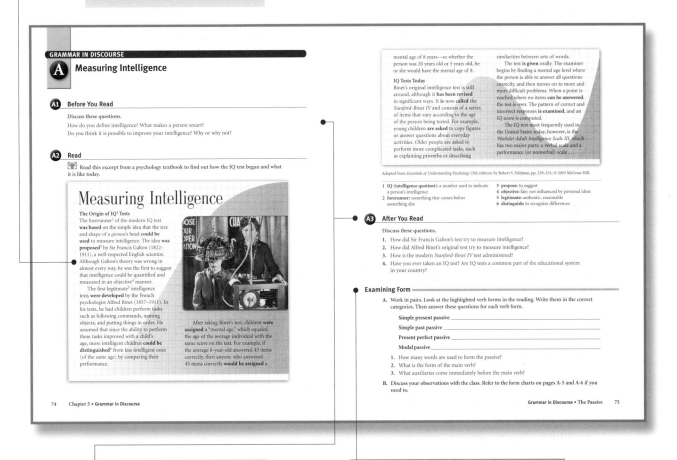

The **Form, Meaning, and Use** section(s) offers clear presentation of the target structure, detailed notes, and comprehensive explanations of how the target structure is used, and exercises to practice using it appropriately.

*Inductive **Examining Meaning and Use** exercises encourage students to analyze how we use the target structure.*

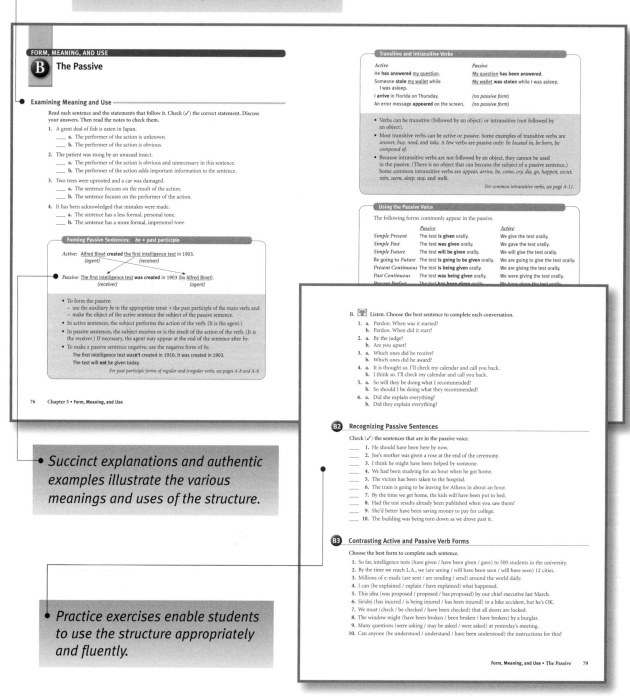

Succinct explanations and authentic examples illustrate the various meanings and uses of the structure.

Practice exercises enable students to use the structure appropriately and fluently.

The **Writing** section guides students through the process of applying their grammatical knowledge to academic writing.

Editing *sections train students to recognize and avoid common errors.*

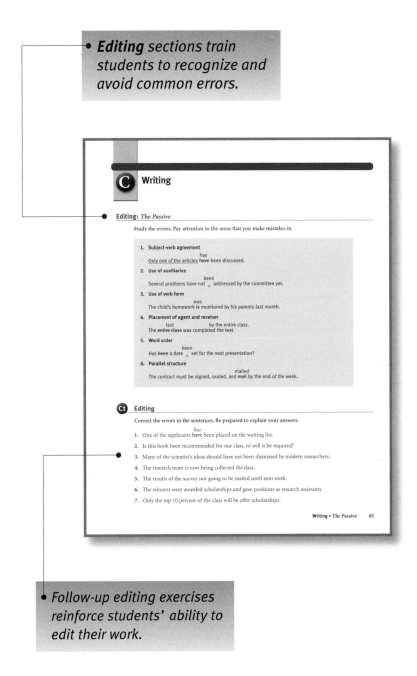

C Writing

Editing: *The Passive*

Study the errors. Pay attention to the areas that you make mistakes in.

1. **Subject-verb agreement**
   has
   Only one of the articles ~~have~~ been discussed.

2. **Use of auxiliaries**
   been
   Several problems have not ∧ addressed by the committee yet.

3. **Use of verb form**
   was
   The child's homework ~~is~~ monitored by his parents last month.

4. **Placement of agent and receiver**
   test   by the entire class.
   The ~~entire class~~ was completed the test.

5. **Word order**
   been
   Has ~~been~~ a date ∧ set for the next presentation?

6. **Parallel structure**
   mailed
   The contract must be signed, sealed, and ~~mail~~ by the end of the week.

C1 Editing

Correct the errors in the sentences. Be prepared to explain your answers.

1. One of the applicants ~~have~~ been placed on the waiting list.
   has
2. Is this book been recommended for our class, or will it be required?
3. Many of the scientist's ideas should have not been dismissed by modern researchers.
4. The research team is now being collected the data.
5. The results of the survey not going to be mailed until next week.
6. The winners were awarded scholarships and gave positions as research assistants.
7. Only the top 10 percent of the class will be offer scholarships.

Writing • The Passive   85

Follow-up editing exercises reinforce students' ability to edit their work.

The **Writing** section provides opportunities for analyzing target structures in the context of model passages, and then constructing a grammatically accurate and appropriate essay.

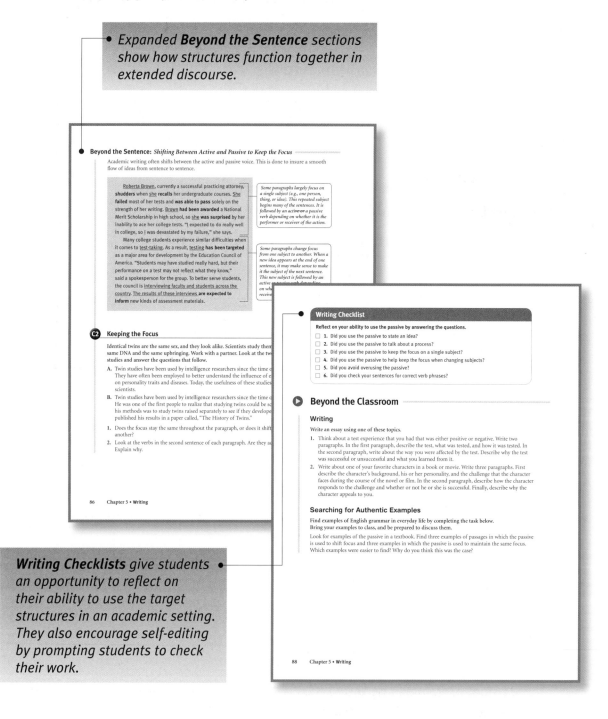

• Expanded **Beyond the Sentence** sections show how structures function together in extended discourse.

Beyond the Sentence: *Shifting Between Active and Passive to Keep the Focus*

Academic writing often shifts between the active and passive voice. This is done to insure a smooth flow of ideas from sentence to sentence.

Roberta Brown, currently a successful practicing attorney, **shudders** when she **recalls** her undergraduate courses. She **failed** most of her tests and **was able to pass** solely on the strength of her writing. Brown **had been awarded** a National Merit Scholarship in high school, so she **was surprised** by her inability to ace her college tests. "I expected to do really well in college, so I was devastated by my failure," she says.

Many college students experience similar difficulties when it comes to test-taking. As a result, testing **has been targeted** as a major area for development by the Education Council of America. "Students may have studied really hard, but their performance on a test may not reflect what they know," said a spokesperson for the group. To better serve students, the council is interviewing faculty and students across the country. The results of these interviews **are expected to inform** new kinds of assessment materials.

Some paragraphs largely focus on a single subject (e.g., one person, thing, or idea). This repeated subject is followed by an active or a passive verb depending on whether it is the performer or receiver of the action.

Some paragraphs change focus from one subject to another. When a new idea appears at the end of one sentence, it may make sense to make it the subject of the next sentence. This new subject is followed by an active or passive verb depending on wh...

C2 Keeping the Focus

Identical twins are the same sex, and they look alike. Scientists study them ... same DNA and the same upbringing. Work with a partner. Look at the tw ... studies and answer the questions that follow.

A. Twin studies have been used by intelligence researchers since the time o ... They have often been employed to better understand the influence of e ... on personality traits and diseases. Today, the usefulness of these studies ... scientists.

B. Twin studies have been used by intelligence researchers since the time o ... He was one of the first people to realize that studying twins could be so ... his methods was to study twins raised separately to see if they develope ... published his results in a paper called, "The History of Twins."

1. Does the focus stay the same throughout the paragraph, or does it shift ... another?
2. Look at the verbs in the second sentence of each paragraph. Are they a ... Explain why.

Writing Checklist

Reflect on your ability to use the passive by answering the questions.

☐ 1. Did you use the passive to state an idea?
☐ 2. Did you use the passive to talk about a process?
☐ 3. Did you use the passive to keep the focus on a single subject?
☐ 4. Did you use the passive to help keep the focus when changing subjects?
☐ 5. Did you avoid overusing the passive?
☐ 6. Did you check your sentences for correct verb phrases?

▶ **Beyond the Classroom**

Writing

Write an essay using one of these topics.

1. Think about a test experience that you had that was either positive or negative. Write two paragraphs. In the first paragraph, describe the test, what was tested, and how it was tested. In the second paragraph, write about the way you were affected by the test. Describe why the test was successful or unsuccessful and what you learned from it.
2. Write about one of your favorite characters in a book or movie. Write three paragraphs. First describe the character's background, his or her personality, and the challenge that the character faces during the course of the novel or film. In the second paragraph, describe how the character responds to the challenge and whether or not he or she is successful. Finally, describe why the character appeals to you.

Searching for Authentic Examples

Find examples of English grammar in everyday life by completing the task below. Bring your examples to class, and be prepared to discuss them.

Look for examples of the passive in a textbook. Find three examples of passages in which the passive is used to shift focus and three examples in which the passive is used to maintain the same focus. Which examples were easier to find? Why do you think this was the case?

Writing Checklists *give students an opportunity to reflect on their ability to use the target structures in an academic setting. They also encourage self-editing by prompting students to check their work.*

Special Sections appear throughout the chapters, with clear explanations, authentic examples, and follow-up exercises.

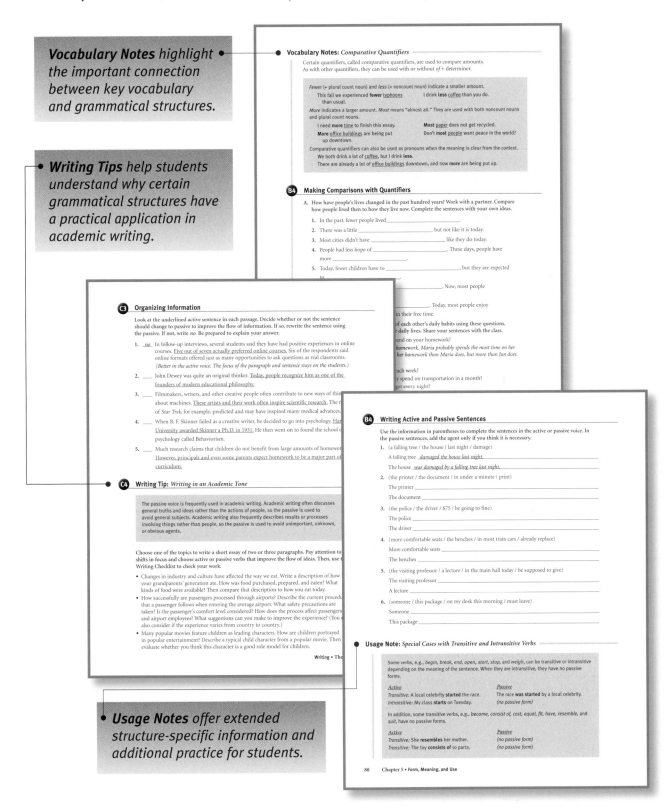

Vocabulary Notes highlight the important connection between key vocabulary and grammatical structures.

Writing Tips help students understand why certain grammatical structures have a practical application in academic writing.

Usage Notes offer extended structure-specific information and additional practice for students.

Vocabulary Notes: *Comparative Quantifiers*

Certain quantifiers, called comparative quantifiers, are used to compare amounts. As with other quantifiers, they can be used with or without *of* + determiner.

Fewer (+ plural count noun) and *less* (+ noncount noun) indicate a smaller amount.
This fall we experienced **fewer** typhoons than usual.
I drink **less** coffee than you do.

More indicates a larger amount. *Most* means "almost all." They are used with both noncount nouns and plural count nouns.
I need **more** time to finish this essay.
More office buildings are being put up downtown.
Most paper does not get recycled.
Don't **most** people want peace in the world?

Comparative quantifiers can also be used as pronouns when the meaning is clear from the context.
We both drink a lot of coffee, but I drink **less.**
There are already a lot of office buildings downtown, and now **more** are being put up.

B4 **Making Comparisons with Quantifiers**

A. How have people's lives changed in the past hundred years? Work with a partner. Compare how people lived then to how they live now. Complete the sentences with your own ideas.

1. In the past, fewer people lived_____.
2. There was a little _____ but not like it is today.
3. Most cities didn't have _____ like they do today.
4. People had less hope of _____. These days, people have more _____.
5. Today, fewer children have to _____, but they are expected to _____.

_____. Now, most people
_____. Today, most people enjoy
in their free time.
of each other's daily habits using these questions.
r daily lives. Share your sentences with the class.

end on your homework?
homework. Maria probably spends the most time on her
her homework than Maria does, but more than Jun does.
ach week?
spend on transportation in a month?
get every night?

C3 **Organizing Information**

Look at the underlined active sentence in each passage. Decide whether or not the sentence should change to passive to improve the flow of information. If so, rewrite the sentence using the passive. If not, write *no*. Be prepared to explain your answer.

1. __*no*__ In follow-up interviews, several students said they have had positive experiences in online courses. Five out of seven actually preferred online courses. Six of the respondents said online formats offered just as many opportunities to ask questions as real classrooms.
   (Better in the active voice. The focus of the paragraph and sentence stays on the students.)
2. ____ John Dewey was quite an original thinker. Today, people recognize him as one of the founders of modern educational philosophy.
3. ____ Filmmakers, writers, and other creative people often contribute to new ways of thinking about machines. These artists and their work often inspire scientific research. The [...] of *Star Trek*, for example, predicted and may have inspired many medical advances.
4. ____ When B. F. Skinner failed as a creative writer, he decided to go into psychology. Harvard University awarded Skinner a Ph.D. in 1931. He then went on to found the school of psychology called Behaviorism.
5. ____ Much research claims that children do not benefit from large amounts of homework. However, principals and even some parents expect homework to be a major part of curriculum.

C4 **Writing Tip:** *Writing in an Academic Tone*

The passive voice is frequently used in academic writing. Academic writing often discusses general truths and ideas rather than the actions of people, so the passive is used to avoid general subjects. Academic writing also frequently describes results or processes involving things rather than people, so the passive is used to avoid unimportant, unknown, or obvious agents.

Choose one of the topics to write a short essay of two or three paragraphs. Pay attention to shifts in focus and choose active or passive verbs that improve the flow of ideas. Then, use the Writing Checklist to check your work.

- Changes in industry and culture have affected the way we eat. Write a description of how your grandparents' generation ate. How was food purchased, prepared, and eaten? What kinds of food were available? Then compare that description to how you eat today.
- How successfully are passengers processed through airports? Describe the current procedure that a passenger follows when entering the average airport. What safety precautions are taken? Is the passenger's comfort level considered? How does the process affect passengers and airport employees? What suggestions can you make to improve the experience? (You [...] also consider if the experience varies from country to country.)
- Many popular movies feature children as leading characters. How are children portrayed in popular entertainment? Describe a typical child character from a popular movie. Then evaluate whether you think this character is a good role model for children.

Writing • The [...]

B4 **Writing Active and Passive Sentences**

Use the information in parentheses to complete the sentences in the active or passive voice. In the passive sentences, add the agent only if you think it is necessary.

1. (a falling tree / the house / last night / damage)
   A falling tree __*damaged the house last night.*__
   The house __*was damaged by a falling tree last night.*__
2. (the printer / the document / in under a minute / print)
   The printer _____
   The document _____
3. (the police / the driver / $75 / be going to fine)
   The police _____
   The driver _____
4. (more comfortable seats / the benches / in most train cars / already replace)
   More comfortable seats _____
   The benches _____
5. (the visiting professor / a lecture / in the main hall today / be supposed to give)
   The visiting professor _____
   A lecture _____
6. (someone / this package / on my desk this morning / must leave)
   Someone _____
   This package _____

Usage Note: *Special Cases with Transitive and Intransitive Verbs*

Some verbs, e.g., *begin, break, end, open, start, stop,* and *weigh,* can be transitive or intransitive depending on the meaning of the sentence. When they are intransitive, they have no passive forms.

Active
Transitive: A local celebrity **started** the race.
Intransitive: My class **starts** on Tuesday.

Passive
The race **was started** by a local celebrity.
(no passive form)

In addition, some transitive verbs, e.g., *become, consist of, cost, equal, fit, have, resemble,* and *suit,* have no passive forms.

Active
Transitive: She **resembles** her mother.
Transitive: The toy **consists of** 10 parts.

Passive
(no passive form)
(no passive form)

80   Chapter 5 • Form, Meaning, and Use

The Present

A   Changes in Language Learning

A1   Before You Read

Discuss these questions.

What foreign languages do students usually choose to study in your country?

Why do students usually choose to study those languages?

A2   Read

Read this magazine article to find out why more and more students are beginning to study Chinese in American schools.

Changes in Language Learning

Becoming aware of the challenges ahead, American students are beginning to study Chinese.

At Dulles High School in Sugar Land, Texas, the roster[1] for Advanced Chinese 5 **begins** with Jason Chao and **ends** with Kathy Zhang. In between the many Chinese names comes an unexpected one: Elizabeth Hoffman. Hoffman, now a 12th grader, **has been studying** Chinese since the 8th grade. She **has spent** a summer abroad in Nanjing and plans to perfect her Mandarin in college. When her peers, who typically take Spanish, ask Elizabeth why she **is learning** Chinese, she asks them, "Why aren't you?"

Chinese is a language spoken by 1.3 billion people worldwide. And as China **rushes** toward superpower status,[2] America's schools and government officials **are echoing**[3] Hoffman's opinion. As one Congressman says, "For reasons of economics, culture, and security we should have much better facility[4] with Chinese

languages and dialects." Even the State Department (the U.S. agency responsible for foreign affairs) **has designated** Chinese a "critical language." But despite these facts, the most recent data **shows** that only 24,000 American students in grades 7 to 12 study it. (More than 1 million students **learn** French, a language spoken by just 75 million people.)

Still, the number of students learning Chinese **is growing**. In Chicago, enrollment in Chinese classes **has skyrocketed**,[5] from 500 students in 1999 to nearly 3,500 students this year—and most are Caucasian, African-American, or Hispanic. In Santa Clara County, California, enrollment has quadrupled[6] during this period.

"People **are** always **trying** to gauge[7] what languages will be useful for the future," says Marty Abbot at the National Council on the Teaching of Foreign Languages. Stephanie Wong, a high school student in California, **has been taking** Chinese so she can speak with her grandfather. (In U.S. homes, Chinese has passed French, German, and Italian to become the third most commonly spoken language, after English and Spanish.) But Wong also predicts that Chinese will be important if she becomes a doctor: her hometown is nearly 80 percent Asian.

Even elementary-school parents **have noticed** the trend. "My children will have a distinct advantage if I can keep them interested in Chinese," says one mother. She **has enrolled** her two children (ages 8 and 9) at a school where 30 percent of students receive math and science instruction in Chinese, starting in kindergarten.

Adapted from *Newsweek*, May 9, 2005, Newsweek, Inc. All rights reserved. Reprinted with permission.

1 **roster:** a list of people
2 **status:** position in the world
3 **echo (an opinion):** to express agreement with an opinion
4 **facility:** an ability to do something well
5 **skyrocket:** to increase very quickly
6 **quadruple:** to become four times as large
7 **gauge:** to measure or judge something

 After You Read

Discuss these questions.

1. The subtitle of the article states that "American students are beginning to study Chinese." In your own words, explain why this trend is happening.

2. What foreign language other than English do you think people should study? Why?

Examining Form

A. Work in pairs. Look at the highlighted verb forms in the reading. Write them in the correct categories. Then answer the questions for each verb form.

Simple present _____

Present continuous _____

Present perfect _____

Present perfect continuous _____

1. What do you notice about the main verb? Is it in the base form or is there an ending?

2. What auxiliary or auxiliaries, if any, come before the main verb?

B. Discuss your observations with the class. Refer to the form charts on page A-3 if you need to.

The Present

Examining Meaning and Use

Read each sentence and the statements that follow it. Check (✓) the correct statement. Discuss your answers. Then read the notes to check them.

1. Over one billion people worldwide <u>speak</u> Chinese.

    ____ **a.** This expresses a general truth.

    ____ **b.** This expresses an ongoing, changing situation.

2. The number of Chinese-language students <u>is growing</u> this year.

    ____ **a.** This expresses a habitual activity.

    ____ **b.** This expresses an ongoing, changing situation.

3. Elizabeth <u>has been studying</u> Chinese since the 8th grade.

    ____ **a.** This situation was completed in the past.

    ____ **b.** This situation continues up to the present.

4. Elizabeth <u>has spent</u> a summer abroad in Nanjing.

    ____ **a.** This situation was completed in the past.

    ____ **b.** This situation continues up to the present.

Simple Present: base form of verb or verb + -s / -es

Habits and Repeated Activities
The board **meets** regularly on the first Tuesday of the month.

Facts and General Truths
Over one billion people worldwide **speak** Chinese.
Young children **learn** foreign languages more easily than adults.

States or Conditions
We **know** a lot about changes in language learning.

- The simple present is used to make general, timeless statements and to talk about repeated or habitual activities. It is often used with stative verbs to talk about states and conditions.

For verbs ending in –s and –es, see page A-6.
For adverbs of frequency, see page A-8.

Present Continuous: *am / is / are* + verb + *-ing*

Activities in Progress Now or Over a Period of Time
It's Tuesday, December 1. The board **is meeting** <u>right now</u>.
Listen. Those people **are speaking** Chinese.
More and more children **are learning** foreign languages in elementary school <u>these days</u>.
* We are knowing a lot about changes in language learning. (INCORRECT)

- The present continuous is used to talk about what is happening at the exact moment of speaking or over an extended period of time *(this week, these days)*. The continuous form can imply that the activity is temporary or changing. Verbs with stative meanings (like *know*, *seem*, and *have*) are not usually used in the continuous.

For verbs ending in –ing, *see page A-7.*
For stative verbs, see pages A-7 and A-8.

Present Perfect: *have / has* + past participle

Activities and States Completed Recently or at an Indefinite Time in the Past
I**'ve** just **visited** China. I know a lot of Chinese words now.
   (His trip is finished. He now knows Chinese words because of the experience.)
He**'s written** <u>30 pages</u> of the book. *(how much)*
I**'ve traveled** to China <u>twice</u>. *(how many times)*

Activities and States Beginning in the Past and Continuing in the Present
I**'ve known** about it <u>since last week</u>. *(how long)*
He**'s had** the same teacher <u>for two years</u>. *(how long)*

- **The present perfect:** The present perfect is used to show how something that happened in the past relates to the present. It provides background information for present events and situations.
- **Recent and indefinite past time:** The present perfect is often used to talk about activities and states that were completed recently or at an indefinite time in the past. These sentences can answer the questions: *How much?* or *How many times?*
- Because it is a present form, the present perfect is not used with specific past time markers. (See Chapter 2, page 19 for a discussion of the present perfect and simple past.)
    - * I've visited China last year. (INCORRECT)
    - * He's written 30 pages of the book last night. (INCORRECT)
- **Continuing past time:** The present perfect can be used to express activities that began in the past and continue up to the present, usually with time expressions like *for, since,* or *all.* These can answer the question: *How long?* Stative verbs (like *be, have,* and *know*) and other verbs that express duration (like *wait* and *keep*) are commonly used with this meaning. Other verbs that express completion are not used with *for* and *since.*
    - * I've read this book for two hours. (INCORRECT)
    For simple past and past participle forms of regular and irregular verbs, see pages A-8 and A-9.

Activities Beginning in the Past and Continuing in the Present

I**'ve been visiting** China, so I'm learning a lot of Chinese words.

>   *(She is still making trips to China, and is continuing to learn Chinese.)*

He**'s been writing** a book. *(He is still writing it or has just completed it.)*

I**'ve been reading** this report for two hours. *(how long)*

* I've been knowing about it since last week. (INCORRECT)

- The present perfect continuous is also used to show how something that happened in the past relates to the present. It is not used as often as the present perfect.

- The present perfect continuous is used to express activities that began in the past and continue up to the present, or activities that were in progress but have just ended. It emphasizes that the activity is ongoing. It can imply that the activity is temporary.

- With time expressions like *for* and *since*, present perfect continuous sentences can answer the question: *How long?* Verbs with stative meanings are not usually used in the continuous.

For verbs ending in –ing, see page A-7.

Different Meanings

I**'ve visited** China. *(completed)* I**'ve been visiting** China. *(ongoing)*

Similar Meanings

She **has studied** Arabic <u>since 8th grade</u>. She **has been studying** Arabic <u>since 8th grade</u>.

The band is popular, so people **have waited** <u>for hours</u> for tickets. *(factual)* People **have been waiting** <u>for hours</u> for tickets. They're freezing! *(emotional)*

- **Different meanings:** The present perfect can express a completed activity. In contrast, the present perfect continuous shows that an activity is ongoing and may or may not be completed.

- **Similar meanings:** When talking about continuing time up to now, there is little difference between the two forms with certain verbs, such as *live, teach, sleep, study,* and *work.*

- The present perfect has a factual and neutral tone. In contrast, the present perfect continuous can add an emotional quality that makes a situation seem more immediate.

A. 🎧 Each sentence in the passage is incomplete. Listen to the entire passage first. Then listen again and put a caret (^) where you hear a missing word. Listen once more to fill in the missing words.

have

Most American universities ^ foreign language requirements. Students usually languages such as French or Spanish that they began in high school. However, more and more university students languages such as Serbo-Croatian, Korean, and Arabic. Government grants it possible for universities to offer a wide variety of less commonly taught languages. Because demand so much, many universities tutorial instruction and intensive summer courses abroad to their programs.

B. 🎧 Listen. Circle the best answer to complete each question.

1. **a.** That's because Pablo has been working in Buenos Aires.
   b. That's because Pablo has worked in Buenos Aires.
2. **a.** Yes, I do. I'm only working full time this week because they need the help.
   b. Yes, I do. I work full time because they need the help.
3. **a.** I'm visiting my grandparents.
   b. I've been visiting my grandparents.
4. **a.** It lasts for two and a half hours.
   b. I've taken it for two and a half weeks.
5. **a.** Yes, and happily. They were together for 18 years.
   b. Yes, and happily. They've been together for 18 years.
6. **a.** I've finished my final exams for the semester.
   b. I've been finishing my final exams for the semester.

B2 **Contrasting Verb Forms**

Choose the best form to complete each sentence.

Simple Present vs. Present Continuous

1. Tell me about yourself. (Do you speak / Are you speaking) any foreign languages? (Habit)
2. The students (listen / are listening) to a lecture in the auditorium right now.
3. (Do you have / Are you having) any trouble with the assignment? You look upset. (Right now)
4. (Do you have / Are you having) any questions about the assignment? (generally)
5. She (isn't / hasn't) been at school since Tuesday.

Simple Present vs. Present Perfect

6. (I love / I've loved) my job since I started working here.
7. She (isn't / hasn't been) dating anyone at the moment.
8. (We live / We've lived) in the same house for ages.
9. I (don't look at / haven't looked at) my English textbook for weeks.

Present Perfect vs. Present Perfect Continuous

10. (I've been living / I've lived) in a beautiful area. I'll never leave it.
11. (Have you visited / Have you been visiting) a foreign country before?
12. How long (have you read / have you been reading) that book?
13. That movie (has won / has been winning) five awards since it came out.

B3 Comparing Simple and Continuous Meanings

A. These verbs have both stative and active meanings. Read each sentence and decide on the meaning. Then complete the sentence with the simple or continuous form of the verb.

[handwritten: no action / Simple Pres]

1. I ___am thinking___ (think) about another solution to your problem. *[handwritten: action]*
2. I ___think___ (think) your answer is correct. *[handwritten: feeling / belief / opinion]*
3. Our son ___has had g. statement___ (have) five classes this semester. *[handwritten: no action]*
4. Out of all his classes, he ___has having___ (have) the most trouble in mathematics. *[handwritten: general / group — no action]*
5. At the moment, the United Nations ___is looking___ (look) for interpreters fluent in English and Arabic.
6. "False friends" are foreign words that ___look___ (look) similar to English words but have different meanings.

B. Choose three verbs below and write about two situations for each verb: one using the stative meaning in the simple present and one using the active meaning in the present continuous.

appear	be	feel	have
look	see	taste	weigh

I need to send this package. It underlineweighs about 15 pounds.
I'm trying to lose weight, so I'm weighing myself every morning these days.

B4 Background Information and Present Situations

Complete each item with appropriate information. Talk about the present situation. Try to use the simple present or present continuous.

1. I've just finished reading for class, so _now I'm starting to write my paper_____.
2. I've been working at the same job for 10 years, so _____.
3. She hasn't eaten in hours, so _____.
4. I've lost my roommate, so _____.
5. He hasn't felt well lately, so _____.
6. I've already finished packing the boxes, so _____.
7. I've been working with a tutor, so _____.

Talking About Accomplishments and Progress

A. Choose an activity that you have already started planning, for example, writing a research paper or applying for a job. Complete the chart with a list of tasks. Then check (✓) if each task is completed, in progress, or not completed.

Activity: _____,_____

TASKS	COMPLETED	IN PROGRESS	NOT COMPLETED
1. _____	☐	☐	☐
2. _____	☐	☐	☐
3. _____	☐	☐	☐
4. _____	☐	☐	☐

B. Write an e-mail to a friend about the activity. Discuss things you have completed, things that are in progress, and things you haven't done yet.

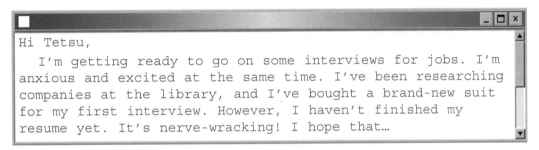

```
Hi Tetsu,
    I'm getting ready to go on some interviews for jobs. I'm
anxious and excited at the same time. I've been researching
companies at the library, and I've bought a brand-new suit
for my first interview. However, I haven't finished my
resume yet. It's nerve-wracking! I hope that...
```

B6 **Using Forms in Combination**

A. Write about each topic. What is the situation like in your country? Think about the following questions.
   • What is the current situation?
   • What has led to this?
   • How has the situation changed or how is it changing?

1. the birthrate
   The birthrate is dropping. Very few people have more than one or two children.
   People are getting married when they are older, so they can't have as many children.
   The government has been encouraging couples to start families earlier.

2. climate change
3. cell phones and personal communication
4. fashion

B. In small groups, take turns sharing your ideas about each situation in part A. How are your ideas about each situation the same? How are they different? Report back to the class.

Read each sentence and the statement that follows it. Write *T* if the statement is true, *F* if it is false, or *?* if there isn't enough information to decide. Then discuss your answers in small groups.

1. Many people think it's important to study a foreign language.

   ____ The number of people with this opinion is growing.

2. Most African people speak several languages.

   ____ This is factual information.

3. Because of the construction, I'm working in the conference room this week.

   ____ I should be able to work in my office next week.

4. The company is looking for people who are bilingual in Chinese and English.

   ____ The company has been looking for people for several months.

5. They've placed a job announcement on the website.

   ____ The announcement is still on the website.

6. He has taken a course in Hindi.

   ____ He'll finish the course soon.

7. He's been taking a course in Hindi.

   ____ He'll finish the course soon.

8. Adult humans have 206 bones in their bodies.

   ____ This describes an unchanging situation.

9. I'm working in my garden quite a bit these days.

   ____ I'm working in the garden right now.

10. He's taking a new medication for his illness.

    ____ He isn't finished with the medication yet.

B8 **Speaking**

Use these steps to discuss your experiences as a speaker of more than one language.

1. Work in pairs. Brainstorm a list of questions to discuss. For example:
   - Where do you use English?
   - What difficulties have you had with English?
   - What obstacles, if any, have you encountered as a bilingual student?
   - What have you been doing to improve your English?

2. Discuss the questions with your partner.

3. Join another pair. Discuss your answers. Then answer this question: What are some of the main problems facing bilingual students?

Writing

Editing: *The Present*

Study the errors. Pay attention to the areas that you make mistakes in.

1. **Subject-verb agreement**

                                           are
    The <u>publishers</u> of the new software ~~is~~ planning to market it internationally.

2. **Use of auxiliaries**

           have
    They ∧ not had much success in learning Chinese this semester.

3. **Parallel structure (two or more main verbs)**

                                 studies
    He attends classes, works nights, and ~~studying~~ hard on the weekends.
    The students haven't written, ~~haven't~~ spoken, or ~~haven't~~ heard German all summer.

4. **Word order**

         have not been
    I ~~have been not~~ feeling well.

5. **Time expression**

                                             recently
    We have been watching Chinese movies in class ~~nowadays~~.

6. **Adverb placement**

                         has always distinguished
    The ability to experiment ~~has distinguished always~~ good language learners.

C1 Editing

Correct the errors in the sentences. Be prepared to explain your answers.

1. Students of Chinese tends to have difficulty with pronunciation.

2. Many schools now teaching Chinese and Urdu.

3. Raoul and Carlos has been working full time and has been attending night classes.

4. Always, I have liked studying a new language.

5. Recently, I been playing guitar.

6. Chung have been not traveling lately.

Beyond the Sentence: *Describing Current Situations*

The various forms of the present are used to describe current situations. The choice of form communicates important information about whether a statement refers to a general idea or a changing situation.

> *The simple present is often used in the topic sentence of a paragraph to establish a present context. It introduces a general idea about the current situation. The present perfect is also frequently used.*

> *Supporting statements in the present perfect show that something began in the past and relates to the present.*

Almost everyone in the United States **is** familiar with Chinese food. Children **grow up** eating fried rice. Employees often **order** take-out Chinese when they have to work late, and Chinese buffets **are** always busy. In recent years, the popularity of Chinese food **has** only **increased**. As people **have become** more interested in the different flavors and styles of Chinese food, chefs **have begun** experimenting with new techniques and ingredients. As a result, Chinese cuisine **has been influencing** other forms of cooking. Many fashionable restaurants **are** now **offering** dishes that are a mixture of western and Asian influences. This new combination of styles is called "fusion."

> *Supporting statements in the simple present expand on the topic by giving further information.*

> *The present continuous is often used to show a situation that is changing. The present perfect continuous can also show a changing situation.*

(C2) Recognizing Present Contexts

A. Read the topic sentences. Think about the sentences that might follow. Check (✓) the sentence if you think it sets up a present context and will be followed by sentences in the present. Put an ✗ next to the sentence if you think it does not set up a present context.

_____ The Internet has made shopping and doing business easier.

_____ The classroom of the future is not necessarily a physical space.

_____ Learning a language has changed me in certain ways.

_____ My state (or country) is different because of the influence of other cultures.

_____ I have traveled to many countries.

_____ My teacher showed us several techniques for learning new vocabulary.

_____ There are many English words in my language.

B. Choose one of the topic sentences you checked in part A and write four different supporting sentences that could follow it. Use the simple present, present continuous, present perfect, and present perfect continuous.

Example: The Internet has made shopping and doing business easier.

1. *Nowadays people <u>shop</u> in their pajamas because they can look at merchandise online.*
2. *Many people <u>are selling</u> their used items over the Internet.*
3. *Online banking <u>has become</u> normal.*
4. *My friend is very busy, so she <u>has been shopping</u> for a car on the Internet.*

Vocabulary Notes: *Time Expressions*

These time expressions are commonly used with these verb forms.

	SIMPLE PRESENT	PRESENT CONTINUOUS	PRESENT PERFECT	PRESENT PERFECT CONTINUOUS
nowadays / these days	✓	✓		
currently	✓	✓		
recently / until recently			✓	✓
up to now			✓	✓
in recent years / months / weeks			✓	✓
over the last few days / weeks / months			✓	✓

C3 Talking About Your Life

Use the time expressions from the box above to write three or four short responses to each question. Then discuss the questions with a partner.

1. Do you play any sports?

   No, actually nowadays I'm not exercising at all.

2. How is your health?

3. Are you making progress in meeting your career goals?

C4 Writing Tip: *Writing About Trends*

A **trend** is a pattern that shows the way a situation is developing. When you write about a trend, you describe changes that may have begun in the past, are occurring in the present, and will probably continue to occur as long as the trend is developing.

Choose one of the topics to write a short essay of two to three paragraphs. Explain a trend that is familiar to you. Then, use the Writing Checklist to check your work.

- Think about a culture or tradition that has influenced you and/or people you know. Describe what you admire about the culture. What changes have you made as a result of what you have learned?

- Think about your own experiences speaking a second or other language. Does functioning in another language change you? In what ways do you behave differently? In what ways do you feel different?

- What evidence have you noticed in the news, the arts, or popular culture that indicates that a particular country is becoming more important globally?

- What cultural or artistic trends have you experienced? Do you listen to Latin music? Do you practice yoga? Do you watch French movies? Do you go to karaoke bars? Describe the trend. Then explain the trend. What evidence do you have that it is trendy?

Beyond the Classroom

Writing

Write an essay using one of these topics.

1. Watch a TV news story, listen to the radio, or read an article about a current trend. Then write two paragraphs. In the first paragraph describe the trend. In the second paragraph give your opinion of the trend. Why is it happening? Is it a good thing?

2. Interview a friend about his or her feelings about life in the 21st century. Ask your friend to think about topics such as technology, family, music, and shopping. What changes has your friend noticed over the past five years? How does he or she feel about these changes? Take notes. Then use your notes to write one or two paragraphs describing your friend's ideas. Be careful to focus on your friend's ideas rather than your own.

Searching for Authentic Examples

Find examples of English grammar in everyday life by completing the task below. Bring your examples to class, and be prepared to discuss them.

Look in a reference book or on the Internet for factual information about a language that is spoken in the world today. Find examples of the simple present and other verb forms related to the present. Why do you think these forms were used?

The Past

Ripening at the Center of the World

A1 Before You Read

Discuss these questions.

What can you learn from traveling to foreign places and meeting people from other countries? How do these kinds of experiences enrich a person's life?

A2 Read

 Read this essay to find out what the author learned while traveling in rural Brazil.

Ripening at the Center of the World

My encounter[1] with the green banana started on a mountain road in Brazil. My ancient jeep **was straining**[2] up through the countryside when the radiator[3] began to leak, 10 miles from the nearest mechanic. The overheated engine **forced** me to stop at the next village. People **gathered** around to look. Three streams of hot water spouted[4] from holes in the radiator. "That's easy to fix," a man said. He **sent** a boy for some green bananas and assured me everything would work out. "Green bananas," he smiled. Everyone agreed.

We chatted while I **was wondering** about the green bananas. I didn't want to appear ignorant, so instead I remarked on the huge rock formations[5] all around us. "Do you see that tall one right over there?" asked the man. "That rock marks the center of the world." I looked to see if he **was teasing** me, but his face was serious. "The center of the world?" I repeated, trying to show interest. He nodded. "The absolute center. Everyone around here knows it."

At that moment, the boy returned with my green bananas. The man sliced one in half and pressed the cut end against the radiator. The banana melted into a glue against the hot metal, plugging[6] the leaks instantly. Everyone laughed at my astonishment. They refilled my radiator and gave me extra bananas to take along. An hour later, after one more application of green banana, my pesky[7] radiator and I reached our destination.

When I returned to the United States, I thought about the meaning of these events. For some time, I **had been wondering** about those experiences which educators call "learning moments," and I realized I **had just had** two of them. First, being North American, I **had never paid** the slightest attention to the green banana. But suddenly on that mountain road, its special potential[8] and my need had come together. And as I reflected further,

I understood that this chance encounter **had shown** me the special genius of those people.

The second learning moment—the importance of the rock marking the center of the world—**took** a while longer to comprehend. Gradually, I realized that we tend to define the center of the world as that place where we are known, where we know others, and where things mean something to us. The lesson was that every place has special meanings for the people in it; in a way, every place represents the center of the world.

Adapted from *Ripening at the Center of the World*, by Donald Batchelder, which first appeared in the 1974 edition of the *Parents League Review*. © 1974 Parents League of New York.

1 **encounter:** unexpected meeting	5 **formation:** an arrangement of things
2 **strain:** to move with great effort	6 **plug:** to fill
3 **radiator:** machinery that cools a car's engine	7 **pesky:** annoying (informal)
4 **spout:** to come out in a stream	8 **potential:** something that can change or develop

 ## After You Read

Discuss these questions.

1. The essay begins with a story. In your own words, retell the main events of the story.
2. What two "learning moments" does the author have because of this experience in Brazil?
3. Have you ever had an experience where you learned an unexpected lesson?

Examining Form

A. Work in pairs. Look at the highlighted verb forms in the reading. Write them in the correct categories. Then answer these questions for each verb form.

Simple past _____

Past continuous _____

Past perfect _____

Past perfect continuous _____

1. What do you notice about the main verb? Is there an ending, or is the verb in its base form?
2. What auxiliary or auxiliaries, if any, come before the main verb?

B. Discuss your observations with the class. Refer to the form charts on pages A-3 and A-4 if you need to.

Simple Past and Past Continuous

Examining Meaning and Use

Read each sentence and the statements that follow it. Check (✓) the correct statement. Discuss your answers. Then read the notes to check them.

1. He was driving up the mountain and listening to the radio.
   ____ **a.** He reached the mountaintop.
   ____ **b.** It's not clear if he reached the mountaintop.

2. He was driving up the mountain when the car broke down.
   ____ **a.** The car broke down after he reached the top.
   ____ **b.** The car broke down before he could reach the top.

3. He drove up the mountain and took some pictures at the top.
   ____ **a.** He drove and took pictures at the same time.
   ____ **b.** He took pictures after he reached the top.

4. He has worked in the mountain village for a few months.
   ____ **a.** He still works there.
   ____ **b.** He doesn't work there anymore.

> **Simple Past:** base form of verb + *-d* / *-ed* or irregular form

Activities and States Completed at a Specific Time in the Past
Last night, she **filled out** the application online. (She completed the application.)
After he **attended** college in Brazil for two years, he **came back** to the United States.
He **knew** the answer right away.

- The simple past is used to talk about activities and states that were completed at a specific time in the past *(yesterday, a month ago, in 1995)*, whether or not the specific time is mentioned.

  For simple past and past participle forms of regular and irregular verbs, see pages A-8 and A-9.

Past Continuous: *was / were* + verb + *-ing*

Activities in Progress During a Specific Time in the Past

Last night, she **was filling out** the application online when the computer crashed.

  (She may or may not have completed the application.)

While he **was living** in Brazil and **attending** college, he met his wife.

* He was knowing the answer right away. (INCORRECT)

- The past continuous is used to talk about past activities (but not states) in progress at a specific moment in the past or over an extended period of time in the past. The past continuous usually shows that one or more actions were in progress when a simple past event occurred.

Comparing Simple Past and Past Continuous

Simple Past	*Past Continuous*
Last night at 6:00, I **ate** dinner.	Last night at 6:00, I **was eating** dinner.
(completed)	*(not completed)*
When the phone rang at 10:00, . . .	she **was** still **working**.

- The simple past is used to express a completed activity. In contrast, the past continuous shows that an activity was ongoing and often incomplete.

- Sentences with one simple past and one past continuous clause usually show that a simple past event interrupted an ongoing past continuous event. Words such as *when*, *while*, and *as* often connect the two clauses.

  For adverb clauses showing time, see page 215.

Comparing Simple Past and Present Perfect

Simple Past	*Present Perfect*
An art exhibit **opened** in town yesterday. *(specific time)*	An art exhibit **has opened** in town. Do you want to see it? *(indefinite time; specific time is unimportant)*
He **lived** in Brazil for six years. *(completed)*	He **has lived** in Brazil for six years. *(continues now)*

- The simple past is used to express an activity completed at a specific time in the past. The present perfect can show an activity completed at an indefinite time in the past.

- Because it is a present form, the present perfect isn't used with specific past time expressions. (See Chapter 1, page 5, for a discussion of the present perfect.)

    * An art exhibit has opened in town yesterday. (INCORRECT)

- When using *for*, both the simple past and the present perfect can answer the question: *How long?* A simple past sentence expresses a completed activity. A present perfect sentence shows an activity that began in the past and continues up to the present.

Listening

A. 🎧 Each sentence in the passage is incomplete. Listen to the entire passage first. Then listen again and put a caret (∧) where you hear a missing word. Listen once more to fill in the missing words.

has opened

An interesting new art exhibit ∧∧ downtown. When I it on Saturday, no one attention

to the beautiful paintings. Instead, everyone out the window at a crowd of demonstrators

across the street. I still why. Meanwhile, I the whole gallery to myself for almost half an hour.

It really quite unusual.

B. 🎧 Listen. Choose the best answer to complete each conversation.

1. **a.** Did he finish it?
   b. When did he finish it?
2. **a.** What exactly annoyed you?
   b. When did you become annoyed?
3. **a.** Which did he do first?
   b. It sounds like he was happy.
4. **a.** Did you drive it to work?
   b. Does it get good gas mileage?
5. **a.** What did you do then?
   b. What were you doing?
6. **a.** When does it end?
   b. Was it interesting?

B2 **Contrasting Verb Forms**

Choose the best answer to complete each conversation.

Simple Past vs. Past Continuous

1. **A:** Where were you when I called last night?
   B: I (had dinner / was having dinner) with friends. (interrupted action)
2. **A:** Why did you apologize?
   B: Because I (was realizing / realized) that I had made a mistake. (situation)
3. **A:** I didn't hear the homework assignment.
   B: That's because you (slept / were sleeping). (interrupted continuous)
4. **A:** Why didn't she win the race?
   B: Right before she crossed the finish line, she (fell / was falling). (One time fall)
5. **A:** How did you break the glass?
   B: I don't know. It just broke when I (was holding / held it).

Simple Past vs. Present Perfect

6. **A:** Do you still see Emily?

    B: Every week. (I knew / I've known) her for 20 years.

7. **A:** When did you arrive in Australia?

    B: (I got / I've gotten) here three weeks ago.

8. **A:** Why won't you try the new restaurant with us?

    B: I don't want to. I (never ate / have never eaten) that kind of food.

9. **A:** How long did you own your home?

    B: (I had / I've had) it for more than 10 years. Now I rent.

Complete

B3 ## Simple Past vs. Present Perfect

Read each conversation. Notice the use of the present perfect in the underlined sentence.
Can the present perfect sentence also be expressed in the simple past without changing the
meaning? Write why or why not.

1. **Athlete:**   Where's Jeff?
    Coach: He's in the hospital. <u>He's broken his leg</u>. You're starting the game tonight.
    Athlete: No problem!

    *Yes. He broke his leg at a specific time in the past, so the simple past can be used. (The present
    perfect also works because the condition is still the same in the present, and a specific time isn't
    mentioned in the sentence.)*

2. **Interviewer:**   Can you tell me something about your current job?
    Interviewee: Well, <u>I've worked there since 2002</u>. I'm the office manager.
    Interviewer: And why do you want to leave that job?

3. **Daughter:**   I've got some big news.
    Mother: What is it, honey?
    Daughter: <u>I've joined the volleyball team</u>. Our first practice is on Tuesday.

4. **Friend 1:**   Do you want to see the Tom Cruise movie?
    Friend 2:   <u>I've already seen it</u>. It's not very good.
    Friend 1:   Really?

5. **Man:**   Do you like it here?
    Woman: I certainly do. <u>I've lived here my whole life</u>. And I don't have any plans to move.
    Man: It does seem like a really nice place.

6. **Friend 1:**   <u>Have you ever seen a UFO?</u>
    Friend 2:   No. Have you?
    Friend 1:   You won't believe this, but I have. One time, I was . . .

Using Time Clauses

In 1986, Christa McAuliffe was an astronaut on the Challenger space shuttle, which exploded 73 seconds into flight. Complete the sentences about her life. Use the simple past or past continuous.

1. As a child, she _____ (become) interested in the space program after she _____ (see) a NASA rocket launch on TV.

2. She _____ (teach) at Concord High School when she _____ (learn) about the NASA "teacher in space" program.

3. After Christa _____ (apply) to the program, NASA _____ (choose) her as the first teacher in space.

4. Before she _____ (leave) on her mission, Christa _____ (meet) with many famous politicians and TV personalities.

Usage Note: *Background Events and Events in Sequence*

> The simple past and the past continuous often occur together in narratives. The past continuous is used at the beginning of the passage to express background information (what was happening before the story began). The simple past is used for events that move the narrative forward in a sequence.

B5 **Describing a Past Event**

A. Think of an event that you witnessed, experienced, or heard about. Use one of the ideas below or your own idea. Think about the questions and make some notes.

an important personal achievement	an accident or a natural disaster
a family celebration	a big sporting event

- When was the experience?
- Where were you?
- Who were you with?

- What was happening at the time?
- What did you do?
- How did you feel?

B. Now write about the event. Discuss what was happening before the event, what happened during the event, and what happened afterward.

It was cold, but the sun was shining on the day of the accident. My sister was driving, and I was riding in the backseat with my little brother. We were listening to music and chatting. Suddenly, the car hit an icy patch. When the car started to slide, my sister screamed. My father grabbed the wheel while my sister tried to . . .

C Past Perfect and Past Perfect Continuous

Examining Meaning and Use

Match the examples with the statements below them. Discuss your answers. Then read the notes to check them.

1. **a.** When I called her, she had packed her suitcase.
   b. When I called her, she had been packing her suitcase.
   ____ She finished packing.
   ____ It's unclear that she finished packing.

2. **a.** By lunchtime, we had written half the article.
   b. By lunchtime, we had been working for five hours.
   ____ This focuses on how long it took.
   ____ This focuses on how much was accomplished.

3. **a.** When we began lunch, she had just turned off her cell phone.
   b. When we began lunch, she turned off her cell phone.
   ____ We began lunch and then she turned off her phone.
   ____ She turned off her phone and then we began lunch.

Past Perfect: *had* + past participle

Earlier Activities and States
The news **had** already **spread** . . .
Because he **hadn't traveled** <u>very much</u>, . . .
We **had been** there <u>for a month</u>, . . .

Later Activities and States
by the time she arrived.
he was nervous about his trip. *(how much)*
so we were ready to leave. *(how long)*

- The past perfect helps show the time relationship between two past situations. It is used to express the earlier (first) activity or state. It provides background information about the later (second) activity or state, which is often in the simple past. Sometimes only a time phrase (e.g., *by noon*) is used to refer to the later situation.

- The past perfect is often used in sentences with *when, by the time, because, although,* and *even though* to connect the past perfect and simple past situations.

- Similar to the present perfect, the past perfect can answer the questions: *How much?* or *How many times?* In sentences with *for, since,* and *all,* it can answer the question: *How long?*

   For simple past and past participle forms of regular and irregular verbs, see pages A-8 and A-9.

Past Perfect Continuous: *had been* + verb + *-ing*

Earlier Activities	*Later Activities and States*
He **had been traveling** for a week . . .	when his car broke down. *(how long)*
Rumors **had been spreading** since May . . .	when she admitted the truth. *(how long)*
* We had been being there for a month, . . .	so we were ready to leave. (INCORRECT)

- The past perfect continuous also shows the time relationship between two past situations. It emphasizes that the earlier (first) activity (but not state) was ongoing. It is most often used in sentences with *for*, *since*, and *all* to answer the question: *How long?* It is not used as often as the past perfect.

For verbs ending in –ing, *see page A-7.*

Comparing Past Perfect and Past Perfect Continuous

Past Perfect	*Past Perfect Continuous*
When I met her, she **had written** the novel.	When I met her, she **had been writing** the novel.
(She finished the novel.)	*(She was not finished.)*

- The past perfect can express a completed activity. In contrast, the past perfect continuous shows an activity that was ongoing and often incomplete.

Comparing Simple Past and Past Perfect

Simple Past	*Past Perfect*
When I **got** to the beach, it **started** to rain. *(First, I arrived at the beach. Second, it rained.)*	When I **got** to the beach, it **had** already **started** to rain. *(First, it rained. Second, I arrived at the beach.)*
I **had** the car for two years before it broke down.	I **(had) had** the car for two years before it broke down. *(unnecessary: time is clear)*

- In sentences with two simple past clauses connected with *when*, the first clause expresses the earlier event. In contrast, in sentences with one simple past and one past perfect clause, the simple past clause expresses the later event.
- The past perfect is often unnecessary if the time sequence is understandable from the context. This is usually true when clauses are connected with *before* or *after*.

C1 Listening

A. 🎧 Listen to each situation. Circle the verb form you hear. (Pay attention to verb endings and unstressed syllables.)

1. **a.** He'd been waiting
   b. He's been waiting
2. **a.** She'd never traveled
   b. She's never traveled
3. **a.** did they decide
   b. had they decided
4. **a.** didn't run
   b. hadn't run
5. **a.** We've worked
   b. We worked
6. **a.** I had
   b. I'd had

B. 🎧 Listen to each sentence. Choose the earlier (first) event or situation.

1. **a.** He struggled hard.
   b. He found the job of his dreams.
2. **a.** I read the directions.
   b. I brought the appliance home.
3. **a.** I went to work.
   b. I felt ill.
4. **a.** We celebrated.
   b. We met the deadline.
5. **a.** He heard the news.
   b. He went on the Internet.
6. **a.** They got married.
   b. They graduated.

C2 Contrasting Verb Forms

Complete the sentences with the simple past, past perfect, or past perfect continuous. Use the words in parentheses. More than one answer may be possible.

1. The movie _had been playing_ (play) for a half hour when we finally got there, so we decided to wait for the next show.
2. I _attended_ (attend) Harvard for two months during the summer. It was a great experience.
3. When I got to work, I realized that I _didn't have / hadn't had_ (not have) my laptop.
4. Melissa didn't call me at noon yesterday because she _hadn't arrived_ (not arrive) yet.
5. The party _had already ended_ (end) by the time I finally got there. I missed the whole thing!
6. The police _checked_ (check) my ID carefully because the day before there _was / had been_ (be) a robbery.
7. Kate _had been waiting_ (wait) for almost 20 minutes at the café when Suzy _arrived_ (arrive).
8. Because Ray _didn't study / had not studied_ (not study) very much, he _was_ (be) unprepared for the test.

Usage Note: *Flashbacks; Missing Information and Conclusions*

> **Flashbacks:** The past perfect and past perfect continuous are often used in narratives for flashbacks—scenes that happened earlier than the main events of the story.
>
> **Missing information and conclusions:** The past perfect is also used at the end of a story to state missing information or to make a concluding comment.

C3 Giving Background Information

A. Complete each paragraph with a flashback of two to three sentences. Use the past perfect and past perfect continuous.

1. When I arrived at my school reunion, I thought there would be no one I knew. I had forgotten all about Gavin Smith!

   Back when we were students, we had shared a dorm and had spent many long evenings studying philosophy together. He had read almost every book there was on the subject, and had received the best grades in our classes.

2. When I left the airport, I was surprised at how cool it was. On my previous visit . . .

   _____

   _____

3. I was in a department store buying a gift. Suddenly, I realized that I didn't have my wallet. I remembered that I'd had it in the morning . . .

   _____

   _____

B. Write two possible endings to each sentence to complete the missing information in the story or to make a concluding comment. Use the past perfect.

1. The tornado approached quickly. We all rushed into the basement to escape. When it was over, I couldn't believe my eyes. The storm . . .

   a. _____

   b. _____

2. We were excited because my aunt was coming to visit. She was due in at 5:00 P.M., but didn't arrive until 10:00 P.M. She said that . . .

   a. _____

   b. _____

3. The neighborhood children were playing outside when I heard a loud crash. I ran outside and saw five-year-old Jimmy standing there, holding a baseball bat. The little guy . . .

   a. _____

   b. _____

Combining Verb Tenses

A. Rosa Parks was known as the "mother of the Civil Rights movement." Read about her life. For each underlined event, write *1* for the action that happened first and *2* for the later event.

1. The year was 1955. Rosa <u>had been working all day as a seamstress</u> when she <u>took a seat on a city bus</u>. She was tired.

2. She <u>was arrested</u> when she <u>refused to give up her seat on the bus to a white person</u>.

3. Rosa was a member of the NAACP.* Before she <u>was arrested</u>, she <u>had been active in the fight for equal rights</u>.

4. Rosa and her lawyers filed a lawsuit. Her case went all the way to the Supreme Court. She <u>was still working as a seamstress</u> when <u>the court ruled in her favor</u>.

5. She soon lost her job. By the time she finally <u>found another job as an administrative assistant</u>, she <u>had been unemployed for eight years</u>.

6. After <u>her husband Raymond died</u>, she <u>founded the Rosa and Raymond Parks Center for Self-Development to help inner-city teenagers</u>.

* NAACP: National Association for the Advancement of Colored People

B. Make up a timeline showing 10–15 important events in your life. Exchange papers with a partner. Use the timeline to write five sentences with time clauses. Use a variety of time clauses introduced by *when, while, as, before, after, until,* or *by the time*.

July 2004	Received a special scholarship
September 2004	Moved to the United States
October 2004	Started school

Farik had already received a special scholarship when he started school in the United States.

_____

_____

_____

_____

_____

Read each sentence and the statement that follows it. Write *T* if the statement is true, *F* if it is false, or *?* if there isn't enough information to decide. Then discuss your answers in small groups.

1. My father called and told me my brother had stopped by.

    ____ My brother was still visiting when my father called.

2. He had been studying philosophy, but he decided he didn't really like it.

    ____ He is still a student of philosophy.

3. The college had intended to hold weekend courses, but they had trouble registering enough students.

    ____ They were unable to hold weekend courses.

4. I was hooking up the video equipment when the power went out.

    ____ I finished the task before the power failure.

5. By the time she graduated, she had found the job of her dreams.

    ____ She graduated, and then she found the job of her dreams.

6. The movie started two hours ago.

    ____ The movie is still playing.

7. When the plane landed, it started to smoke.

    ____ There was smoke after the plane landed.

C6 **Speaking**

Use these steps to discuss people, events, and decisions that have been important in your life.

1. Work in pairs. Look at the questions below. Brainstorm a list of five questions to discuss for each of the other two topics: a significant event and a significant decision.

    Significant Person

    1. Which person had the greatest influence on you when you were a child?
    2. How did you know this person? What did you do together?
    3. What was an important moment in your relationship?
    4. How did your life change after you met this person?
    5. What lasting effect has the person had on you?

2. Choose a category—significant person, significant event, or significant decision—that interests you the most. Interview your partner.

3. Prepare a brief summary of your interview and report back to the class. Use a variety of past forms. If you shift from talking about the past to talking about the present, give a signal. Some good signals are *now, currently, more recently, today,* and *since then.*

D Writing

Editing: *The Past*

Study the errors. Pay attention to the areas that you make mistakes in.

> 1. **Use of auxiliaries**
>   did   wait
>   How long ∧ you and your friend ~~waited~~ for them?
>
> 2. **Parallel structure (two or more main verbs)**
>   listening
>   She was <u>driving</u> along and ~~listened~~ to the radio.
>   They had been <u>laughing</u> and ~~had been~~ talking all morning.
>
> 3. **Subject-verb agreement**
>   were
>   The two men in the speeding car ~~was~~ waving at us.
>
> 4. **Time clause fragments**
>   test when
>   Annie learned the results of the ~~test. When~~ she got home.
>
> 5. **Word order**
>   they missed
>   Why had ~~missed they~~ the exam?
>
> 6. **Adverb placement**
>   frantically calling
>   The nurse had been ~~calling frantically~~ for the doctor.

D1 Editing

Correct the errors in the sentences. Be prepared to explain your answers.

1. When they returned to the city. It was raining and the wind blew.

2. Al had been not sleeping enough, so he not do well on the exam.

3. How long Professor Levine and his colleague was traveling in Brazil?

4. He was traveling and lead tours. Until he injured his back two years ago.

5. The employees brought immediately a list of complaints to their new boss.

6. The team didn't finish their investigation or announced their findings.

7. By the time the storm arrived, residents of the coastal town been evacuated.

8. Why they didn't finish after they had eaten and had rested?

Beyond the Sentence: *Shifting Between Past and Present*

A written passage begins with a specific time frame in mind, for example, the past or the present. Sometimes writers choose to maintain a single time frame, but often they choose to shift between times. (See Chapter 3: Shifting Between the Past, Present, and Future, page 47)

> *A time in the past is often established by using the simple past or the past continuous.*

A small event during my first few weeks as a teacher **taught** me an important lesson about first impressions. I **had** recently **graduated** from college and **gotten** a job in an ESL program. I **had been planning** lessons all summer, and I was nervous but excited to begin.

> *Background information may be included with past perfect forms.*

As a new teacher, I wanted my students to like me. It is generally true that the ESL classroom **is** a friendly place, and my class was no different. The students were good-natured and eager to participate. There was one exception, however. Her name was Maria. Maria sat in the back of the classroom and scowled at me. I was intimidated, but it did not occur to me to ask her about my concerns.

> *The simple present is used to make a general comment or explain something. In this case, it is not necessary to mark the time change with a time expression.*

> *The past perfect is used to give background information about the event or situation.*

One day, a small joke in class caused everyone to laugh. I glanced nervously at Maria. She smiled, then quickly covered her mouth. Suddenly, I realized she **had not been** upset with me at all. Maria **hadn't been smiling** all that time because she had two heavy rows of braces across her teeth.

> *Statements in the past offer examples that support the general idea. Time expressions (in the past, last year) or time clauses signal the change of time.*

The ability to communicate **is** one of the most important skills a teacher can have. When I **was** a student, my teacher often **told** us, "You must never trust your assumptions in the classroom; always investigate." Until my experience with Maria, I had never really understood my teacher's advice. After that, I learned to ask my own questions in class.

> *The simple present or present perfect may be used to introduce a general idea at the beginning of a paragraph (again, without a time expression).*

Recognizing Shifts in Time

Read the passages. Write *past* for a single past time frame, *present* for a single present time frame, or *past to present* or *present to past* for a shifting time frame.

1. _past to present_   Ten years ago the country was in trouble. Unemployment was rising, and the crime rate was increasing. Last year, the government changed. In my opinion, new leadership is certainly making a difference.

2. _____   The sudden rain caused some flooding, but it had a positive effect on the vegetation. The area's trees and plants look healthy and green again.

3. _____   After the Civil War ended, many northerners moved to the south in search of opportunities. These people were called carpet-baggers because they carried bags made of carpet.

4. _____   Penicillin is an antibiotic that fights against infectious diseases. It saves lives on a daily basis.

5. _____   The use of wind power as an alternative energy source is controversial. Last year, for example, voters in six coastal towns opposed plans for offshore windmill projects.

D3 **Practicing Shifts in Time**

Complete each passage with a comment or an explanation in a different time frame. Write several sentences for each passage. You may shift time again after the first sentence you write.

1. My time management has improved a lot. In the past, . . . *In the past, I had trouble computing tasks. I was using my time poorly. I took a time-management class, and today . . .*

2. I used to sit around and watch TV. But then I started going to the gym. Nowadays, . . .

3. I used to travel a lot. Now . . .

4. I often left my door unlocked when I took my dog for a walk. Then I got robbed. Now, . . .

5. My taste in music has changed. A few years ago, . . .

6. When I was younger, I hadn't experienced much. Now that I'm older . . .

D4 **Writing Tip:** *Writing About Learning Moments*

A learning moment is a moment of sudden understanding. Learning moments can come from personal experiences or from a new or sudden insight into something you have heard or read. When you write about a learning moment, use past tenses to describe the situation that led to it. Use present tenses to explain your new understanding.

Choose one of the topics. Write two or three paragraphs. Explain a learning moment from your past. Then, use the Writing Checklist to check your work.

• Good manners are important. Agree or disagree with the statement and explain why. Describe experiences from your past that led to your opinion.

- Write about an insight that you had while traveling. Tell the story of how you arrived at your new understanding and state what you learned.
- Think of a time you rejected good advice and later regretted it. What did you learn from the experience? Tell the story of what happened and what you learned.

Writing Checklist

Reflect on your ability to use past tenses and shift to present time by answering the questions.

- [ ] **1.** Did you use the simple past and the past perfect to show the sequence of two past situations?
- [ ] **2.** Did you use the past continuous and the past perfect continuous to emphasize an activity that was ongoing?
- [ ] **3.** Did you use time clauses?
- [ ] **4.** Did you shift between past and present to support ideas or contrast information?
- [ ] **5.** Did you use present tenses to make a general comment or explain something?
- [ ] **6.** Did you check your verb phrases for correct form?

▶ Beyond the Classroom

Writing

Write an essay using one of these topics.

1. Life events such as immigration, marriage, or the birth of a child can change people in a dramatic way. Think about an experience that has changed you. Then write three paragraphs. In the first paragraph, write about your life before the experience. In the second paragraph, briefly describe the experience and your life after it. Finally, write a concluding paragraph explaining what you have learned as a result of your experience.

2. Choose an important invention that had an effect on society as a whole. Consider scientific, medical, or technological fields. Then write a short essay. First, describe the invention and how it changed society. Then, go back in time and describe what life was like before the invention. Finally, write a brief concluding paragraph. Say if you think the invention has had a mainly positive or negative effect.

3. Think about a world leader that you know about and feel strongly about. The person can be from the distant or more recent past. Then write a short essay analyzing this leader. What were the most significant events in the leader's life? What kind of impact has the leader had on his/her country or the world? In your final paragraph, comment on the leader's goals and whether they were or have been achieved.

Searching for Authentic Examples

Find examples of English grammar in everyday life by completing the task below. Bring your examples to class, and be prepared to discuss them.

Watch a news broadcast on television and listen for six examples of past forms. Try to include at least one sentence with a time clause and as many different tenses as possible. Which past tense did you hear the most?

The Future

The Secret Treasures of Zeugma

 ## Before You Read

Read the information. Then discuss the questions.

> Zeugma was one of the great cities of the Roman Empire. Founded around 300 B.C.,
> this city became wealthy because of its bridge across the Euphrates River, which made it
> an important trading city. In the summer of 2000, the ancient ruins of Zeugma disappeared
> under the waters of a new dam. But before they did, an enormous effort was made by
> archaeologists to rescue some of the important historical artifacts.

Have you ever heard of Zeugma? Can you name any other important archeological finds?

 ## Read

Read these excerpts from the script of a television documentary about the archaeologists'
fight to save Zeugma's artifacts.

WEEK 1

AT THE ZEUGMA EXCAVATION SITE
NARRATOR: The story you **are going to hear**
takes place in a remote region of eastern
Turkey on the banks of the Euphrates River.
Over the past four years, French and Turkish
archaeologists have been exploring the
ancient city of Zeugma. However, the site
has never been properly excavated.[1] This
is the team's last chance to search the site;
in six weeks the area you see here will be
flooded.

NEARBY, AT BIRECIK DAM
NARRATOR: I'm standing at Birecik Dam,
which is now close to completion. It **is
going to produce** electricity and provide
water for a huge area of farmland, but
these benefits will come with a cost. When

the dam is finished, the whole valley **will become** a reservoir.[2] The dam will flood villages and displace[3] more than 30,000 people. The hidden treasures of Zeugma will disappear forever unless archaeologists can get to them first. The team has only six weeks to collect the artifacts. Their work **begins** later today.

WEEK 3

AT THE EXCAVATION SITE
NARRATOR: The team thinks it has found something significant—a villa, possibly filled with incredible mosaics.[4]

INSIDE THE VILLA
NARRATOR: Archaeologists now know they have found a wealthy house. As they brush away mud from the wall, brightly colored paintings are appearing. The archaeologists **are going to clean** them and remove them from the site. Then specialists will restore[5] the paintings so they won't deteriorate.[6]

WEEK 6

INSIDE THE VILLA
NARRATOR: Time is almost up. By the end of the week, the team **will have been working**

for 42 days without rest. With only two days left, they have discovered a beautifully designed mosaic floor. Luckily, they have been given more time to excavate, so they**'re going to remove** the mosaic and transport it to a local museum. Over the next three months, the waters of the Euphrates **will be gathering** behind the dam.

A FEW WEEKS LATER

NARRATOR: Work on the site **is ending** soon. With the waters rising around the villa, archaeologists have found more stunning mosaics, but there is only time to save some of them. These mosaics will be sent to the local museum as well. There the mosaics will hold a place of honor and give visitors a unique perspective on the culture of the valley in ancient times.

A MONTH LATER

NARRATOR: The newly uncovered villa has disappeared under water. By October, the whole area will have become a calm lake, and much of Zeugma **will have vanished** forever.

Adapted from *The Secret Treasures of Zeugma*, © Dedeon Programmes, by permission of Terranoa, Paris.

1 **excavate:** to uncover by digging
2 **reservoir:** a body of water held back by a dam
3 **displace:** to remove people from their homes
4 **mosaic:** a piece of art made of small pieces of colored stone

5 **restore:** to bring back to a better condition
6 **deteriorate:** to become worse

 After You Read

Discuss these questions.

1. What positive and negative effects will Birecik Dam have on the region?
2. What does the reading tell us about the origin and fate of the mosaics?
3. In your opinion, how important is it to protect historical sites? Is it more important to meet modern needs?

Examining Form

A. Work in pairs. Look at the highlighted verb forms in the reading. Write them in the correct categories. Then answer these questions for each verb form.

Simple future _____

Be going to future _____

Future continuous _____

Present continuous as future _____

Simple present as future _____

Future perfect _____

Future perfect continuous _____

1. What do you notice about the main verb? Is it in the base form, is there an ending, or is the verb in another form?
2. What auxiliary or auxiliaries, if any, come before the main verb?
3. Which future forms begin with *will*? How is the future indicated without *will*?

B. Discuss your observations with the class. Refer to the form charts on pages A-3 and A-4 if you need to.

FORM, MEANING, AND USE

B The Future

Examining Meaning and Use

Read each sentence and the statements that follow it. Check (✓) the correct statement. Discuss your answers. Then read the notes to check them.

1. Without special care, these artifacts are going to decompose quickly in the hot sun.
   _____ a. This is a prediction.
   _____ b. This is an informal plan.

2. When you arrive, they'll have been taking pictures for over an hour.
   _____ a. They'll still be taking pictures.
   _____ b. They'll be finished taking pictures.

3. There's something wrong with this computer. I'll go and check the connection again.
   _____ a. This is a plan made in advance.
   _____ b. This is a decision made at the moment of speaking.

Overview: Basic Future Forms

Simple Future
(will + *verb*)

Maybe we **will take** a trip next week.

Be Going To Future
(am / is / are + going to + *verb)*

We**'re going to visit** our parents.

Future Continuous
(will be + *verb* + -ing
or am / is / are + going to + be + *verb* + -ing)

We**'ll be visiting** them all week.

Present Continuous as Future
(am / is / are + *verb* + -ing + *time expression*)

We**'re visiting** our parents <u>next week</u>.

Simple Present as Future
(simple present form + time expression)

We **leave** at 8:00 <u>tomorrow morning</u>.

- All forms refer to a specific time in the future.
- In sentences with time clauses expressing future time, the time clause usually uses a present form. The main clause uses a future form.

   Before we <u>leave</u> for Turkey, we're going to visit our parents.

- Adverbs such as *maybe, perhaps, possibly, probably,* and *definitely* are often used with the simple future, *be going to,* or the future continuous to show the speaker's certainty.

For verbs ending in –ing, see page A-7.

Plans vs. Quick Decisions

Planned Future Activities
I**'m** probably **going to visit** some friends in Turkey next year.
I think I**'m going to stay** in Istanbul for two weeks.

Quick Decisions
I wonder how much plane tickets to Turkey cost. I think I**'ll check out** the fares right now.
Don't worry about the hotel reservations, I**'ll make** them for you.

- **Planned future activities:** Typically, *be going to,* not *will,* is used to talk about activities that have been planned in advance.
- **Quick decisions:** The simple future *(will)* is often used to express a decision made at the moment of speaking, such as a promise or an offer to help. The speaker's decision is spontaneous.

Planned Future Activities

I**'m going** to Turkey next month. I'll buy you a souvenir when I'm there.

I**'m staying** in Istanbul for two weeks. I know a great hotel there.

At this time tomorrow, I**'ll be flying** to Istanbul. *(emphasizes an ongoing activity)*

Scheduled Activities

My flight for Turkey **leaves** at eleven o'clock tonight.

- **Planned future activities:** The present continuous as future is also used to talk about activities that have been arranged in advance. The meaning is often the same as *be going to*, but the present continuous as future is sometimes used when the plan is more definite.

- The future continuous is also used to talk about planned activities. The meaning is similar to *be going to*, but the future continuous emphasizes that the planned activity will be ongoing. The form is often used in sentences with time clauses.

- **Scheduled activities:** The simple present as future is usually used to express things scheduled on a formal timetable (such as airplane schedules and store hours).

  For more information on time clauses and other adverb clauses, see Chapter 13, pages 240–250.

Predictions About Future Activities or States

I bet tomorrow **is going to be** a really busy day.

Energy costs **are going to rise** next year.

I think someday we **aren't going to use** cell phones.

I bet tomorrow **will be** a really busy day.

Energy costs **will rise** next year.

I think someday we **won't use** cell phones.

Predictions About Future Activities in Progress

While you're relaxing, I**'m going to be running** around all day tomorrow.

Energy costs **will be rising** all through next year.

I think someday we **won't be using** cell phones.

- **Predictions about future activities or states:** The simple future *(will)* or *be going to* can be used to talk about things that the speaker thinks might be true in the future, or things that the speaker expects to happen. These may refer to future facts, general truths, habits, states, or activities.

- *Be going to*, not *will*, is used to predict things that are going to happen in the very immediate future. The speaker feels there is evidence it will happen.

    Don't move. The equipment **is going to fall.**

    * Don't move. The equipment will fall. (INCORRECT)

- **Predictions about future activities in progress:** The future continuous emphasizes that the predicted or expected activity will be ongoing over a period of time in the future.

> **Future Perfect:**   *will / be going to* **+ have + past participle**
> **Future Perfect Continuous:**   *will / be going to* **+ have been + verb + -ing**

Earlier Events	Later Events
She**'ll have lived** here for two years . . .	by the end of the summer.
She**'ll have been living** here for two years . . .	by the end of the summer.
The class **will have read** most of the book . . .	when they see the play.
They**'ll have been reading** the book for a week . . .	when they see the play.
We**'ll have finished** the meeting . . .	by the time he gets here.
We**'ll have been meeting** all morning . . .	by the time he gets here.

- The future perfect and the future perfect continuous are used to show a time relationship between two future situations. These forms are not used as often as the other future forms.

- The future perfect and future perfect continuous are used to express the earlier (first) event. The later (second) event is expressed with a time clause (in the simple present) or a time phrase (e.g., *by the end of the summer*).

- The future perfect continuous emphasizes that the first (earlier) event was ongoing and often incomplete. This form cannot be used with verbs that have a stative meaning.
  When the president steps down, he **will have been** in office for two terms.
  * When the president steps down, he will have been being in office for two terms.
  (INCORRECT)

For verbs ending in –ing, see page A-7.
For past participle forms of regular and irregular verbs, see pages A-8 and A-9.

B1 Listening

A. Each sentence in the passage is incomplete. Listen to the entire passage first. Then listen again and put a caret (∧) where you hear a missing word. Listen once more to fill in the missing words, and correct the punctuation.

will be collecting

Over the next three months, the waters of the Euphrates ∧∧∧ behind the dam. In just

over a month, the area a reservoir, and two weeks after that, the newly discovered villa, too.

The story of Zeugma government policy? Only time, but archaeologists hope it people more

aware of the need to protect ancient ruins. Next month, officials from over 40 nations in

Turkey to discuss this important issue.

B. 🎧 **Listen. Choose the best answer to complete each conversation.**

1. **a.** I help you with it.
   b. I'll help you with it.
2. **a.** When did they make up the schedule?
   b. Why didn't they make up a schedule?
3. **a.** That's a wise plan.
   b. That's a kind offer.
4. **a.** Too bad, then he won't know what to expect.
   b. Good, then he'll know what to expect.
5. **a.** I guess she likes it here.
   b. Why did she move away?
6. **a.** I like that promise.
   b. That's a safe prediction.

B2 Contrasting Verb Forms

A. **Choose the best form to complete each sentence.**

1. I promise that (I'll sign / I sign) the contract tomorrow.
2. Look out! (The cat will knock / The cat is going to knock) the glasses over.
3. I can't help you right now. Ask Joanna. (She'll do / She's going to do) it.
4. We're going to have our film developed immediately when (we get / we're going to get) home.
5. I've decided to remain in my current position a while longer. (I don't leave / I'm not leaving) this job yet.
6. At this time next week, (I'm going to relax / I'll be relaxing) on a beach in California.
7. Is everyone ready? The president (will start / is going to start) the meeting now.
8. How (will life change / is life changing) in the next century?
9. By the time we get to the airport, their plane (will have landed / will have been landing) and they'll be waiting in the terminal.
10. By ten o'clock, (you'll be working / you'll have been working) for over twelve hours, so (I'll be happy / I'll have been happy) to take over.

B. **Complete these sentence beginnings in your own words.**

1. I'll be seeing . . .

   I'll be seeing my brother on Friday so I'll ask him if he can help.

2. At this time next Saturday, I . . .

   _____

3. By the time I get home this evening, . . .

   _____

4. I bet tomorrow . . .

   _____

5. I'll have finished . . .

_____

6. I'm probably going to . . .

_____

Contrasting Simple and Continuous Future Forms

Use the context to decide which answers are possible. You may circle one, two, or all three responses.

1. Set the alarm clock for 6:00 A.M. and make sure all your things are packed. We need to wake up early because _____ first thing in the morning.
  a. we leave
  b. we're leaving
  c. we'll be leaving

2. _____ the ladder for me, please? It's a little shaky.
  a. Are you holding
  b. Are you going to hold
  c. Will you hold

3. I expect that _____ with most of the work tonight.
  a. they'll be finished
  b. they're finished
  c. they're going to be finished

4. _____ with the team from 3:00 onward. We have a lot to discuss.
  a. I'm meeting
  b. I'll be meeting
  c. I'm going to meet

5. At this time next year, _____ a book about famous archaeological digs.
  a. I'll write
  b. I write
  c. I'll be writing

6. A century from now, the dam _____ water to the region.
  a. is still providing
  b. will still be providing
  c. is still going to be providing

7. When you visit, _____ you around to all the famous sites.
  a. I'll take
  b. I'm going to take
  c. I'll be taking

8. Watch out! That glass _____!
  a. breaks
  b. will break
  c. is going to break

A. Elisa is going to Chile to study Spanish in a year-long language program. She took notes at an orientation meeting and is now planning her trip. Put the phrases in the correct order. Use the time words in parentheses to write sentences about her plans.

> 1. book ticket to Chile
>   make sure passport is still valid
> 2. study key vocabulary
>   buy a Spanish phrase book
> 3. make sure to pack the right clothing
>   check the weather in Chile
>
> 4. arrive in Chile
>   register at new school
> 5. finish the program
>   be fluent in Spanish

1. (before)

Before Elisa books her ticket to Chile, she's going to make sure her passport is still valid.

OR *She's going to make sure her passport is still valid before she books her trip to Chile.*

2. (once)

3. (after)

4. (as soon as)

5. (by the time)

B. Imagine you are going to take a trip. Think about the reason for your trip and what you will need to do to prepare. Make some notes and then write about your trip. Use time clauses in some of your sentences.

Destination _____

Purpose of trip _____

Itinerary _____

Preparations before departure _____

> *I'm traveling to Hawaii next month. I'm going for vacation. I plan to take surfing lessons while I'm there. My flight leaves at 6:00 P.M. on July 22, and I arrive the next morning. Before I leave, I'm going to buy a wetsuit. I'm also going to find out where I can rent a surfboard.*

Usage Note: Be Going To *and* Will *in Longer Discourse*

In paragraphs or conversations about the future, *be going to* is often used to introduce a situation. Once the context is set, *will* is usually used to add further details.

*The archaeologists **are going to start** their work tomorrow. First they **will survey** the site. Then they **will draw** a plan of the area. At that point, the excavation **will be** ready to begin . . .*

B5 Making Plans with *Be Going To* and *Will*

A. Read this excerpt about the temples of Angkor in Cambodia. Then follow the instructions.

> All around the village of Siem Reap, Cambodia, are the temples of Angkor. These beautiful and unique structures were built between the 9th and 13th centuries. In the 19th century, French explorers rediscovered them in the jungle. Although some of the larger temples are open to the public, many smaller ones are closed because they are in disrepair. But even if more temples were open, many tourists wouldn't visit them because the area is dangerous. Another problem is that the temples are being taken apart. Smugglers are stealing artifacts from the temples and selling them to art dealers. The art dealers then sell the artifacts to art collectors.

B. Work in pairs. Imagine that you are representatives for the Cambodian government. How would you address the issues outlined in the excerpt? Make suggestions about the topics below. Introduce your ideas with *be going to*. Then use *will* to add details.

- the smaller temples
  We're going to raise money to fix the smaller temples.
  Then we'll hire archaeologists and artists to help restore them.
- security concerns
- smugglers
- art dealers
- art collectors

C. Work in small groups. Take turns sharing your ideas and decide on the best suggestions. Then work together to write a press release for the local newspaper about the situation in Angkor and future plans for the site.

The temples around Siem Reap have been neglected for many decades, but a new plan to save them is starting to take shape . . .

B6 **Making Predictions with *Be Going To*, *Will*, and the Future Continuous**

A. Think about your neighborhood or hometown. How do you think it will change in the next 20 years? Write your predictions about some of the topics in the box or write about ideas of your own. Use *be going to, will* or the future continuous.

office buildings	public transportation system	parks
stadiums	streets and highways	

> *I think they're going to improve the public transportation system in my city.*
> *They will probably build a light-rail system that connects the suburbs*
> *and downtown. I believe there will also be changes to . . .*

B. Work in pairs. Describe your neighborhood or hometown and share your predictions. Discuss these questions.
   1. How are your neighborhoods or hometowns similar or different?
   2. If your predictions come true, will your neighborhoods or hometowns be better places to live? Why or why not?

B7 **Talking About Future Goals with the Future Perfect**

Read the list of lifetime goals and add some of your own. Then choose six goals to write about. Decide when you think they will happen and write about them in order. Use the future perfect or the future perfect continuous and the time expressions in the box

LIFETIME GOALS		TIME EXPRESSIONS
be married	have an interesting job	At this time next year, I . . .
have a family	travel to many countries	When I turn _____ , I . . .
graduate	buy a house	By the time I _____ , I . . .
_____	_____	_____ years from now, I . . .
_____	_____	

At this time next year, I will have already graduated and . . .

1. _____

2. _____

3. _____

4. _____

5. _____

6. _____

Speaking

Follow these steps for making a short presentation about a classmate's future goals.

1. Choose a person in the class to interview about his or her lifetime goals. Brainstorm a list of questions. Use a variety of future forms and time expressions, such as *when, as soon as, after,* and *by the time.*

    What are you going to do after you graduate?

    Do you think you will have decided on a career by the time you graduate?

    Will you still be living at home when you get married?

2. Use your questions to interview your classmate. Ask follow-up questions to get more details about his or her goals. Take notes.

3. Prepare a brief presentation about your classmate's plans and present your findings to the class.

B9 **Thinking About Meaning and Use**

Read each sentence and the statement that follows it. Write *T* if the statement is true, *F* if it is false, or *?* if there isn't enough information to decide. Then discuss your answers in small groups.

1. By the time we finally get to see it, they'll have finished the project.
    _____ We'll see the project before it is completed.

2. Turn on the radio. The news is coming on at 10:00.
    _____ It's probably just before 10:00.

3. When the new recruits arrive, our group will have been training for five months.
    _____ Our group's training period is finished.

4. I'm going to spend next summer studying in Rome.
    _____ The speaker made her plans a long time ago.

5. At this time next week, we'll be graduating.
    _____ The speaker expects this to happen.

6. That car is going to crash!
    _____ The speaker has just seen the car.

7. I think she'll definitely win the race.
    _____ This prediction will come true.

8. School begins on August 28th this year.
    _____ School always starts before September.

Writing

C

Editing: *The Future*

Study the errors. Pay attention to the areas that you make mistakes in.

1. **Use of auxiliaries**

   have
   He will ∧ renovated the house by Christmas.

2. **Use of verb form**

   is going to solve
   Venice ~~solves~~ the problem of rising sea levels soon.

3. **Parallel structure (two or more main verbs)**

   restored
   The artists will have completed six murals and ~~restore~~ 10 others by the end of the project.

   The group is going to meet the artist and ~~is going to~~ inspect the murals later today.

4. **Subject-verb agreement**

   is
   A team of experts ~~are~~ going to carry out the tests.

5. **Word order**

   not be performing
   The lead actor will ~~be not performing~~ in tonight's production.

6. **Use of tenses in dependent clauses**

   freezes
   When the lake ~~will freeze~~ over, we will go ice-skating.

7. **Time clause fragments**

   finished, it
   When the dam is ~~finished. It~~ will begin operations.

Editing

Correct the errors in the passage. Be prepared to explain your answers.

Hundreds of architectural and cultural sites worldwide are in danger. Across the world,
unless
archaeological sites, valuable buildings, and works of art will disappear forever. ~~Unless~~ we act
now to save them. Many organizations are working hard to raise public awareness. For example,
next month the World Monuments Watch will going to publish a list of 100 threatened sites.
In many cases if immediate measures are not taken, these artifacts won't survive. But if even
only one site is saved, the organizations feel their efforts will have been not wasted.

Money will be necessary. Unless the organizations will be able to raise funds, they will not
be able to rescue or won't protect many recognized historical treasures. Cooperation among
nations, government officials, and researchers are going to be even more vital. If society can
rescue this valuable cultural heritage, then it will has preserved an important legacy.

Beyond the Sentence: *Shifting Between the Past, Present, and Future*

The topics of many written passages include past, present, and future contexts. Often time will
shift within one passage.

> *The present perfect is often used to transition from past to future. It shows that an event or circumstance is not resolved.*

> *Present and future forms can be used together. Again, time expressions are often unnecessary to shift to the future.*

Neighbors in a shady older section of Houston are used to a quiet life. Long-time homeowners like to sit on their porches and tell stories. Recently, however, these homeowners became alarmed in response to the news that 11 historic bungalows **have been slated** for demolition. **Next year**, their tree-lined block of small houses with large porches **will have** a new look.

The developer that **purchased** the property **is going to build** town houses. The developer **says** it **plans to incorporate** architectural features **that will preserve** the spirit of the neighborhood's history, but residents **are** not convinced. The new houses will have more square footage, but smaller porches and yards. Many trees **will be cut** down.

Opponents say that American history is in danger. One 68-year-old resident (who has lived on the block all her life) stated, "Today is just the beginning. **In the past**, we **battled** storms, poverty, and disease. We **are not going to let** a few builders tear down our heritage without a fight."

> *Past and future forms can be used together. Time expressions are often unnecessary to shift to the future*

> *Time expressions are usually used for shifts to past time to maintain clarity.*

A. Read the passages. Write *future* for a single future time frame. Write *shift* if there is a change in time frame.

1. _____ The city's urban landscape has changed so rapidly that many local residents will not recognize areas when they visit them.

2. _____ The psychology department is conducting a study on risk next weekend. Volunteers will participate in a parachute jump.

3. _____ The mayor has plans to expand the freeways. He's going to add two new lanes to the Interstate.

4. _____ The river will not be diverted because too many people complained.

5. _____ The anthropology course is going to fill up rapidly because it will include a trip to South America.

6. _____ Many working people have said they would like to live closer to downtown. The cost of housing in this area will continue to go up as demand increases.

B. Work with a partner. Write supporting sentences for the following main idea sentences. Use future tenses.

1. A vaccination to cure some forms of cancer has been discovered.
   Many people will be cured as a result.
2. I made a big mistake my first semester of college, but it taught me a lesson.
3. Automotive companies are developing new cars that run on alternative fuels such as ethanol.
4. A sports apparel company has developed an interesting advertising campaign.
5. The economy is improving.
6. I met with my boss about a raise, and we reached an agreement.

Vocabulary Notes: *Future Time Expressions*

Some future time expressions refer to events or plans that will take place at a specific time.
   By five o'clock next Saturday, I'll have given the presentation.
   I'm going to see my doctor **next Tuesday**.

Other future time expressions are vague and the time of the plan or event is not definite.
   One day all my dreams will come true.
   Don't worry! I'll go see my attorney **at some point.**

Talking About Plans

A. Read the sentences. Write *specific* or *vague* next to the sentence depending on the time expression.

1. _____*specific*_____ **Next month**, the city will begin work on a bike trail in our neighborhood.

2. _____ **One of these days**, the bridge will have to be widened.

3. _____ The winner will have crossed the finish line **by this time tomorrow**.

4. _____ Patients will have many alternatives to surgery **in the future**.

5. _____ **Someday**, a massive earthquake will hit the northwest coast of America.

6. _____ The president will address the public at a press conference **next week**.

B. What would you like to accomplish over the next five years? Write three sentences about specific goals you have and three sentences about vague goals you have. Use future time expressions.

Someday, I'm going to learn to play the piano.

Writing Tip: *Writing Predictions*

> Making a prediction is a key component of the learning process and an important element in writing. When you write about a prediction, use the future to state the prediction. Use present and past forms to describe present circumstances and past situations that support your predictions.

Choose one of the topics to write a short essay of two or three paragraphs. Include a variety of past, present, and future tenses. Remember to include time expressions when necessary. Then, use the Writing Checklist to check your work.

• What will the ideal home of the future look like? Describe the significant features of homes of past decades. How have homes changed? Based on these changes, what desires and needs do you expect homes of the future to fulfill?

• Many people find comfort in learning about and remembering historical eras. What events, conditions, fashions, art works, pieces of music, and/or architecture of today will people remember affectionately in 25 years?

• Select a current event from the news that you think is going to have a significant impact on people. It can be political, scientific, or environmental. Describe the event and then write an extended prediction about how you think the event will affect the future.

• Transportation has been a major factor in shaping civilization. For example, early cities appeared along rivers so goods and passengers could travel by ship. Today, transporting people and products remains a challenge. What are the current challenges of transportation? What predictions can you make about the future of transportation?

Beyond the Classroom

Writing

Write an essay using one of these topics.

1. Read a newspaper or listen to the news. What is a specific change that is taking place in your city or neighborhood? Write a short essay analyzing this change. First describe the change and what caused it. Then discuss how people are responding to the change. Finally, write how you think the change will affect the city in the future. Will the effect be positive or negative?

2. The desire to explore new worlds has always been a characteristic of human beings. We have traveled to the ice caps, the bottoms of oceans, and into space. Write a short essay giving your views of exploration. First write about explorations that you know about. Why were they done? What were the risks and benefits involved? Then write your thoughts on the next step for explorers. What places are left to be explored? Why are they worth (or not worth) learning about? What risks and benefits might come from these future expeditions?

Searching for Authentic Examples

Find examples of English grammar in everyday life by completing the task below. Bring your examples to class, and be prepared to discuss them.

Look for six examples of future forms in newspaper or magazine articles discussing innovations in technology (e.g., advances in medical treatments, computers, and toys). Why do you think the particular forms were used? Are there other forms that could replace them?

Modals

A Astrology and Psychology

 A1 **Before You Read**

Discuss these questions.

Do you read your horoscope every day? Do you believe it?

Why do you think so many people believe in horoscopes?

 A2 **Read**

 Read this article about astrology and the people who believe in it.

ASTROLOGY AND PSYCHOLOGY

IT'S true, last week you **may have wasted** your time being in a bad mood, but that's all in the past. Today is a new day. Some new financial opportunities **may be coming** your way soon. Because of this, you **must get** organized. Don't make any big purchases unless you have to. If you're still single, there **could be** a change on the horizon.[1] It may come from an unexpected direction, so be prepared.

Why do so many people seem to believe in the zodiac[2] to such a great degree? Could it be that astrological charts really can tell us something about our personalities? Can they answer that age-old question: What **should** I **do** with my life?

Research psychologists chuckle[3] when asked these questions. While they readily admit that checking one's horoscope from time to time **might be** entertaining, they stop cold[4] at the suggestion that astrology can be used effectively as a tool for predicting the future.

Researchers have studied the behavior of people who believe in horoscopes. In doing so, they have discovered some interesting facts about human behavior. Research shows that often people desperately want the statements that are made in their horoscope to be true. This desire **can lead** them to find evidence in their own lives to support the information. They may even distort[5] it to fit their own lives better. Because the language used in most horoscopes is overly general, it is not difficult to find something in one's life that will support what's written.

In comparing different kinds of horoscopes, research has revealed another interesting result: A majority of people tend to believe those horoscopes that say they have been "created especially for you." Psychologists smile at this finding. They are not quite sure why this phenomenon[6] occurs—they need more time to study it.

One man said that, while he didn't have to consult his charts for everything, when it came to major decisions, he "always relied on it." However, this same man may have missed out on his dream house because of this dependence.[7] He was close to buying the house, but his horoscope had warned him, "You**'d better wait** until the full moon passes before you make any big purchases." By the time that had happened, it was too late: someone else had bought the house.

"Obviously, he **shouldn't have relied** on astrology so much," says one researcher. "I think his case **could have had** a happier outcome if he'd relied on good old common sense."[8]

---

1 **on the horizon:** in the near future
2 **zodiac:** a system of signs used in astrology
3 **chuckle:** to laugh quietly
4 **stop cold:** to stop suddenly and completely
5 **distort:** to change or alter
6 **phenomenon:** a fact or event
7 **dependence:** the need for something
8 **common sense:** the natural ability to make good decisions

A3 After You Read

Discuss these questions.

1. According to the research, why do people believe in horoscopes? What characteristics of horoscopes can help make them more believable?
2. Why did the man miss out on his dream house?
3. What do you think of the study? What do the findings suggest about human behavior?

Examining Form

A. Work in pairs. Look at the highlighted verb forms in the reading. Write them in the correct categories. Then answer the questions for each verb form.

Simple modal _____

Continuous modal _____

Past modal _____

1. Do these modals change form to show number or person?
2. What do you notice about the main verb? Is there an ending, or is the verb in its base form?
3. What other auxiliary, if any, comes before the main verb?

B. Discuss your observations with the class. Refer to the form charts on page A-4 if you need to.

B Modals of Advice, Necessity, Prohibition, and Obligation

Examining Meaning and Use

Read each sentence and the statements that follow it. Check (✓) the correct statement. Discuss your answers. Then read the notes to check them.

1. It's raining. We could leave now to give ourselves a few more minutes. What do you think? This advice . . .
   _____ **a.** is polite and tentative.
   _____ **b.** warns of possible bad consequences.

2. Visitors must check all photographic equipment at the front desk. This sounds . . .
   _____ **a.** informal.
   _____ **b.** official.

3. You don't have to pay by check, but you can if you want to. Paying by check is . . .
   _____ **a.** allowed, but not required.
   _____ **b.** not allowed.

4. You should stay in touch with your relatives when you move out of town. This tells what you . . .
   _____ **a.** are prohibited from doing.
   _____ **b.** are expected to do.

Modals of Advice:	Present / Future:	modal + base form of verb
	Past (or Perfect):	modal + *have* + past participle

Present / Future Advice

Weaker	• could, might	
↕	• should(n't), ought to	
Stronger	• had better (not), have to, have got to, must	

Present / Future Context

I don't like my job. I want to quit.

You **could talk** to your boss. Maybe she can help.
You **shouldn't quit** until you find another job.
You**'d better keep** your job. You need the money.
You**'ve got to** keep your job.

Past (or Perfect) Advice

Weaker	• could have, might have	
↕	• should(n't) have, ought to have	
Stronger	• had better (not) have	

Past Context

I didn't like my job, so I quit.

You **could have talked** to your boss instead.
You **should have waited** until you found another job.
You **had better have found** another job first.

Continued

- Modals can be used to give advice. The choice of modal depends on the strength of a person's attitude or opinion.
- Present and future forms are used to give advice and opinions about a current situation. Past (or perfect) forms express opinions about missed opportunities or regrets about past actions. They mean something was a good idea but it didn't happen.
- Weaker modals—*could (have)* and *might (have)*—often sound more polite. Words such as *maybe, perhaps,* and *I think* are also sometimes used with weaker modals of advice.
- *Had better (not)* and *had better (not) have* are used to give advice with a warning of possible bad consequences if the advice isn't followed.
- *Have to, have got to,* and *must* are also used to give very strong advice—something the speaker thinks is necessary.

For past participle forms of regular and irregular verbs, see pages A-8 and A-9.

Modals of Necessity: modal + base form of verb

Present / Future Necessity

You **must pay** before entering the park. That's the rule.

He **has to be** at the meeting by 10:00, so he**'s got to take** a taxi.

Past Necessity

You **had to pay** before entering the park. Unfortunately, I'd left my wallet at home.

He **had to be** at the meeting by 10:00, so he **had to** take a taxi.

- Modals can be used to talk about necessity or something that is required. *Must* expresses the strongest necessity, and is used in formal or official situations—often to talk about laws or rules. *Have to* is used in formal or informal situations. *Have got to* is informal.
- Only *had to* is used to express past necessity. Notice that unlike past modals of advice, *had to* does not express regret.

    She **had to quit** her job. It was driving her crazy.

- *Have to* and *have got to* change form to show agreement in the present and future.

Present / Future Prohibition

You **must not bring** anything into the exam room.

You **may not use** the gym equipment.

You **can't eat** on the subway.

Past Prohibition

I **couldn't bring** anything into the exam room.

I **couldn't use** the gym equipment.

I was surprised you **couldn't eat** on the subway.

Present / Future Lack of Necessity

She **doesn't have to go** to work tomorrow. It's a holiday.

Past Lack of Necessity

She **didn't have to go** to work yesterday, but she went anyway.

- **Prohibition:** *Must not, may not,* and *can't / cannot* are used to indicate that something is prohibited or not allowed. *Must not* is strong. It is used in formal situations. *May not* is formal, but not as strong. *Can't / cannot* are used in formal or informal situations

- Only *couldn't* is used to express past prohibition.

- *Can't / cannot* is also used to give very strong advice—something the speaker wants to prohibit.

    You **can't quit** your job. You need it!

    You **cannot smoke** in here! It's a hospital!

- **Lack of necessity:** *Don't have to* means that something is not necessary—there is a choice of whether to do it or not. *Didn't have to* means that something was unnecessary, whether it happened or not.

Present / Future Obligation

I**'m supposed to cook** dinner tonight. It's my turn.

You **shouldn't** eat on the bus, but a lot of people do.

Past Obligation

I **was supposed to cook** dinner last night, but I had to stay late at work.

You **weren't supposed to eat** on the bus, but I did. I hadn't eaten all day!

- **Present / future obligation:** *Should(n't)* and *be (not) supposed to* are used to express present or future obligation when we feel we are expected to do something (but we may or may not do it).

- **Past obligation:** Only *was / were (not) supposed to* is used to express past obligation. It means that something was expected, but it didn't happen.

A. Each sentence in the passage is incomplete. Listen to the entire passage first. Then listen again and put a caret (^) where you hear a missing word. Listen once more to fill in the missing words, and correct the punctuation.

In ancient times, astrology was often used by rulers to advise them what they ^*could* do. It was based on the idea that there a correlation between events like famine or war and cosmic events. Unlike the way astrology is used today, common people astrology. Instead, only their leaders about their fate. Since a quarter of the Earth's population still believes in astrology today, some interesting questions remain: How astrology so long? Interest by now? What makes people think that there a connection between their lives and the sun, moon, stars, and planets?

B. Listen. Choose the best sentence to complete each conversation.

1. a. Yes, you're allowed to.
   b. Yes, you're required to.
2. a. I know. It's optional.
   b. I know. It's not allowed.
3. a. I'm happy I did.
   b. I'm sorry I didn't.
4. a. I'm glad you suggested that.
   b. I'm glad you required that.
5. a. Yes, documents don't have to remain in the library.
   b. Yes, documents must remain in the library.
6. a. You could have saved your files.
   b. You'd better save your files first.

B2 Contrasting Modal Forms

Choose the best modal to complete each sentence.

1. We (could / ought to) get there early. Otherwise, we won't get seats.
2. You (might have / had better have) already finished everything. You won't have time to do it later.
3. Lisa was feeling sick, but she still came to class. She (had better stay / should have stayed) home.
4. You (might have gone / were supposed to go) to the movie with us. Where were you?
5. We (must / had to) leave at 6 A.M. because the boat sailed at 7 A.M.
6. You (couldn't / shouldn't) drive fast around here. There are a lot of police.
7. I (could / have got to) turn in my paper today. The professor said she wouldn't take late papers.
8. You (don't have to / must) register now or you can't take the course.
9. Teenagers have to make their own decisions. You (can't / had better) control everything they do.
10. We (couldn't / must not) take any photos because it was against the regulations.
11. You (don't have to / may not) enter the building without permission.
12. They (had to / were supposed to) close down their restaurant. They went broke.
13. You (don't have to / must not) take sunscreen to the pool. They have some there.
14. (I may not / I'm not supposed to) eat eggs, but I couldn't resist the ones they served today.

Complete each conversation with an appropriate modal or phrasal modal. More than one answer may be possible.

1. **A:** Excuse me. Can I use my laptop?

   B: No, I'm sorry. You ___*cannot / must not / may not*___ use your laptop until the plane takes off.

2. **A:** I don't think my boss likes me very much. And I don't want to lose my job.

   B: You __should / had better__ take fewer breaks. He gets angry when you're not at your desk. *(advice)*

3. **A:** I can't make any changes to this document. The program won't let me. What's wrong?

   B: First you __must / have to / should (advice)__ save it as a new file. Then you can make changes. *(necessity)*

4. **A:** What can I bring to the party on Saturday?

   B: You __don't have to__ bring anything, but you could pick up some drinks if you want to. *(Lack of necessity)*

5. **A:** Those people are on their cell phones. Is that OK?

   B: No, they __are not supposed to__ be using their cell phones in the theater. *(expected or obligation)*

6. **A:** How long did you wait in the emergency room?

   B: I __didn't have to__ wait at all. They saw me right away. *(Lack of necessity)*

7. **A:** I e-mailed my sister about something important, and she still hasn't responded.

   B: You __should have__ called her. You know she's never online. *(Past advice)*

8. **A:** Why wasn't anyone in the office yesterday afternoon?

   B: We __had to__ close early. Some repairs were being done on the building. *(Past necessity)*

9. **A:** I have to admit: I knew about the surprise party.

   B: What? You __were not supposed to__ find out about it! Who told you? *(obligation)*

10. **A:** What was your favorite TV program when you were younger?

    B: I __couldn't__ watch TV when I was a kid. My parents wouldn't let me. *(Past Prohibition)*

A. Read the rules for employees at a restaurant. Circle the best modals to complete the rules.

THE RED CAFÉ
Rules and Requirements for Employees

1. Employees (had to / might / must) treat customers with courtesy and respect.
2. Employees (cannot / do not have to / have to) work without the proper uniform.
3. Employees (could / have to / shouldn't) maintain a neat and clean appearance at all times.
4. After using the restroom, employees (couldn't / must / must not) wash their hands before returning to work.
5. Employees (do not have to / have to / may not) give customers complimentary items without the manager's approval.
6. Employees (do not have to / must not / must) eat food intended for customers.
7. Waiters (do not have to / have to / should not) prepare drinks. Bartenders will do all drink preparation.
8. Employees (do not have to / may not / must) punch in other employees' timecards.
9. Part-time employees (couldn't / do not have to / have to) work overtime. All other employees are required to when they are asked.
10. Full-time employees must be present at monthly staff meetings. Part-time employees (cannot / do not have to / must) attend, but are encouraged to do so.

B. Work in pairs. Joe is a full-time waiter at The Red Café. He is the café's worst employee. Read about his behavior and take turns answering these questions for each situation.

- What did he do wrong?
- What was he supposed to or not supposed to do?
- What do you think he could have or should have done instead?

1. Joe forgot to bring the pants for his uniform, so he worked in his jeans. The manager noticed and sent him home.
   A: Joe shouldn't have worked in his jeans. He was supposed to wear a uniform.
   B: He should have told the manager about his problem. The manager might have let him go home and get his pants.
2. A customer was rude to Joe, so Joe yelled at the customer.
3. Joe hadn't eaten all day, so he ate some French fries from a customer's plate.
4. Some of Joe's friends came to the restaurant to celebrate a birthday. Joe wanted to do something nice for them, so he gave them some free appetizers.
5. Joe didn't show up at the monthly staff meeting. Later he told the manager that he also had a part-time job and he had to work there.
6. Joe's car wouldn't start, and he was going to be late for work. He called the restaurant and asked a friend to punch his timecard.

A. Work with a partner. Read each situation and write advice. First say what you think the people should have or could have done instead. Then say what they should do now. Make notes of your ideas.

1. Paul was caught cheating on a test. Now he's afraid he's going to fail the course.

   He shouldn't have cheated. He could have asked for help from a friend before the test.
   He'd better apologize. And he ought to study extra hard for the next test.

2. Rose was supposed to be promoted at work. She had been with the company for five years and did her job well. However, the job was given to a man who had been at the company for only one year. Rose quit, and now she's unemployed.

3. Ed was at dinner in a restaurant with two friends and their five-year-old son. The child was screaming, running around the table, and disturbing everyone in the restaurant. His parents were doing nothing. Finally, Ed picked up the boy, put him in his seat, and told him to be quiet. His friends were furious and left the restaurant.

4. A group of pedestrians threw some trash on the ground outside of Sue's house. Sue picked up the trash, ran after them, and threw it back at them. Now the people are harassing her by throwing trash into her yard every night.

5. Andrew was driving when another car suddenly pulled in front of him. Andrew honked his horn and started yelling. Then he sped up and got right next to the other car. When he looked over, he saw that the other driver was his good friend, Tom. Tom looked embarrassed and quickly drove away. They haven't spoken for two weeks.

B. Join another pair and compare your ideas. Decide on the best advice for each problem.

C. Now discuss three of the issues below and brainstorm different solutions. Say what should or could be done about the situation. Give reasons for your opinions.

What should be done about . . . ?

- cheating
- gender discrimination
- bad parenting
- littering
- road rage

   A: If it's their first time, people who cheat should be given a second chance. They're probably under a lot of pressure to succeed in school.

   B: I don't agree. Even young children should know that it's wrong to cheat . . .

A. Complete these sentences using your own ideas

1. I had to _____ last week.

2. I've got to _____ in the next few days, even though I don't want to.

3. I should _____ as soon as I can.

4. I ought to have _____ before I came to school today.

5. I was happy that I didn't have to _____ last month because _____.

6. If you don't understand a grammar point, you could _____ or you might _____.

7. You shouldn't tell _____ about _____.

8. Everyone in our school has to _____.

9. People appreciate it when you _____, even though you don't really have to.

10. One time I forgot to do something important. I was supposed to _____, but it completely slipped my mind.

11. When I was a kid, I couldn't _____ because my parents wouldn't let me.

12. I could have _____ when I was younger, but _____.

13. I shouldn't have _____ because now _____.

B. Compare your answers from part A with a partner. Ask follow-up questions about your partner's statements.

A: I had to finish a paper for art history last week.
B: What was the paper about?

Modals of Possibility

Examining Meaning and Use

Match the examples with the statements. Discuss your answers. Then read the notes to check them.

a. The package has got to have arrived. I saw the delivery truck.

b. The package might have arrived. We'll have to check in the mailroom.

c. The package ought to have arrived. It was expected this morning.

____ I don't know if it arrived.

____ I'm certain that it arrived based on the evidence.

____ I'm fairly certain, but not positive, that it arrived.

Modals of Possibility

Present / Future
(*modal + base form of verb*)   You **could talk** to your boss. He **might help**.
(*modal + be + verb + -ing*)   I **should be arriving** around six.

Past (or Perfect)
(*modal + have + past participle*)   You **could have talked** to your boss.
(*modal + have been + verb + -ing*)   They **must have been driving** all night.

- Modals and phrasal modals are often used to talk about different levels of certainty.

Weaker Certainty

Weaker Certainty in the Present / Future
Helen isn't here yet. She **might not be coming**, or she **could be** stuck in traffic.
Don't serve steak tonight. Joe **may not eat** meat.

Weaker Certainty in the Past
Helen isn't here yet. She **might have forgotten** about the party.
Joe looks upset. Something bad **may have happened.**

- *Could, might (not), may (not)*, and their past forms are used to make guesses about situations when there isn't much proof. *Could* and *might (not)* sometimes show less certainty than *may*, especially when they express more than one possibility.

Assumptions in the Present / Future

It takes a while to drive there. If I leave now, **I should be arriving** by around six.

The weather report said this storm won't last long. It **ought to pass** quickly.

Assumptions in the Past

The game **shouldn't have ended** yet. It's only 9:30.

I think it **ought to have stopped** raining by now. Let's go outside.

- *Should(n't), ought to,* and their past forms are used to make assumptions about situations based on knowledge or experience. It means you are fairly certain of something, but not positive.

- The past forms—*should(n't) have* and *ought to have*—are not very often used with this meaning.

Strong Certainty

Strong Certainty in the Present / Future

Look at that man on the side of the road. He **must need** some help.

Exams **have got to be starting** soon. A lot of students are in the library.

Strong Certainty in the Past

I'm sorry you're confused. I **must not have been** very clear.

I **must have been doing** something wrong. My computer crashed again.

- *Must (not), have to, have got to,* and their past forms are used to make conclusions when there is strong certainty.

- *Must (not), have to,* and *have got to* are not usually used to express certainty about the future unless they are used with a continuous verb. More typically, we use *will* to express strong certainty about the future.

     I'll probably **be** late tonight. I have a meeting at five.

- *Have to* and *have got to* change form to show agreement.

Impossibility

Impossibility in the Present / Future

You all did very well on the test. I **couldn't be** more pleased.

Impossibility in the Past

You speak Japanese so well! That **can't have been** an easy language to learn.

- *Can't, couldn't,* and their past forms are used when it is certain something is unlikely or impossible. They often are used in sentences that express surprise or disbelief.

Listening

Listen. Choose the best sentence to complete each conversation.

1. **a.** Why do you believe it?
   b. Why don't you believe it?

2. **a.** Why are you so certain?
   b. What makes you think that?

3. **a.** When will you be sure?
   b. Are you sure?

4. **a.** Yes, that's a possibility.
   b. Yes, that's the only reasonable conclusion.

5. **a.** Good. Then we can leave.
   b. Too bad. Then we'd better not leave.

6. **a.** She must be staying up late.
   b. She should be staying up late.

C2 **Restating Sentences with Modals of Possibility**

Rewrite the underlined sentences using modals of possibility.

Present / Future Modals of Possibility

1. Should I bring an umbrella? It's possible that it's going to rain today.

   It might rain today.

2. Jack injured his ankle in practice, but I assume that he will be playing on Friday.

   He should be playing on Friday

3. He barely smiled at me when I waved. I'm certain that he doesn't remember me.

   100% cert   He must not remember me

4. It's impossible that our trip is canceled. I've been looking forward to it for months.

   Our trip can't be cancelled

5. Maybe Bill is trying to call us. Is your phone on?

   Bill may/might be trying.

Past Modals of Possibility

6. I'm positive that he knew I was waiting for him. I told him I'd be there at four o'clock.

   he must have known I was waiting.

7. His answer was strange. It's possible he was lying. Or perhaps he was exaggerating.

   he could/may have been lying

8. By now, I expect that he has found the note I left. I hope he's not worried.

   He should have found the note

9. He looked embarrassed. It's very unlikely that it was easy for him to admit his mistake.

   can't could   It couldn't have been easy

10. I don't know if she's guilty. I think there's a small chance that she didn't do it.

    She might / may not don it

C3 Expressing Possibility About the Present
_____

A. Read these situations. How many guesses, assumptions, and conclusions can you make? Write sentences with modals of present possibility. Add sentences to explain what you mean if necessary. Then compare your ideas with a partner. Who thought of the most sentences?

1. Gina is trying to call her sister, but every time she dials she gets the wrong person. She's checked the number twice.

   Gina should be able to reach her sister if she has the right number.
   Her sister may have a new number.

2. The clock says it's 8:30, and John isn't home from work. The store that he works at closes at 7:30, and he's always home by 8:00.

3. Ron has gone to visit his friend Sean. When he knocks on the door, he hears someone moving around, but no one answers.

4. Paul has just received three large boxes. He looks really pleased.

5. Jill just got a new computer. It worked fine yesterday, but now it won't start up.

B. Choose five friends or family members. What do you think they might be doing right now? Write a few sentences about each person using modals of present possibility. Give reasons for your ideas.

I think my father may be working in the yard. I know he had to do some work there and it's his day off today. If he isn't there, he's probably having a cup of coffee with my mom at home.

C4 Expressing Possibility About the Future
_____

A. Consider the questions below and think about your plans for the future. What are you sure you will do? What do you think you might do? Write six to eight sentences about your plans.

What plans do you have regarding . . . ?

- your next vacation
- your job
- your free time
- your hobbies
- your home
- your studies
- your family

I'll definitely be going to Canada next year. I want to see Montreal.
I should be hearing about a promotion at work soon. If I get it, I'll have a lot more responsibility.
I might take dance classes if I can find a friend to come with me.

B. Work with a partner. Take turns asking about your plans. Ask follow-up questions to get more information.

A: *What plans do you have for your next vacation?*
B: *I may be going on a hiking trip in the Adirondacks.*
A: *Great! How long is the hike?*

C5 Expressing Possibility About the Past

A. Work in small groups. Read the situations and answer the questions that follow. Use past modals of possibility. Then choose your best explanations to share with the class.

1. You were having dinner at your friend Terry's house last night when she got a phone call. She grabbed her purse and then asked you if you had any money. You gave her $20. She said she had to go and ran out the door. What do you think happened?

   Terry might have gotten a call from the police. Someone she knows could have gotten arrested.

2. You got home early yesterday. You surprised your neighbor, who was standing in front of your house trying to look in through the window. He seemed nervous. What do you think he was doing?

3. You were home alone last Saturday night. It was around midnight, and you were getting ready for bed. Suddenly, your dog started barking at the front door. You checked outside and there was no one there, but he wouldn't stop barking for 15 minutes. Why was the dog barking?

4. A week ago, you left your bike locked up outside. The next day, your bike was gone, and you assumed it had been stolen. Then yesterday, you went outside and your bike was back! It was locked up right where it was before. What happened?

B. Write another past situation like the ones in part A. Then exchange situations with another group and write explanations.

C6 Thinking About Meaning and Use

Read each sentence and the statements that follow it. Check (✓) the sentence that is most likely to follow. Then discuss your answers in small groups.

1. I couldn't see James when I went to the hospital.
   - ✓ **a.** Only family members are allowed in the patient's room.
   - ____ **b.** I think he may have been visiting another patient.

2. Two days after Tom lost his wallet and keys someone broke into his house and robbed him.
   - ✓ **a.** That's awful. It must have been the person who found his wallet and keys.
   - ____ **b.** That's awful. It may have been the person who found his wallet and keys.

3. You don't have to take notes during the lecture.
   - ____ **a.** Note-taking is not allowed.
   - ✓ **b.** Note-taking is optional.

4. Helen majored in computer technology in college.
   - ✓ **a.** She should be able to figure out this new software.
   - ____ **b.** She might be able to figure out this new software.

5. Excuse me. Could you put out that cigarette, please?

_____ **a.** You could not smoke in here.

_____ **b.** You're not supposed to smoke in here.

6. Sorry I'm so late. I had to take a phone call.

_____ **a.** It was an emergency.

_____ **b.** I love to talk on the phone.

7. Because he didn't have a lawyer, he lost his case.

_____ **a.** He shouldn't have hired a lawyer.

_____ **b.** He ought to have hired a lawyer.

8. My parents must be having a hard time finding a parking space.

_____ **a.** They've been gone for a few minutes.

_____ **b.** They've been gone for over an hour.

C7 ## Speaking

A. **Think about the questions. Then write one or two statements about each problem.**

- What is the current situation like in your community?
- How has the situation changed, or how is it changing?

1. pollution

There's a lot of pollution in my community because there are too many cars on the street. It's going to get worse because they're opening a new mall so even more cars will come into the area.

2. unemployment

3. illiteracy

4. healthcare

B. **Work in small groups. Take turns sharing your ideas about each problem in part A. Choose one of the problems that you feel strongly about. Discuss the questions below. Make notes of your answers.**

- What are the possible causes of the situation?
- What could or should have been done in the past?
- What should or must be done now?

The highways are too crowded. The traffic must come from people driving through the neighborhood to avoid the highway. All the new construction could be happening because . . .

There should have been better city planning. The highways could have been modernized years ago. I think a law should be passed to . . .

C. **Summarize your ideas and report back to the class.**

D Writing

Editing: *Modals*

Study the errors. Pay attention to the areas that you make mistakes in.

1. **Use of verb form**

                serve
   Noncitizens may not ~~to serve~~ on a jury.

           to
   Every citizen ought ∧ serve on a jury once in their lives.

2. **Use of tenses**

     should have studied
   I ~~should study~~ harder when I was in college.

3. **Parallel structure**

                         discussing
   The jury might be going over the case again and ~~discuss~~ all the evidence.

4. **Subject-verb agreement**

          has
   Each jury member ~~have~~ to participate in every part of the process.

5. **Word order**

        should we pay
   How much ~~we should pay~~ court-appointed lawyers?

D1 Editing

Correct the errors in the passage. Be prepared to explain your answers.

     Deciding when to tell children the truth about Santa Claus can ~~to~~ be difficult for parents. Currently, as many as 700 million children worldwide believe in Santa. Many of these children have looked forward to Santa's visit since they could first walk and talked. In addition, many parents think that children ought believe in Santa for as long as possible. They maybe having fond memories of their own childhood beliefs. They think, "Why not should my children believe?"

     Older children in particular, however, may experience negative effects. First of all, parents is supposed to tell the truth. If a child feels tricked, he may not believe anything they tell him for some time. Second, the child might have resented his parents, especially if his belief in Santa causes embarrassment.

This is exactly what happened to Kevin Glover. Now 21, he still recalls the day he told his 11-year-old friends that he'd asked Santa for a bike. "They laughed at me," says Kevin. "I ran home and screamed at my parents for lying to me. I really think they should not waited so long to tell me the truth."

Beyond the Sentence: *Reacting to Situations with Advice, Guesses, and Conclusions*

The various functions of modals—in the past, present, and future—are often used in combination to talk about a single situation. Writers often shift among these uses in order to react to situations with advice, guesses, or conclusions.

Modals can be used to explain possible situations or suggest different alternatives.

Modals can be used to make guesses or draw conclusions about a situation.

Modals can be used to express predictions about a future situation.

Modals can be used to make suggestions and give advice and opinions about a situation.

Some things never change from generation to generation. Who has not met a child who has been bullied at school? Most of us have. Every school has a bully who feels he or she **must try to control** others. He or she **might be** bigger and stronger than their peers, but they **don't** always **have to be**. An effective bully **may be able to intimidate** in other ways. For example, he or she **could use** threats or insults to pressure classmates.

The best way to deal with a bully starts with understanding. The truth is that most bullies feel insecure. A bully **might have been** a victim in the past, and **may feel** that he or she needs to treat others the same way to gain respect. But bullies **should not** be permitted to act this way. Often kids **may be able to stop** a bully simply by being polite to him or her. If that doesn't work, they **must demand** respect for themselves. The next time a bully tries to intimidate them, they **should** simply say, "You **can't talk** to me like that," and walk away.

The results are often surprising. Classmates **might see** "the bully" the next day and discover that he has had a complete change of attitude overnight.

A. Read the situations and the sentences that follow. For each sentence, write *G* if it is a possible explanation or guess, *A* if it is advice, or *C* if it is a conclusion.

Situation 1

Demand for organic food products is changing agricultural methods.

____ 1. This will be very good for the planet.

____ 2. The recent media reports on pesticides might be influencing consumers.

____ 3. The government should subsidize organic farming to help domestic growers remain competitive.

Situation 2

Research suggests that exercise has a positive effect on a person's mental health.

____ 1. Depressed people ought to exercise regularly.

____ 2. There must be a closer relationship between the mind and body than people realize.

____ 3. They may have studied people with mental illnesses.

B. Choose two of the situations below. Then write three sentences for each. Use modals to write a possible explanation or guess about the situation, to give advice, and to draw a conclusion.

1. People are buying smaller, more fuel-efficient cars.

2. After World War II ended, there was a dramatic increase in the birthrate.

3. The World Cup is gaining popularity in the United States.

4. Last year, 10 percent fewer new students started college.

Vocabulary Notes: *Adverbs*

These adverbs are often used with or in place of modals.

When giving advice with modals, *maybe*, *perhaps*, and *probably* can soften the advice.

Maybe you could ask Jill for help.

You **probably** ought to call first.

Certainly and *definitely* can strengthen advice.

You **definitely** should have called first.

When talking about possibility, *maybe*, *perhaps*, *probably*, *certainly*, and *definitely* can often replace modals.

Maybe he's embarrassed. *(He may be embarrassed.)*

He's **probably** on his way now. *(He should be on his way now.)*

He's **definitely** gotten lost. *(He must have gotten lost.)*

Write answers to the questions using adverbs with modals or adverbs in place of modals.

1. Who will be the next person in your class to get married?
2. Where will you be living in 10 years?
3. My brother is trying to decide on a profession. What advice would you give him?
4. Who will have e-mailed you when you next check your messages?
5. What should you do when you have trouble sleeping?
6. My brother and sister don't get along. How can I help?

Writing Tip: *Supporting Ideas with Modals*

We often use modals to examine many different possibilities, explanations, or courses of action. Because most modals express different degrees of certainty and possibility, they allow us to suggest one idea while not eliminating others.

Choose one of the topics to write a short essay of two or three paragraphs. Use modals to suggest various explanations that support your topic. Use adverbs of time if necessary for clarification. Then, use the Writing Checklist to check your work.

• Write about a place that makes you feel uncomfortable. Describe the place, why you have to go there, and what happens when you are there. Then write several possible explanations about why that place makes you feel uncomfortable.

• Many people use the word "cool" to describe someone they like or admire. Yet it is difficult to define what "cool" is and why some people are "cool" and others are not. Write a definition that you think explains "cool", and then speculate about the features that a "cool" person has and an "uncool" person does not.

• Addiction is a strong need or craving to do or have something. Think of a behavioral or physical addiction that you know about such as gambling, shopping, or smoking. What makes these habits addictive? Why are some people able to quit and some people not, even when their health or livelihood is in danger?

Writing Checklist

Reflect on your ability to use modals by answering the questions.

☐ **1.** Did you use modals to explain possible situations or make guesses?
☐ **2.** Did you use modals to draw conclusions?
☐ **3.** Did you use modals to give advice or suggest a possible course of action?
☐ **4.** Did you use modals to make predictions about a future situation?
☐ **5.** Did you use adverbs with or in place of modals?
☐ **6.** Did you check your verb phrases for correct form?

Beyond the Classroom

Writing

Write an essay using one of these topics.

1. Think about a mistake that someone you know made in the past. Write two paragraphs. In the first paragraph, describe the person's mistake and the circumstances in which that person made it. In the second paragraph, write about what the person could have done differently. Finally, write about how the person's life would have been different as a result.

2. Brainstorm about a challenge that you face in a relationship that you have with another person. Write three paragraphs. In the first paragraph, describe your relationship and the challenge that you have with that person. In the second paragraph, explore possible courses of action that can help you address this challenge. In the final paragraph, draw conclusions about what you should or must do. Also consider explaining what you think will happen if you take your own advice.

3. Sometimes students drop out of school. Write an essay in which you explore the factors that may cause a student to stop attending. In the first paragraph, describe the demands and difficulties that college students face. In the second paragraph, speculate about the reasons why they drop out. Finally, suggest some ways that schools and teachers can support students so that they do not drop out. What will happen as a result?

Searching for Authentic Examples

Find examples of English grammar in everyday life by completing the task below. Bring your examples to class, and be prepared to discuss them.

Look for modals in a newspaper editorial or a letter to the editor. Why do you think each modal is used? What other expressions does the writer use to express degrees of certainty or necessity?

The Passive

A Measuring Intelligence

A1 Before You Read

Discuss these questions.

How do you define intelligence? What makes a person smart?

Do you think it is possible to improve your intelligence? Why or why not?

A2 Read

Read this excerpt from a psychology textbook to find out how the IQ test began and what it is like today.

Measuring Intelligence

The Origin of IQ[1] Tests

The forerunner[2] of the modern IQ test **was based** on the simple idea that the size and shape of a person's head **could be used** to measure intelligence. The idea **was proposed**[3] by Sir Francis Galton (1822–1911), a well-respected English scientist. Although Galton's theory was wrong in almost every way, he was the first to suggest that intelligence could be quantified and measured in an objective[4] manner.

The first legitimate[5] intelligence tests **were developed** by the French psychologist Alfred Binet (1857–1911). In his tests, he had children perform tasks such as following commands, naming objects, and putting things in order. He assumed that since the ability to perform these tasks improved with a child's age, more intelligent children **could be distinguished**[6] from less intelligent ones (of the same age) by comparing their performance.

After taking Binet's test, children **were assigned** a "mental age," which equaled the age of the average individual with the same score on the test. For example, if the average 8-year-old answered 45 items correctly, then anyone who answered 45 items correctly **would be assigned** a mental age of 8 years—so whether the person was 20 years old or 5 years old, he or she would have the mental age of 8.

IQ Tests Today

Binet's original intelligence test is still around, although it **has been revised** in significant ways. It **is** now **called** the *Stanford-Binet IV* and consists of a series of items that vary according to the age of the person being tested. For example, young children **are asked** to copy figures or answer questions about everyday activities. Older people are asked to perform more complicated tasks, such as explaining proverbs or describing similarities between sets of words.

The test **is given** orally. The examiner begins by finding a mental age level where the person is able to answer all questions correctly, and then moves on to more and more difficult problems. When a point is reached where no items **can be answered**, the test is over. The pattern of correct and incorrect responses **is examined**, and an IQ score is computed.

The IQ test most frequently used in the United States today, however, is the *Wechsler Adult Intelligence Scale III*, which has two major parts: a verbal scale and a performance (or nonverbal) scale . . .

Adapted from *Essentials of Understanding Psychology* (5th edition) by Robert S. Feldman, pp. 229–231; © 2003 McGraw Hill.

1 **IQ (intelligence quotient):** a number used to indicate a person's intelligence
2 **forerunner:** something that comes before something else
3 **propose:** to suggest
4 **objective:** fair; not influenced by personal ideas
5 **legitimate:** authentic, reasonable
6 **distinguish:** to recognize differences

A3 **After You Read**

Discuss these questions.

1. How did Sir Francis Galton's test try to measure intelligence?
2. How did Alfred Binet's original test try to measure intelligence?
3. How is the modern *Stanford-Binet IV* test administered?
4. Have you ever taken an IQ test? Are IQ tests a common part of the educational system in your country?

Examining Form

A. Work in pairs. Look at the highlighted verb forms in the reading. Write them in the correct categories. Then answer these questions for each verb form.

Simple present passive _____

Simple past passive _____

Present perfect passive _____

Modal passive _____

1. How many words are used to form the passive?
2. What is the form of the main verb?
3. What auxiliaries come immediately before the main verb?

B. Discuss your observations with the class. Refer to the form charts on pages A-5 and A-6 if you need to.

B The Passive

Examining Meaning and Use

Read each sentence and the statements that follow it. Check (✓) the correct statement. Discuss your answers. Then read the notes to check them.

1. A great deal of fish is eaten in Japan.
   - ____ **a.** The performer of the action is unknown.
   - ____ **b.** The performer of the action is obvious.

2. The patient was stung by an unusual insect.
   - ____ **a.** The performer of the action is obvious and unnecessary in this sentence.
   - ____ **b.** The performer of the action adds important information to the sentence.

3. Two trees were uprooted and a car was damaged.
   - ____ **a.** The sentence focuses on the result of the action.
   - ____ **b.** The sentence focuses on the performer of the action.

4. It has been acknowledged that mistakes were made.
   - ____ **a.** The sentence has a less formal, personal tone.
   - ____ **b.** The sentence has a more formal, impersonal tone.

Forming Passive Sentences: *be* + past participle

Active: <u>Alfred Binet</u> **created** <u>the first intelligence test</u> in 1903.
     (agent)   *(receiver)*

Passive: <u>The first intelligence test</u> **was created** in 1903 (by <u>Alfred Binet</u>).
       (receiver)   *(agent)*

- To form the passive:
  - use the auxiliary *be* in the appropriate tense + the past participle of the main verb; and
  - make the object of the active sentence the subject of the passive sentence.
- In active sentences, the subject performs the action of the verb. (It is the agent.)
- In passive sentences, the subject receives or is the result of the action of the verb. (It is the receiver.) If necessary, the agent may appear at the end of the sentence after *by*.
- To make a passive sentence negative, use the negative form of *be*.

  The first intelligence test was**n't** created in 1910. It was created in 1903.

  The test will **not** be given today.

  For past participle forms of regular and irregular verbs, see pages A-8 and A-9.

Active	*Passive*
He **has answered** <u>my question</u>.	<u>My question</u> **has been answered**.
Someone **stole** <u>my wallet</u> while I was asleep.	<u>My wallet</u> **was stolen** while I was asleep.
I **arrive** in Florida on Thursday.	*(no passive form)*
An error message **appeared** on the screen.	*(no passive form)*

- Verbs can be transitive (followed by an object) or intransitive (not followed by an object).
- Most transitive verbs can be active or passive. Some examples of transitive verbs are *answer, buy, need,* and *take.* A few verbs are passive only: *be located in, be born, be composed of.*
- Because intransitive verbs are not followed by an object, they cannot be used in the passive. (There is no object that can become the subject of a passive sentence.) Some common intransitive verbs are *appear, arrive, be, come, cry, die, go, happen, occur, rain, seem, sleep, stay,* and *walk.*

For common intransitive verbs, see page A-11.

The following forms commonly appear in the passive.

	Passive	*Active*
Simple Present	The test **is given** orally.	We give the test orally.
Simple Past	The test **was given** orally.	We gave the test orally.
Simple Future	The test **will be given** orally.	We will give the test orally.
Be going to *Future*	The test **is going to be given** orally.	We are going to give the test orally.
Present Continuous	The test **is being given** orally.	We are giving the test orally.
Past Continuous	The test **was being given** orally.	We were giving the test orally.
Present Perfect	The test **has been given** orally.	We have given the test orally.
Past Perfect	The test **had been given** orally.	We had given the test orally.
Simple Modal	The test **may be given** orally.	We may give the test orally.
Past Modal	The test **may have been given** orally.	We may have given the test orally.

- The passive is used when you want to focus on the result (or the receiver) of the action instead of the performer (or agent) of the action.
- Using the passive form does not change the meaning of the sentence. The various tenses and forms express the same meanings discussed in Chapters 1–4 (e.g., the simple present is still used to talk about habitual behavior). But the passive form changes the way we think about the information in the sentence.
- The passive is used much less often than the active voice. It should not be used in contexts where active sentences are more direct and easier to understand. It is used most often in academic writing and in more formal contexts.

The Agent in Passive Sentences

Agent Is Not Used

Unimportant Agent	Binet's original intelligence test **has been revised** significantly. *(Who revised it is unimportant.)*
Unknown Agent	The man **had been hurt** during the riot. *(We don't know who or what hurt him.)*
Obvious Agent	A lot of tea **is drunk** in England. *(The tea is obviously drunk by English people.)*
General Subject	**Can** music **be used** to enhance learning? *(Active: Can <u>people</u> use music to enhance learning?)*
Avoiding Blame	IQ tests **have been misused** at this school. *(The speaker deliberately doesn't say who has misused them.)*

Agent Is Used

Completes the Meaning	Most of our climate change **can be explained** <u>by global warming</u>. *(Without the agent, the meaning is vague and incomplete.)*
Adds Important Information	The man **was injured** badly <u>by a falling tree</u>. *(The agent adds <u>how</u> he was injured.)*
Surprising Agent	The surgery **was** successfully **completed** <u>by a robot-guided laser</u>. *(The agent is kept because it is unexpected.)*

- Because passive sentences focus on the receiver of the action, they do not usually need to mention the agent at all.

- Sometimes it is necessary to include the agent. Inanimate or nonhuman agents are often included because they are unexpected. (Most omitted agents are human or living.)

B1 **Listening**

A. 🎧 Listen to the conversations. Choose the answer with the words you hear.

1. **a.** She's being offered
   b. She's been offered

2. **a.** I'll be contacted
   b. I've been contacted

3. **a.** When are the pictures taken?
   b. When were the pictures taken?

4. **a.** The food has all been eaten
   b. The food had all been eaten

5. **a.** It's being repaired.
   b. It's been repaired.

6. **a.** No, it was rescheduled
   b. No, it's rescheduled

B. 🎧 **Listen. Choose the best sentence to complete each conversation.**

1. **a.** Pardon. When was it started?
   b. Pardon. When did it start?

2. **a.** By the judge?
   b. Are you upset?

3. **a.** Which ones did he receive?
   b. Which ones did he award?

4. **a.** It is thought so. I'll check my calendar and call you back.
   b. I think so. I'll check my calendar and call you back.

5. **a.** So will they be doing what I recommended?
   b. So should I be doing what they recommended?

6. **a.** Did she explain everything?
   b. Did they explain everything?

B2 ## Recognizing Passive Sentences

Check (✓) the sentences that are in the passive voice.

____ 1. He should have been here by now.
____ 2. Joe's mother was given a rose at the end of the ceremony.
____ 3. I think he might have been helped by someone.
____ 4. We had been studying for an hour when he got home.
____ 5. The victim has been taken to the hospital.
____ 6. The train is going to be leaving for Athens in about an hour.
____ 7. By the time we get home, the kids will have been put to bed.
____ 8. Had the test results already been published when you saw them?
____ 9. She'd better have been saving money to pay for college.
____ 10. The building was being torn down as we drove past it.

B3 ## Contrasting Active and Passive Verb Forms

Choose the best form to complete each sentence.

1. So far, intelligence tests (have given / have been given / gave) to 500 students in the university.
2. By the time we reach L.A., we (are seeing / will have been seen / will have seen) 12 cities.
3. Millions of e-mails (are sent / are sending / send) around the world daily.
4. I can (be explained / explain / have explained) what happened.
5. This idea (was proposed / proposed / has proposed) by our chief executive last March.
6. Siridej (has injured / is being injured / has been injured) in a bike accident, but he's OK.
7. We must (check / be checked / have been checked) that all doors are locked.
8. The window might (have been broken / been broken / have broken) by a burglar.
9. Many questions (were asking / may be asked / were asked) at yesterday's meeting.
10. Can anyone (be understood / understand / have been understood) the instructions for this?

Use the information in parentheses to complete the sentences in the active or passive voice. In the passive sentences, add the agent only if you think it is necessary.

1. (a falling tree / the house / last night / damage)

    A falling tree _damaged the house last night._

    The house _was damaged by a falling tree last night._

2. (the printer / the document / in under a minute / print)

    The printer _prints the document in under a minute_

    The document _was printed (by the printer) in under a minute_

3. (the police / the driver / $75 / be going to fine)

    The police _is going to fine the driver $75_

    The driver _is going to be fined $75 by police_

4. (more comfortable seats / the benches / in most train cars / already replace)

    More comfortable seats _have already replaced the benches in most train cars_

    The benches _have already been replaced by more comfortable seats in most_

5. (the visiting professor / a lecture / in the main hall today / be supposed to give)

    The visiting professor _is supposed to give a lecture in the main hall_

    A lecture _is supposed to be given by the visiting professor in the main hall today_

6. (someone / this package / on my desk this morning / must leave)

    Someone _must have left this package on my desk this morning_

    This package _must have been left on my desk by someone this morning_

Usage Note: *Special Cases with Transitive and Intransitive Verbs*

Some verbs, e.g., *begin, break, end, open, start, stop,* and *weigh,* can be transitive or intransitive depending on the meaning of the sentence. When they are intransitive, they have no passive forms.

Active	*Passive*
Transitive: A local celebrity **started** the race.	The race **was started** by a local celebrity.
Intransitive: My class **starts** on Tuesday.	*(no passive form)*

In addition, some transitive verbs, e.g., *become, consist of, cost, equal, fit, have, resemble,* and *suit,* have no passive forms.

Active	*Passive*
Transitive: She **resembles** her mother.	*(no passive form)*
Transitive: The toy **consists of** 10 parts.	*(no passive form)*

Changing Sentences from Active to Passive

Change these active sentences to passive sentences where possible. If a sentence cannot be changed, write *Can't be changed* and explain why.

1. The play begins at eight o'clock sharp.
   Can't be changed. "Begin" is intransitive in this sentence.
2. Police stopped three men who were driving a car through Oregon. *Three man were stopped by Police*
3. I had to laugh when he fell down. *Verb can not be follow (No change)*
4. That shirt really suits you! *Verb follow object (can't chang)*
5. Doctors always encourage their patients to exercise. *Patients are always encourage to exercise*
6. The accident surprised and scared my mother *was surprised & scared by the accident doctor*
7. The baby weighed seven pounds at birth. *(can't change)*
8. The nurse weighed the baby. *was weighed by nurse.*
9. I will be staying in a hotel on the Seine in Paris. *(can't change)*
10. By this time next year, we'll have upgraded all of the office computers. *By this time next year, all the office computers will have been upgraded*
11. Real estate in Manhattan costs a lot. *(No change)*
12. In fact, they could solve the problem. *In fact, the problem could be solved by them*
13. They are going to open an investigation early next year. *An investigation is going to be opened early next year*
14. We may have to talk about this problem later. *This Problem may have to be talked by latter by us*
15. Everyone in the room suddenly became aware of the strange shadow. *(can't change)*

Omitting or Including Agents

Change the underlined sentences in each paragraph to the passive voice. Decide whether to include or omit the agent if there is one. Be prepared to explain your decisions.

1. <u>They identified Mount Everest as the world's highest mountain in 1852.</u> It wasn't until 1953, however, that the New Zealander Sir Edmund Hillary and the Nepalese Sherpa Tenzing Norgay reached the summit of the mountain. Previously, several British teams had made attempts to climb to Everest's summit. <u>Unfortunately, bad weather and the dangers of the high altitude had turned all of these teams back.</u>

2. <u>In the United States, individual states issue drivers' licenses.</u> In most states, people must submit proof of identity and residency in order to obtain a license. <u>Most, but not all, states accept a passport, birth certificate, or a Social Security card as proof of identity.</u> However, some states require more than one form of identification.

3. <u>We don't know the identity of the inventors of many everyday objects.</u> For example, no one remembers the names of the inventors of the wheel or paper—if anyone ever knew them in the first place. <u>Even today, people overlook the identities of inventors of world-changing items like the microchip.</u>

4. The Internet has dramatically changed the way researchers gather information. <u>Researchers can find the answers to many basic questions through a simple web search. For more specific information, they can consult a variety of online databases.</u>

A. Work in pairs. Rewrite the sentences in the passive to describe how the Melissa Virus worked.

1. Someone programmed the Melissa Virus into a Word document.
2. Then this person uploaded the document to an Internet newsgroup.
3. People downloaded it from the newsgroup site because it looked important.
4. When people opened the document, it triggered the virus.
5. The virus created 50 new e-mails using the computer's address book.
6. The virus attached the document to these e-mails.
7. Then it sent the e-mails.
8. When people opened these new e-mails, the virus created 50 more e-mails.
9. It forwarded these 50 new virus-infected e-mails to 50 more people, and so on.
10. The virus overwhelmed e-mail systems, so companies had to shut them down.

B. Work in small groups. Choose one of the processes below and describe it. Use passive sentences where you want to focus on the receiver instead of the performer of the action. Think about whether or not you need to include the agent.

1. How a tire on a car is changed

   The correct equipment must be used. First the nuts on the wheel should be loosened with a wrench. Next the car needs to be raised off the ground. A jack can be used to do this . . .

2. How a favorite dish is prepared
3. How laundry is done
4. How a surprise party or wedding reception is planned
5. How a song is written
6. How weather is predicted

Usage Note: *Introducing New Information with* It

The passive can be used after *it* with various verbs to introduce an idea objectively. The *it* subject indicates that the belief, idea, or opinion is held by a group or by people in general, for example, *it is assumed that, it is believed that, it is considered that, it is expected that, it is known that, it is said that, it is reported that, it is thought that.*

It is believed that the candidate is winning. = People generally believe that . . .
It is reported that the company will shut down. = Journalists report that . . .

A. Rewrite the sentences using *it* subjects and passive reporting verbs. (Make sure you put the reporting verb in the correct tense.)

1. In the past, people believed that the Earth was flat.

   In the past, it was believed that the Earth was flat.

2. Journalists are reporting that tourism has increased in the region.

   _____

3. We know that pollution is affecting many rainforests around the world.

   _____

4. Research has shown that this drug decreases the desire to smoke cigarettes.

   _____

5. Previously, people had thought that the economy would recover quickly.

   _____

6. People assume that scientists will one day find a cure for cancer.

   _____

B. In small groups, discuss your knowledge, opinions, and beliefs about these topics. Then write as many sentences as you can, using *it* subjects and passive verbs. Use a variety of verbs in your sentences.

1. dinosaurs

   It is believed that dinosaurs were once the dominant form of life on Earth.

   It is thought that many early dinosaurs walked on two legs.

   It is known that several dinosaurs could fly . . .

2. the role of women in society

   _____

   _____

3. superstitions

   _____

   _____

4. care of the elderly

   _____

   _____

5. a healthy diet

   _____

   _____

6. outer space

   _____

   _____

Read each sentence and the statements that follow it. Choose the statement that best explains the meaning of the sentence.

1. Uniforms are required for all students at this school.
    a. The students require the uniform.
    b. The school requires the uniform.

2. It is thought that the ancient Egyptians had advanced knowledge of geometry.
    a. I think that the ancient Egyptians had advanced knowledge of geometry.
    b. People think that the ancient Egyptians had advanced knowledge of geometry.

3. This restaurant has been called one of the best in the city.
    a. People call this restaurant one of the best in the city.
    b. This restaurant calls itself one of the best in the city.

4. The researchers were asked to repeat the experiment.
    a. Someone asked the researchers to repeat the experiment.
    b. The researchers asked someone to repeat the experiment.

5. Her research paper was accepted for publication by the journal.
    a. A journal will publish her work.
    b. She will publish a journal.

6. We were told by the professor that we should leave our papers on his desk.
    a. The students told the professor that their papers were on his desk.
    b. The professor told the students to leave their papers on his desk.

B10 **Speaking**

A. Work in small groups. Choose a neighborhood that you all know. Think about these questions and take some notes.

1. How has the neighborhood changed in the past few years?
2. What is supposed to happen to the neighborhood in the next few years?
3. Are you happy or upset with the changes and plans? Why?
4. What would you like to see happen in the neighborhood?

    The neighborhood around our school

    The old bank was torn down two years ago. A new mall is supposed to be built on the site. We don't think a mall should be built. We have three in the city already. We think a park should be put in for the community . . .

B. Prepare a brief summary of your ideas and report back to the class. Use a variety of passive and active forms.

    The area around the school has changed significantly in the past few years. Several landmark buildings have been torn down . . .

C Writing

Editing: *The Passive*

Study the errors. Pay attention to the areas that you make mistakes in.

> 1. **Subject-verb agreement**
>
>   has
>   Only one of the articles ~~have~~ been discussed.
>
> 2. **Use of auxiliaries**
>
>   been
>   Several problems have not ∧ addressed by the committee yet.
>
> 3. **Use of verb form**
>
>   was
>   The child's homework ~~is~~ monitored by his parents last month.
>
> 4. **Placement of agent and receiver**
>
>   test   by the entire class.
>   The ~~entire class~~ was completed the ~~test~~.
>
> 5. **Word order**
>
>   been
>   Has ~~been~~ a date ∧ set for the next presentation?
>
> 6. **Parallel structure**
>
>   mailed
>   The contract must be signed, sealed, and ~~mail~~ by the end of the week.

C1 Editing

Correct the errors in the sentences. Be prepared to explain your answers.

                 has
1. One of the applicants ~~have~~ been placed on the waiting list.

2. Is this book been recommended for our class, or will it be required?

3. Many of the scientist's ideas should have not been dismissed by modern researchers.

4. The research team is now being collected the data.

5. The results of the survey not going to be mailed until next week.

6. The winners were awarded scholarships and gave positions as research assistants.

7. Only the top 10 percent of the class will be offer scholarships.

Beyond the Sentence: *Shifting Between Active and Passive to Keep the Focus*

Academic writing often shifts between the active and passive voice. This is done to insure a smooth flow of ideas from sentence to sentence.

Roberta Brown, currently a successful practicing attorney, **shudders** when she **recalls** her undergraduate courses. She **failed** most of her tests and **was able to pass** solely on the strength of her writing. Brown **had been awarded** a National Merit Scholarship in high school, so she **was surprised** by her inability to ace her college tests. "I expected to do really well in college, so I was devastated by my failure," she says.

Many college students experience similar difficulties when it comes to test-taking. As a result, testing **has been targeted** as a major area for development by the Education Council of America. "Students may have studied really hard, but their performance on a test may not reflect what they know," said a spokesperson for the group. To better serve students, the council is interviewing faculty and students across the country. The results of these interviews **are expected to inform** new kinds of assessment materials.

Some paragraphs largely focus on a single subject (e.g., one person, thing, or idea). This repeated subject begins many of the sentences. It is followed by an active or a passive verb depending on whether it is the performer or receiver of the action.

Some paragraphs change focus from one subject to another. When a new idea appears at the end of one sentence, it may make sense to make it the subject of the next sentence. This new subject is followed by an active or passive verb depending on whether it is the performer or receiver of the action.

C2 Keeping the Focus

Identical twins are the same sex, and they look alike. Scientists study them because they share the same DNA and the same upbringing. Work with a partner. Look at the two paragraphs about twin studies and answer the questions that follow.

A. Twin studies have been used by intelligence researchers since the time of Sir Francis Galton. They have often been employed to better understand the influence of environment versus genetics on personality traits and diseases. Today, the usefulness of these studies is being questioned by some scientists.

B. Twin studies have been used by intelligence researchers since the time of Sir Francis Galton. He was one of the first people to realize that studying twins could be scientifically useful. One of his methods was to study twins raised separately to see if they developed differently. In 1875, he published his results in a paper called, "The History of Twins."

1. Does the focus stay the same throughout the paragraph, or does it shift from one subject to another?

2. Look at the verbs in the second sentence of each paragraph. Are they active or passive voice? Explain why.

Look at the underlined active sentence in each passage. Decide whether or not the sentence should change to passive to improve the flow of information. If so, rewrite the sentence using the passive. If not, write *no*. Be prepared to explain your answer.

1. *no* In follow-up interviews, several students said they have had positive experiences in online courses. <u>Five out of seven actually preferred online courses.</u> Six of the respondents said online formats offered just as many opportunities to ask questions as real classrooms. *(Better in the active voice. The focus of the paragraph and sentence stays on the students.)*

2. ____ John Dewey was quite an original thinker. <u>Today, people recognize him as one of the founders of modern educational philosophy.</u>

3. ____ Filmmakers, writers, and other creative people often contribute to new ways of thinking about machines. <u>These artists and their work often inspire scientific research.</u> The makers of *Star Trek*, for example, predicted and may have inspired many medical advances.

4. ____ When B. F. Skinner failed as a creative writer, he decided to go into psychology. <u>Harvard University awarded Skinner a Ph.D. in 1931.</u> He then went on to found the school of psychology called Behaviorism.

5. ____ Much research claims that children do not benefit from large amounts of homework. <u>However, principals and even some parents expect homework to be a major part of the curriculum.</u>

C4 **Writing Tip:** *Writing in an Academic Tone*

> The passive voice is frequently used in academic writing. Academic writing often discusses general truths and ideas rather than the actions of people, so the passive is used to avoid general subjects. Academic writing also frequently describes results or processes involving things rather than people, so the passive is used to avoid unimportant, unknown, or obvious agents.

Choose one of the topics to write a short essay of two or three paragraphs. Pay attention to shifts in focus and choose active or passive verbs that improve the flow of ideas. Then, use the Writing Checklist to check your work.

- Changes in industry and culture have affected the way we eat. Write a description of how your grandparents' generation ate. How was food purchased, prepared, and eaten? What kinds of food were available? Then compare that description to how you eat today.

- How successfully are passengers processed through airports? Describe the current procedure that a passenger follows when entering the average airport. What safety precautions are taken? Is the passenger's comfort level considered? How does the process affect passengers and airport employees? What suggestions can you make to improve the experience? (You may also consider if the experience varies from country to country.)

- Many popular movies feature children as leading characters. How are children portrayed in popular entertainment? Describe a typical child character from a popular movie. Then evaluate whether you think this character is a good role model for children.

Writing Checklist

Reflect on your ability to use the passive by answering the questions.

☐ **1.** Did you use the passive to state an idea?

☐ **2.** Did you use the passive to talk about a process?

☐ **3.** Did you use the passive to keep the focus on a single subject?

☐ **4.** Did you use the passive to help keep the focus when changing subjects?

☐ **5.** Did you avoid overusing the passive?

☐ **6.** Did you check your sentences for correct verb phrases?

▶ Beyond the Classroom

Writing

Write an essay using one of these topics.

1. Think about a test experience that you had that was either positive or negative. Write two paragraphs. In the first paragraph, describe the test, what was tested, and how it was tested. In the second paragraph, write about the way you were affected by the test. Describe why the test was successful or unsuccessful and what you learned from it.

2. Write about one of your favorite characters in a book or movie. Write three paragraphs. First describe the character's background, his or her personality, and the challenge that the character faces during the course of the novel or film. In the second paragraph, describe how the character responds to the challenge and whether or not he or she is successful. Finally, describe why the character appeals to you.

Searching for Authentic Examples

Find examples of English grammar in everyday life by completing the task below.
Bring your examples to class, and be prepared to discuss them.

Look for examples of the passive in a textbook. Find three examples of passages in which the passive is used to shift focus and three examples in which the passive is used to maintain the same focus. Which examples were easier to find? Why do you think this was the case?

Nouns and Noun Modifiers

A Business Investment Worldwide: Costa Rica

 Before You Read

What do you know about Costa Rica? Choose your answers (more than one answer may be possible).

1. What activities can visitors to Costa Rica do?
   a. rafting   **b.** skiing   **c.** golfing   **d.** birdwatching
2. What are some products that Costa Rica is known for?
   a. gold   **b.** coffee   **c.** fish   **d.** cattle
3. What investment opportunities in Costa Rica do you think will be mentioned in the article?
   a. tourism   **b.** technology   **c.** education   **d.** finance

 Read

 Read this interview to find out about business opportunities in Costa Rica.

BUSINESS INVESTMENT WORLDWIDE: COSTA RICA

Part 2 of our series on investing in Latin America focuses on the growing business opportunities in Costa Rica. On a balmy evening in June, we sat down to talk with Mr. Ben Garcia from the Costa Rica Investment and Development Board (CINDE).

BUSINESS INVESTMENT WORLDWIDE: First of all, Mr. Garcia, what is the Costa Rica Investment and Development Board?

BEN GARCIA: It's just what the name says. CINDE is a nonprofit organization that provides **information** and gives advice to foreigners looking to invest in our country.

BIW: So, why should someone invest in Costa Rica? What are some of the **advantages**?

GARCIA: There are several reasons. First of all, our country is a peace-loving nation. Did you know that we have no armed forces—we operate without a military? Also, we have a strong education system and a healthy **democracy**. We support free trade. Our economy is built on a solid foundation and it's growing.

BIW: What exactly is the "solid foundation" you're talking about? Could you be more explicit?[1]

GARCIA: Traditionally, our economy was based on agriculture. We were known for our production of coffee, **bananas**, and

cattle. But things are different today.

BIW: How so?

GARCIA: Well, today our economy is strongly supported by **tourism**. People come from all over the world for scuba diving, golfing, white-water rafting, bird watching . . . . About the only thing you can't do in Costa Rica is go skiing.

BIW: And the natural habitat itself is a big draw for tourists, isn't it?

GARCIA: Yes, that's right. Many travelers come here to spend time in our extraordinary rainforests. The government has gone to great lengths[2] to protect our biodiversity:[3] You can see more than 600 **species** of birds as well as **monkeys**, turtles, and the famous three-toed sloth. So, the tourism sector definitely provides a phenomenal opportunity for investment.

BIW: What about investment opportunities in more traditional industries?

GARCIA: There are also opportunities in technology. We're encouraging high-tech industries to locate in Costa Rica, where they can take advantage of our computer-literate[4] and productive workforce.

BIW: OK, let's say I'm interested in learning more about investing in Costa Rica. What's the next **step** I should take?

GARCIA: I'd recommend that you do some research. You can contact our **organization** as well as the Costa Rican–American Chamber of Commerce (AMCHAM). After that, I'd recommend that you hop on a flight to San José and check out the business climate here firsthand. And take some time off to visit our beautiful, old cities and our lush, wild rainforests—you'll be glad you did!

---

1 **explicit:** clear and exact
2 **gone to great lengths:** made a great deal of effort
3 **biodiversity:** wide variety of plants and animals
4 **literate:** well-educated

(A3) After You Read

Discuss these questions.

1. What are the three areas of industry mentioned in the article?
2. How is Costa Rica's economy changing?
3. What did you learn about Costa Rica? Would you like to visit or invest there?

Examining Form

A. Work in pairs. Look at the highlighted nouns in the reading. Write them in the correct categories.

Singular: _____.

Plural: _____.

B. Look at the nouns you wrote in part A. Then answer these questions.

1. Do all the singular nouns have corresponding plural forms?
2. Do all the plural nouns have corresponding singular forms?
3. One of the words has the same form for both the singular and plural. Which word?

B Nouns

Examining Meaning and Use

Read each sentence and the statements that follow it. Check (✓) the statement that best describes the underlined words. Discuss your answers. Then read the notes to check them.

1. I read <u>a report about crime</u>. It was very disturbing.
   a. These nouns refer to the specific title of something.
   b. These nouns refer to things and ideas, but not to a specific name.

2. We give <u>advice</u> to <u>foreigners</u> who want to invest.
   a. The first noun can be counted individually; the second cannot.
   b. The second noun can be counted individually; the first cannot.

3. Let's install <u>a light</u> in the closet.
   a. This refers to light in general.
   b. This refers to a specific example.

Overview: Proper Nouns and Common Nouns

Proper Nouns	*Common Nouns*
Cambodia, "Over the Rainbow," *Of Mice and Men*, Cornell University	a house, some equipment, the president, things *(concrete)*
Tuesday, January 17th, British, Farsi, Christmas, Buddhism, the President of Egypt	accounting, confusion, dreams, information language, thoughts *(abstract)*

- **Proper nouns** are names of specific people, places, or things. Proper nouns always begin with capital letters. (Titles use capitals for all longer words. Short words like *and*, *of*, and *the* are not usually capitalized unless they are the first word of a title or name.)

- Proper nouns are usually singular and take singular verbs. This includes titles, names of organizations, and proper nouns ending in *-s*.

  <u>Of Mice and Men</u> **is** a novel by John Steinbeck.

  <u>The United Nations</u> **is** voting on proposed resolutions.

- All other nouns are **common nouns**. These also refer to people, places, or things, but not to specific names. Common nouns may be concrete (e.g., *house, equipment*) or they may be abstract (e.g., *confusion, thoughts*). Common nouns can be count or noncount.

Count Nouns

Singular Count Nouns		*Plural Count Nouns*
one job, one key, one party	⟶	two jobs, three keys, five parties
an audience, a committee, a jury *(collective)*	⟶	audiences, committees, juries
a child, a person, a tooth, a woman	⟶	children, people, teeth, women *(irregular plural)*
an aircraft, a deer, a fish	⟶	aircraft, deer, fish *(same plural)*
		jeans, savings, troops *(always plural)*

- **Count nouns** refer to things that can be counted individually. (They can be used with numbers.) Count nouns have both a singular and plural form.

- **Singular count nouns** are used with third-person singular verbs and pronouns. They always occur with *a / an / the* or other determiners (words that come before nouns such as *my, this, each*).

   <u>A party</u> **is** fun when you know the guests, but <u>it</u> can be boring when you don't.

- Some singular nouns are called **collective nouns**. They refer to groups of people or animals. Since collective nouns are countable, they have plural forms. Singular collective nouns are usually used with third-person singular verbs but take both singular and plural pronouns. One notable exception is *police*, which takes a plural verb.

   <u>The committee</u> **is meeting** next Tuesday. I don't know when **it'll/they'll** meet again.

   <u>The police</u> **help** the community in many important ways.

- **Plural count nouns** usually end in *-s* or *-es*. They are used with plural verbs and pronouns. Plural count nouns can occur with *the*, with other determiners (e.g. *my, these, some*), or alone.

   <u>Parties</u> **are** uncomfortable experiences for some people, but <u>they</u> can be fun for others.

- Some count nouns have irregular plural forms. Others have the same form for both singular and plural, or have only a plural form.

   For regular plural nouns, see pages A-11 and A-12.
   For irregular plural nouns, see pages A-12 and A-13.
   For collective nouns, see page A-13.

Here are some common noncount nouns and their categories.

Abstract nouns: advice, beauty, crime, fun, hate

Solids, such as food or materials: cheese, fruit, pasta, cotton, wool

Liquids: blood, cream, honey, milk, oil

Gases: air, oxygen, smoke, steam

Grains and powders: cereal, detergent, dust, flour, rice

Natural phenomena: electricity, gravity, humidity, weather

Areas of study: biology, dentistry, education, engineering, mathematics

Activities: camping, chess, football, gymnastics, reading

General categories: candy, clothing, education, equipment, food

- **Noncount nouns** cannot be counted individually or used with numbers. Noncount nouns don't have plural forms. They are used with third-person singular verbs and are replaced by the pronoun *it*.
- Some noncount nouns end in *-s* (e.g., *news, gymnastics, politics*). They are singular and still take third-person singular verbs.
- Noncount nouns can occur with *the*, with determiners (e.g., *my, this, some*), or alone.

    The news <u>is</u> disappointing.

    Do you have **insurance** for your **jewelry**?

    Pollution <u>is</u> a major problem in urban areas, but <u>it</u> <u>has been reduced</u> in many cities.

For more noncount nouns, see pages A-14 and A-15.

Count Meaning	*Noncount Meaning*
A **crime** was committed on my street.	Many people never think seriously about **crime**.
Why did I eat all those **chocolates**?	I don't like **chocolate**.
My citizenship **papers** arrived today!	More people use recycled **paper** these days.

- Many nouns have both count and noncount meanings. The count meaning of a noun typically refers to a particular example. The noncount meaning of a noun typically refers to something in general.

Making Noncount Nouns Countable

Expressions + of	*Containers* + of	*Measurements* + of
a piece of <u>advice</u>	**a glass of** <u>water</u>	**three feet of** <u>silk</u>
the sheet of <u>paper</u>	**the can of** <u>soda</u>	**two liters of** <u>orange juice</u>
a little bit of <u>honey</u>	**a box of** <u>detergent</u>	**four teaspoons of** <u>oregano</u>
the cloud of <u>smoke</u>	**the bag of** <u>popcorn</u>	**a gallon of** <u>milk</u>
two kinds of <u>ice</u>	**a pack of** <u>chewing gum</u>	**an ounce of** <u>perfume</u>

- You can talk about specific quantities of noncount nouns by using expressions with *of*. Many of these expressions use container or measurement words.
- If the expression is singular, then it is usually used with a third-person singular verb. If it is plural, it is usually used with a plural verb.

  The cloud of smoke <u>was</u> slowly <u>drifting</u> north.

  Two kinds of ice <u>are found</u> on Mars.

- These expressions can be followed by *the* or by determiners (e.g., *my, this, some*), or they may come directly before the noncount noun.

  <u>a bit of</u> **the chocolate**   <u>pieces of</u> **paper**

  <u>an item of</u> **your** dry cleaning.

- In addition to being used with noncount nouns, some phrases with *of* can be used with plural count nouns when the nouns refer to groups of things:

  two kinds of <u>nuts</u>   **a pile of** <u>papers</u>

  For expressions with of *for measuring and counting nouns, see pages A-15 and A-16.*

B1 Listening

A. 🎧 Each sentence in the passage is incomplete. Listen to the entire passage first. Then listen again and put a caret (∧) where you hear a missing word. Listen once more to fill in the missing words.

                years

For the past few ∧ , I've been visiting Costa Rica regularly for and for. My trips began

when I had to start there. At that time, I quickly tried to find about the Costa Rican

economy. It was only by, however, that I also found a perfect place for, relaxation, and fun.

B. 🎧 Listen. Choose the best answer to complete each conversation.

1. **a.** An education.
   b. Education.

2. **a.** It's an inquiry about opportunities in Costa Rica.
   b. *An Inquiry About Opportunities in Costa Rica.*

3. **a.** Four or five sheets.
   b. Four or five items.

4. **a.** Just a little bit.
   b. Just a few grains.

5. **a.** Yes, a paper.
   b. Yes, paper.

6. **a.** No, it's too hard on my ankles.
   b. No, they're too hard on my ankles.

Choose the best answer to complete each sentence.

1. Gymnastics (is / are) being offered at the local community center.
2. This bit of news (is / are) spreading all over the office.
3. Could you hand me (a / those) scissors, please?
4. In the '50s, many kinds of entertainment (was / were) replaced by watching TV.
5. The team (has been / have been) playing well since the beginning of the season.
6. You need four cups of (sugar / sugars) for this recipe.
7. The troops (is / are) being defeated by the enemy.
8. They really liked a couple of your (idea / ideas).
9. I think your help could really make a (difference / differences).
10. Your advice (was / were) helpful.
11. The group (takes off / take off) from O'Hare Airport.
12. Several bags of popcorn (have been / has been) spilled all over the theater.
13. There (is / are) a lot of calories in this recipe.
14. The police (don't / doesn't) know where he went.

B3 Using Different Types of Nouns

Complete the sentences with your own ideas. Use the noun type that is given.

1. They are very interested in English _____. They've studied it for years. (noncount)
2. The two _____ crossed the _____ with great difficulty. (count)
3. I really can't stand the summers in _____. (proper)
4. My brother has a nice _____ of friends. (collective)
5. Her _____ has not been good lately. (noncount)
6. The _____ had extraordinarily large _____. (count)
7. I really enjoy reading _____ when I can. (proper)
8. The _____ can't seem to make a good decision. (collective)
9. He didn't have the _____ to finish the project. (noncount)
10. I want to spend a lot of time near my _____ this winter. (count)
11. They are taking a class called _____ at _____ this semester. (proper)
12. The _____ is losing a lot of money this year. (collective)

A. Read the career description for sports equipment designers. Decide how each underlined noun is used. Write *C* above the noun if it is a count noun and *N* if it is a noncount noun.

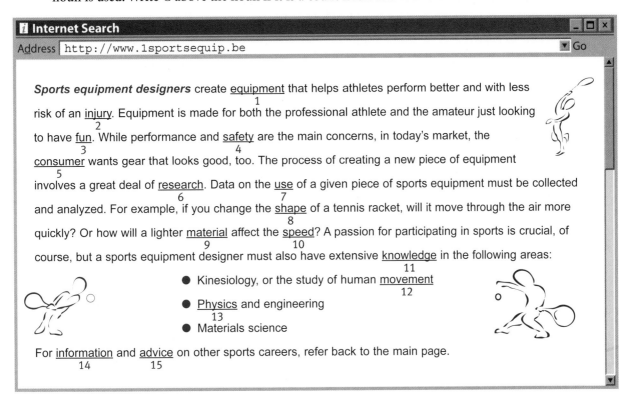

Internet Search   _ □ ×

Address `http://www.1sportsequip.be`   ▼ Go

Sports equipment designers create <u>equipment</u> that helps athletes perform better and with less
                                         1

risk of an <u>injury</u>. Equipment is made for both the professional athlete and the amateur just looking
        2

to have <u>fun</u>. While performance and <u>safety</u> are the main concerns, in today's market, the
     3   4

<u>consumer</u> wants gear that looks good, too. The process of creating a new piece of equipment
 5

involves a great deal of <u>research</u>. Data on the <u>use</u> of a given piece of sports equipment must be collected
                 6   7

and analyzed. For example, if you change the <u>shape</u> of a tennis racket, will it move through the air more
                                    8

quickly? Or how will a lighter <u>material</u> affect the <u>speed</u>? A passion for participating in sports is crucial, of
                      9   10

course, but a sports equipment designer must also have extensive <u>knowledge</u> in the following areas:
                                              11

● Kinesiology, or the study of human <u>movement</u>
                              12

● <u>Physics</u> and engineering
   13

● Materials science

For <u>information</u> and <u>advice</u> on other sports careers, refer back to the main page.
   14   15

B. These nouns have both count and noncount meanings. Read each sentence pair. Write *C* if the underlined noun is a count noun. Write *N* if it is a noncount noun.

1. ____ **a.** <u>Freedom</u> means different things to different people.

    ____ **b.** Free speech is a <u>freedom</u> which many people in the United States take for granted.

2. ____ **a.** The <u>light</u> on the corner of Fifth and Main hasn't been functioning.

    ____ **b.** The way <u>light</u> traveled through space was once a great mystery.

3. ____ **a.** Psychology is the study of the human mind and <u>behavior</u>.

    ____ **b.** Smoking is a <u>behavior</u> that develops over time.

4. ____ **a.** The new <u>democracy</u> will need help to succeed.

    ____ **b.** He left his country because he believes in <u>democracy</u>.

5. ____ **a.** It's against the <u>law</u> to ride your bike on the highway.

    ____ **b.** My local congressman is trying to pass a new <u>law</u> to control street noise.

C. Choose five nouns below and write two sentences for each word: one using the count meaning and one using the noncount meaning.

coffee	education	experience	fish	life
pizza	religion	space	television	time

B5 Using Expressions with *Of*

A. How many logical phrases can you make? Use phrases and words from each line.

a piece of, a pile of, a sheet of, an item of

clothing, ice, mail, music, news, paper

a piece of paper

B. Complete the sentences. Use the singular or plural form of the words in the box + *of*.

branch ✓	bunch	flash	game	liter
pair	period	pinch	pot	set

1. He's interested in studying one of the newer _____*branches of*_____ medicine, like genetics.

2. I made you another _____ keys to replace the ones you lost.

3. I brought a few _____ grapes to snack on.

4. This tastes pretty good, but I think it could use a _____ salt.

5. I'm just making a fresh _____ coffee. Would you like some?

6. We had to play several _____ chess before I won.

7. That _____ lightning startled me!

B6 Subject-Verb Agreement with Nouns

Complete the excerpts from magazine and news articles. Use the correct form of the verbs in parentheses.

1. Over the past 50 years, the United States _____ (have) had a troubled political relationship with Cuba. However, this period of hostility _____ (seem) like it could be ending. A report in the *New York Times* _____ (explain) how economics _____ (be) helping.

2. Spenser University's football team _____ (have) lost a record 50 games in a row. The university _____ (want) to keep the team, but at least one group _____ (think) otherwise. It argues that sports _____ (be) not important and that the money _____ (be) being wasted.

3. Some environmentalists believe that the issue of global warming _____ (be) unsolvable. They say that statistics _____ (show) that we have done irreparable damage to the Earth. However, several pieces of research _____ (have) shown that there is hope—if we act now. While many different kinds of pollution _____ (threaten) the Earth's natural environment, their effects are reversible.

C Noun Modifiers

Examining Meaning and Use

Read each sentence and complete the statement that follows it. Discuss your answers. Then read the notes to check them.

1. Do you have a battery-operated radio? The question is about a type of . . .
   - **a.** battery
   - **b.** radio
2. The man had only 100-dollar bills in his wallet. He had . . .
   - **a.** more than 100 dollars
   - **b.** exactly 100 dollars
3. She bought a lamp for a table. The lamp is a . . .
   - **a.** table lamp
   - **b.** lamp table
4. Dr. Kay's poems are well known. This refers to . . .
   - **a.** the poems of Dr. Kay
   - **b.** poems about Dr. Kay

Adjective and Noun Modifiers

Quality/Opinion	Size	Age	Shape	Color	Origin	Material	Kind/Purpose	Noun
	large		round				conference	table
stylish				black			running	shoes
beautiful		old			Japanese	ceramic		bowl

- Nouns can be modified (or described) by adjectives or other nouns. Modifiers usually come immediately before the nouns they describe.
- If two or more modifiers come before a noun, they usually follow the order above. Most modifiers are adjectives. The modifiers of *material* and *kind / purpose* are often nouns.
- Native speakers rarely use more than three or four modifiers before a noun.
- Sometimes more than one adjective from certain categories is used before a noun. When that happens, the adjectives must be separated by either a comma or *and*. With adjectives describing colors or materials, separate the adjectives with *and*. With adjectives describing qualities or opinions, use a comma or *and*.

   My homepage has a unique **black and white** design. *(color)*

   I just bought a new **glass and metal** table. *(material)*

   She is a **kind, helpful** person. / She is a **kind and helpful** person. *(quality)*

He ran a **five-mile** <u>race</u>. *(The length of the race was five miles.)*
This sales job requires a **high-energy** <u>person</u>.
Chocolate-covered <u>peanuts</u> are my favorite candy.
I know a lot of **open-minded** <u>people</u>.

- Compound modifiers are two or more descriptive words put together to present information in a compact form instead of in a longer phrase. They function as adjectives before nouns in the same way as other adjective or noun modifiers.
- Compound modifiers are often made up of these combinations:
  number + noun: a **five-mile** race, a **two-man** tent, **hundred-dollar** bills
  adjective + noun: **high-energy** drink, a **stainless-steel** pipe, **big-time** politicians
  adjective/adverb + participle: an **unusual-looking** woman, a **far-reaching** decision
  adjective + noun + -ed: an **open-minded** person, a **three-legged** donkey
  noun + participle: **chocolate-covered** peanuts, an **awe-inspiring** view
- Compound modifiers are usually spelled with hyphens when they come before nouns.
- The *-ed* ending is added to adjective and noun combinations that relate to characteristics of people, animals, or objects.
- Plural nouns in compound modifiers become singular. This most often occurs in modifiers with numbers.
  * He ran a five-miles race. (INCORRECT)

Count Nouns	*Noncount Nouns*
credit card, bookstore, baby-sitter	scuba diving, data processing
washing machine, swimming pool	dry cleaning, old age, takeout

- Compound nouns are two or more words put together to present information in a more compact form. They function as single nouns with unique meanings.
- Many compound nouns are two nouns or an adjective + a noun. The first word describes the second word, which is the head or main noun. If the first word is a noun, it is almost always singular.
- Compound nouns can also consist of a verb + preposition or particle.
- Some compound nouns are spelled with hyphens. Others are spelled as one word.
- A compound noun can usually be made plural if the head noun is countable. If the head noun is noncount, the compound noun usually has no plural form.
  credit **cards**, washing **machines**   * scuba divings, * dry cleanings (INCORRECT)

Nouns Followed by the Preposition of
a <u>list</u> **of complaints** *(= a list consisting of complaints)*
a <u>story</u> **of courage** *(= a story about courage)*
the <u>Science section</u> **of the** *Times (= the Science section that is part of the* Times*)*
the <u>wealth</u> **of the company** *(= the wealth that belongs to the company)*
the <u>essays</u> **of Mark Twain** *(= the essays created by Mark Twain)*
the <u>production</u> **of energy** *(= the act of producing energy)*
the <u>success</u> **of the movie** *(= the success resulting from the movie)*

Nouns Followed by Other Prepositions
to: <u>damage</u> **to the building**, <u>answers</u> **to the question**, the <u>road</u> **to Chicago**
for: <u>scholarships</u> **for students**, the <u>search</u> **for extraterrestrial life**
on: a <u>tax</u> **on gas**, a <u>reliance</u> **on scientific theory**
with: <u>photos</u> **with captions**, the <u>girl</u> **with red hair**, an <u>argument</u> **with my sister**
about: <u>a book</u> **about insects**, <u>doubt</u> **about the future**
in: <u>interest</u> **in the future**, <u>belief</u> **in democracy**, <u>talent</u> **in art**
against: <u>an argument</u> **against taxes**, <u>a reaction</u> **against the past**

- Prepositional phrases that follow nouns modify them by making their meanings more specific in many different ways. They are most often used with inanimate nouns. Phrases beginning with *of* are the most common.
- Some nouns are modified by prepositions other than *of*.
- Prepositional phrases with *of* that show belonging or who created something can often be expressed with the possessive *'s* instead.

  the company's wealth   the movie's success   Mark Twain's essays

Listening

A. 🎧 Each sentence in the passage is incomplete. Listen to the entire passage first. Then listen again and put a caret (^) where you hear a missing word. Listen once more to fill in the missing words.

    air quality
Poor ^^ is one of the major problems well-insulated. Fortunately, a solution is. Studies show

that help clean air. They remove and add oxygen. Plants fuzzy leaves may also remove smoke and

grease particles.

C1 **B.** 🎧 **Listen. Choose the best answer to complete each conversation.**

1. **a.** What floor is it on?
   b. How many rooms does it have?

2. **a.** In the boathouse.
   b. In the houseboat.

3. **a.** About arthritis?
   b. For arthritis?

4. **a.** The curly-haired one.
   b. The curly hair.

5. **a.** Was it on sale?
   b. What shape is it?

6. **a.** No, does it really produce tests?
   b. No, does it really test generators?

C2 ## Using Adjective and Noun Modifiers

A. Read these four excerpts. Put the words in parentheses in the correct order. Where do you think these excerpts come from?

1. Seeking a _____ (CEO / tall / handsome) type. I'm a
   _____ (fun-loving / teacher / English / petite) who likes
   the outdoors.

2. On sale: _____ (three-ringed / binders / multi-colored / plastic)
   and _____ (paper / legal-sized / extra-bright).

3. Police are looking for a _____ (young / Caucasian / stocky / man)
   wearing a _____ (wool / black-and-white / distinctive) cap.

4. The good witch waved her wand and suddenly Cinderella's ragged dress was transformed
   into a _____ (long / gown / diamond-studded / green).

B. Write your own excerpts from one of these sources. Use adjective and noun modifiers in your writing where possible.

personal ad	office supply catalog	police report	fairy tale

_____

_____

_____

Working on Compound Modifiers

A. Rewrite each phrase using a compound modifier.

    1. an apartment on the first floor = _a first-floor apartment_ _____

    2. a presentation that takes 15 minutes = _____

    3. a commitment for a long term = _____

    4. a business owned by a family = _____

    5. a street that runs two ways = _____

    6. an instruction booklet with 18 pages = _____

    7. a loan for a small business = _____

    8. a discount ticket for 10 dollars = _____

    9. a wild animal that looks strange = _____

    10. the college that is known best = _____

    11. a diamond that is two karats = _____

    12. an artist who is famous around the world = _____

B. Write sentences with five of the compound modifiers.

I wouldn't rent a first-floor apartment. They don't get enough sunlight during the day.

C4 **Recognizing Adjectives vs. Compound Modifiers**

These sentences each contain several adjectives and/or compound modifiers. Read each
sentence. Add a comma (,), *and*, or a hyphen (-) where needed. If the sentence is OK, write *OK*.

  1. These days, computer ˄ generated animation looks more and more realistic.

  2. The watch had a very unusual ˄*and* elegant design.

  3. The prize winning film was a Spanish movie called *The Sea Inside.*

  4. My aunt has a couple of miniature toy dogs.

  5. The group of skiers was caught in an unexpected powerful avalanche.

  6. The lamp was made of a strange looking yellow plastic.

  7. This surprising new medical discovery could save many lives.

  8. Beth is the most hardworking supportive helpful volunteer we have.

  9. The wings on the butterfly were a beautiful light green color.

10. I saw an interesting new French film last night.

11. I just found a cool leather chrome chair at the thrift store.

12. Some loud mouthed guy interrupted the politician's speech.

A. Circle the compound nouns in these sentences. (Each sentence contains at least one.)

1. Meet me at the (drugstore) across from the (movie theater).
2. As an actor or writer, it's nearly impossible to break into show business.
3. Global warming is largely caused by the burning of fossil fuels.
4. I love scuba diving in Aruba. The coral is beautiful.
5. My cousin John is a security guard at a local bank.
6. I was marked down for handing in homework late.
7. You'll need your flashlight and sleeping bag for the camping trip.
8. I'm trying not to eat a lot of junk food, like French fries and sugary desserts.

B. Read the sentences. Match words from each box to make the compound noun that the sentence describes. (The spaces show you if the compound is one word, two words, or hyphenated.)

common	death	food	attack ✓	house	up
green	heart ✓	sit	order	out	penalty
mail	solar	storage	poisoning	sense	system
take			unit		

1. Doctors recommend that patients take aspirin to help prevent this health problem.
   _____*heart*_____ _____*attack*_____

2. If you don't like to cook, you probably get a lot of this. _____

3. Even in winter, you can grow things in a _____.

4. I really need to get a _____ _____. I have too much stuff.

5. If you do foolish things, you probably don't have a lot of this. _____
   _____

6. Many people oppose this kind of severe punishment. _____ _____

7. If you eat bad sushi, you may get this illness. _____ _____

8. Our planet's _____ _____ is part of the Milky Way galaxy.

9. Some people don't like to go to stores. They prefer to shop this way. _____
   _____

10. An exercise for strengthening abdominal muscles is a _____ _____.

C. Choose six compound nouns from parts A and B. Try to write a paragraph using all six nouns. Be creative.

I work as a <u>security guard</u> *in a small* <u>drugstore</u>. *Late one evening, I was taking a break and eating some* <u>junk food</u> *in the back of the store when the lights went out. Surprised, I got out my* <u>flashlight</u> *and started walking toward the front of the store . . .*

C6

A. Use the correct prepositions from the box to complete the sentences.

for	in	of ✓	of	of
of	of	on	to	with

1. I was stunned by the beauty _____*of*_____ the landscape.

2. There has been a decrease _____ the rate of crime.

3. He had written his address on the back _____ the envelope.

4. I'm very lucky to have the support _____ my parents.

5. I did not like her reply _____ my question.

6. My mother has never gotten over her fear_____ flying.

7. Someday medical researchers will find a cure _____ cancer.

8. The paintings _____ Picasso have always confused me.

9. Lydia had a date _____ a new guy last night.

10. We have to reduce our reliance _____ oil and oil products.

B. Which sentences can easily be rewritten using a possessive *'s* instead? Rewrite the sentences.

C. Complete these sentences using your own ideas.

1. I have an interest in _____.

2. _____ could be the cause of _____.

3. I couldn't believe the reaction to _____.

4. I really don't like people with _____.

5. I think the solution to _____ is _____.

D. Compare your answers with a partner. Ask follow-up questions about your partner's statements.

A: I have an interest in art and music.
B: What kind of art do you like?

C7 **Using Modifiers Effectively**

These sentences use noun phrases that are too long. Rewrite the sentences. Replace the underlined phrases with noun compounds, possessives, or compound modifiers.

1. Robbers broke into the <u>house of the family named Smith</u> last night and stole the <u>computer belonging to the family</u>.

   Robbers broke into the Smith family's house last night and stole the family's computer.

2. A new <u>book about the history of the world</u> has been published by a <u>professor of history</u> from Oxford University.

3. The meeting is with the <u>chancellor of the university</u> and the <u>president of the government of the students</u>.

_____

4. The <u>Department of Journalism of the university</u> plans to hire several new <u>members of its faculty</u>.

_____

5. The <u>committee of the city council for public works</u> has approved a <u>facility costing one million dollars for the treatment of water</u>.

_____

C8 Working on Pronoun Agreement

A. Complete the sentences with the correct pronouns. If the pronoun refers to a modified noun, remember that it needs to agree with the head noun.

1. The committee is meeting next week. Then _____ will choose a committee head.

2. All the members of the team are strong athletes. I am sure _____ will do well.

3. I posted photos of the party online. You can see _____ when you log on later.

4. I need a 10-foot ladder to paint that wall. I want _____ to reach the ceiling.

5. The list of complaints is available to everyone. _____ can be picked up at the front desk.

6. The class was interesting. _____ had an interesting mix of people.

7. The reports about the war sounded troubling. I was disturbed to hear _____.

C9 Thinking About Meaning and Use

Read each sentence and choose the correct response.

1. I'll have a large coffee, please.
   ____ **a.** OK. Here's a large can.
   ____ **b.** Would you like anything else with that?

2. My sister Jane majored in economics when she was an undergraduate.
   ____ **a.** Did she enjoy studying it?
   ____ **b.** Where did she study them?

3. The company's earnings have increased in the past two months.
   ____ **a.** It's increased much more than expected.
   ____ **b.** They've increased almost 10 percent.

4. We only spoke very briefly, but she gave me some good advice.
   ____ **a.** Are they helping you?
   ____ **b.** Is it helping you?

5. This species of insect is pretty rare.

　　____ **a.** Where are they usually found?

　　____ **b.** What's its Latin name?

6. We'll need a five-foot ladder to reach the ceiling.

　　____ **a.** Why do you need so many?

　　____ **b.** Do you think that's high enough?

7. Did you watch any news broadcasts yesterday?

　　____ **a.** No, I missed them.

　　____ **b.** No, I missed it.

8. Has the success of the environmental group been recognized?

　　____ **a.** Yes, they have. In several articles.

　　____ **b.** Yes, it has. In several articles.

C10 Speaking

A. The 1989 *Oxford English Dictionary* defines a time capsule as "a container used to store for posterity a selection of objects thought to be representative of life at a particular time." What would you bury in a time capsule to represent your way of life today? Think about these and other categories:

- pictures of things
- pieces of memorabilia
- types of publications
- kinds of technology
- books of a particular author
- examples of entertainment

B. Join a partner. Compare your lists and discuss your choices. Say why you chose each thing. Agree on five items and share your ideas with the class

C. Now work with another partner. What would you each put in a time capsule to represent your own lives so far? Would the things be different from those you chose in part A? Take turns to find out the reasons for your partner's choice of objects.

A: I'd put a recording of my parents' voices in the time capsule.

B: That's interesting. Why?

A: So that in many years' time I'd be able to hear how they sounded, and let my children hear their grandparents' voices.

D Writing

Editing: *Nouns and Noun Modifiers*

Study the errors. Pay attention to the areas that you make mistakes in.

> **1. Use of noncount nouns**
>
> research
> I have followed her ~~researches~~ with great interest.
>
> **2. Use of compound nouns and modifiers**
>
> shoe
> On the way to work, I stopped at the ~~shoes~~ store.
>
> year
> I want to show you a picture of my five-~~years~~-old son.
>
> **3. Subject-verb agreement**
>
> was
> Collective noun: They told us that the group ~~were~~ waiting for us in the lab.
>
> is
> Noncount noun: Mathematics ~~are~~ a difficult subject for many people.
>
> is
> Noun + prepositional phrase: The gang of thieves ~~are~~ still at large.
>
> are
> Noun + *and/or* + noun: Education and crime ~~is~~ the big issues of this political campaign.

D1 Editing

Correct the errors in the passage. Be prepared to explain your answers.

A local conservation team have received a three-years grant to study the effects of urban development on local plant species. The first of the four phases have already been completed. The goal of phase one was to collect informations. Phase two can now begin. It will require researchers to categorize the data from phase one. Plant growth, soil, and air quality is the main categories the team seeks to examine. Phase three will measure changes in the plants, soil, and surrounding airs over time. The final phase will involve analysis of these changes. The analysis are going to be used to plan wildlife preserves.

Beyond the Sentence: *Avoiding Repetition Using Pronouns and Synonyms*

Writers often use pronouns and synonyms to avoid repetition and to maintain clarity.

Pronouns can replace previously mentioned nouns to avoid repetition. This is done when it is clear what noun is being referred to. (People = Everyone = They; a stamp = it; shipping = it.)

People pay attention when your hobby is stamp collecting. **Everyone** gets involved in your pastime. **They** make special trips to the local post office for you when they visit other countries. A stamp is an easy gift to bring back to someone. Or even better, **it** can just be sent home on a postcard. There is no additional charge for shipping; **it's** included in the price of the stamp!

The best part about being a **stamp collector** is you can call yourself a **philatelist**. This is just another way of saying stamp collector, but it sounds more impressive.

My favorite philatelist was my father. He tried to get me to collect when I was young, but it wasn't interesting to me then. Only after I inherited his four large **binders of stamps** did I realize the value of his hobby. My father's treasured **notebooks** have stamps from all over the world. When you look at **the stamps**, you can see not only personal memories of trips taken, but also history.

Do not overuse pronouns. In this sentence, the writer repeats "the stamps" instead of using "them." Otherwise, the reader would not know if the pronoun stands for notebooks or stamps.

The writer also uses synonym pairs (stamp collector / philatelist; binders of stamps / notebooks) to avoid repetition.

D2 Using Pronouns and Synonyms

Read these news items. Rewrite the paragraphs. Replace the underlined expressions with appropriate pronouns or synonyms.

1. The corporation's plan to develop a huge section of downtown is moving forward because the city council approved <u>the corporation's plan</u>, saying that <u>the section of downtown</u> was in urgent need of improvement.

   The corporation's plan to develop a huge section of downtown is moving forward because the city council approved <u>it</u>, saying that <u>the area</u> was . . .

2. The police raided several Internet cafés to gather evidence for their investigation. <u>The police</u> said <u>the evidence</u> would be used in an upcoming trial.

3. Famous fashion model Katie Krass will be throwing a huge party on the island of Ibiza to celebrate her upcoming wedding to rocker Johnnie Apples. <u>The huge party</u> will be held on Ibiza because <u>Katie Krass</u> loves Ibiza and because <u>Katie Krass</u> first met <u>rocker Johnnie Apples</u> on Ibiza.

4. It seems that a group of world-renowned scientists cannot agree on how many planets there are in our solar system. <u>The scientists</u> are meeting for a four-day conference in Belgium, where <u>the scientists</u> will spend <u>the four-day conference</u> discussing <u>how many planets there are</u>.

Adding details to your writing enables you to explain ideas more clearly and to paint a more vivid picture for your reader. This engages the reader and makes your writing more interesting.

Choose one of the topics to write a short essay of two or three paragraphs. Use details to explain how you feel about the topic. Then, use the Writing Checklist to check your work.

- Everyone has a favorite hobby or pastime. For some, it's a sport and for others, an area of study or a creative art. Write about a hobby or interest you have. Explain the different materials or equipment you use, how you do it, and what makes it interesting.
- Machines often make our lives easier. If you could invent a new machine to make your life easier, what would it be and why? Explain your invention. What are the different parts of your machine? Why is it useful? What materials is it made out of? What does it look like?

Writing Checklist

Reflect on your ability to use nouns and noun modifiers by answering the questions.

- ☐ **1.** Did you capitalize all proper nouns?
- ☐ **2.** Did you check for subject-verb agreement with nouns?
- ☐ **3.** Did you use plurals correctly with compound nouns and modifiers?
- ☐ **4.** Did you use synonyms and pronouns to avoid repetition?
- ☐ **5.** Did you use pronouns and antecedents clearly?
- ☐ **6.** Did you add details to your writing?

▶ Beyond the Classroom

Writing

Write an essay using one of these topics.

1. There is a saying, "There is a solution for every problem." Describe in detail a problem that exists in the world today. What do you feel are the causes of this problem? What do you think is the solution to this problem? Who needs to be involved in the solution to make it work?

2. We often go through life without really looking at things. We may walk past certain places every day, but never really notice that they are there. On your way home today, find something that you have paid little attention to in the past. This time, stop and look at it. What do you see? Try to describe it in complete detail. What does it feel like?

Searching for Authentic Examples

Find examples of English grammar in everyday life by completing the task below. Bring your examples to class, and be prepared to discuss them.

Browse the Internet for information about a country that you are interested in. Look for three examples each of compound nouns and adjectives. Can you paraphrase them using prepositional phrases or other types of expressions? Can you find any noncount nouns used with specific quantity expressions? Why do you think they were used?

Articles and Other Determiners

A Manifesto for a Livable City

A1 Before You Read

Think about the city you live in or one you know well. Discuss these questions.

What aspects of city living are satisfying? What are some problems with city living?
What would make your city a nicer place to live in (or more "livable")?

A2 Read

A *manifesto* is a public statement of intentions or ideas. People often write manifestos in reaction to an issue they feel strongly about. Read this excerpt from a manifesto about a livable city.

A MANIFESTO FOR A LIVABLE CITY

The **news** is often full of pessimistic[1] predictions about the future of our urban centers: The experts warn us of an increase in population and traffic congestion as well as a decrease in convenience and overall quality of life. It's certainly true that many **challenges** face us as our cities continue to grow in the 21st century. However, these challenges do not have to paralyze[2] us. By planning early, we can prevent many of the negative consequences.

We believe that we *can* make our city more livable, and we will present some of our **advice** and recommendations in this manifesto.

Key Idea #1: We support the development of strong, healthy neighborhoods. **Neighborhoods** are the backbone for the entire city. They are not only the places where we live, shop, and spend time with our families, but also sanctuaries[3] we retreat to for rejuvenation.[4] A **healthy neighborhood** should contain those amenities[5] that its **residents** truly need: restaurants, laundromats, cafés, and the like. To strengthen our neighborhoods, we propose the **construction** (or upgrade) of a **public park** and a public library in every neighborhood by 2012.

Key Idea #2: A more walkable city is a healthier city. You may have a car and drive to work every day, but you are also a pedestrian—we all are. We believe that the pedestrian needs to be protected and supported. To encourage **travel** on foot, **sidewalks** should be widened and trees need to be planted to make walking a more pleasurable experience. We also suggest building neighborhoods "up" rather than "out," which will result in areas of greater population density. More potential customers living in a smaller area will increase the **foot traffic** in local businesses and result in greater profits for those business owners.

Key Idea #3: It's expensive to live here. If we truly want our city to grow and prosper, we need to build more **affordable housing**. The city benefits enormously from having people of many economic levels living here: artists, business professionals, immigrant workers, families, and students. For that **trend** to continue,

housing prices must stabilize so that these people are able to stay here. We support an increase in the gas tax; the **revenues** earned from this tax can then be used to invest in the building of housing for all income levels.

We have a vision of our city as one that will welcome productive workers from all over this country and from overseas: a **city** that will not only cultivate[6] its economic base, but strengthen its communities as well; a city that will not lose its **friendly attitude** as the population swells in the coming decades, ushering in an era of new challenges. Won't you join us in this quest[7] for a better tomorrow?

---

1 **pessimistic:** having a negative attitude
2 **paralyze:** to make immobile or unable to take action
3 **sanctuary:** a safe place
4 **rejuvenation:** getting new life or energy

5 **amenity:** something provided for your use and convenience
6 **cultivate:** to develop
7 **quest:** a search for something; an undertaking

A3 **After You Read**

Discuss these questions.

1. What is the main idea presented in the manifesto?
2. In your own words, summarize the three key ideas in the excerpt.
3. Is the manifesto's overall tone positive or negative? How can you tell?
4. What other points would you add to this list of key ideas?

A. Work in pairs. Look at the highlighted nouns and adjectives + nouns in the reading. Which ones are preceded by *a / an, the,* or no article (Ø)? Which are preceded by other determiners (e.g., *my, this*)? Write them in the correct categories.

A / an _____

The _____

Ø _____

Other determiners _____

B. Which kinds of nouns follow the articles or determiners: singular count nouns, singular noncount nouns, or plural count nouns? Discuss your observations with the class. Refer to the notes on pages 115–116 and 120 if you need to.

Indefinite and Definite Articles

Examining Meaning and Use

Read each sentence and the statements that follow it. Check (✓) the correct statement. Discuss your answers. Then read the notes to check them.

1. A *manifesto* is a public statement of ideas.
    ____ **a.** This sentence describes what a manifesto is.
    ____ **b.** This sentence identifies a specific manifesto.

2. I'm looking for a new cell phone, but I don't know what kind to buy.
    ____ **a.** The speaker has a specific phone in mind.
    ____ **b.** The speaker doesn't have a specific phone in mind.

3. I looked at a very affordable apartment yesterday.
    ____ **a.** The speaker has a specific apartment in mind.
    ____ **b.** The listener has a specific apartment in mind.

4. If you go out tonight, don't forget to lock the door.
    ____ **a.** The speaker and the listener have a specific door in mind.
    ____ **b.** Only the speaker has a specific door in mind.

Singular Count Nouns

It's **a story** about small-town America.

It's **the story** of my childhood in small-town America.

Plural Count Nouns

There are **(Ø) policemen** downstairs. What's going on?

Even **the policemen** have no idea what happened.

Noncount Nouns

He really needs **(Ø) advice** if he's going to succeed.

He never listens to **the advice** I give him.

- Articles and other determiners are used to introduce, describe, and classify common nouns. They come immediately before a noun or an adjective + a noun.

  a <u>story</u>   **an** <u>interesting story</u>

- **Singular count nouns** must always occur with *a / an / the* or other determiners (e.g., *this, my, Tom's*). They cannot occur alone.

- **Plural count nouns and all noncount nouns** can occur alone (Ø), with *the* or with other determiners (e.g., *this, my, Tom's*).

- Indefinite articles *a / an* or no article (Ø) are used to classify a noun; they are used to say what kind of thing the noun is. The definite article, *the*, is used to identify or pick out a particular noun; it can often answer the question: *Which one(s)?*

  Dr. Lee is <u>a</u> professor. *(what kind)*   Dr. Lee is <u>the</u> professor I like most. *(which one)*

Singular Count Nouns

I heard **an interesting story** while I was at **a café** last night.
  (The listener doesn't know what story the speaker heard or what café he heard it in.)

Plural Count Nouns

I need to buy new **(Ø) shoes** and **(Ø) socks** before our next training session.
  (Neither the speaker nor the listener has specific shoes or socks in mind.)

Noncount Nouns

I don't have **(Ø) time** to play **(Ø) tennis** with you today.

- The indefinite articles *a / an* or no article (Ø) are used when the person you are speaking to (the listener) doesn't know the specific noun you are talking about. In some cases, the noun is not specific for the speaker either.

- Indefinite articles are often used to introduce nouns when they are first mentioned.

- *A / an* are never used with plural count nouns or noncount nouns. However, *some* and *any* often act like indefinite articles with plural count nouns or noncount nouns.

  I need to buy **some** new shoes and socks.   I don't have **any** time to play tennis.

You and the person you are speaking to know the specific noun you are talking about when . . .

it's been mentioned before: We attended <u>a lecture</u> on assertiveness in the workplace. **The lecture** was required for all employees.

I've had <u>some interesting discussions</u> with my advisor about my future. **The conversations** have really helped me.
(A synonym also becomes specific: discussions = conversations.)

you can see, hear, or easily identify it: **The traffic** <u>on Main Street</u> has never been worse.
The man <u>who is signing the books</u> is Frank Calloway.
Do you see **the icons** on **the screen**? Click on **the little folder**.
(A prepositional phrase, relative clause, or adjective may identify the noun.)

it's general knowledge: All employees attended a course on business ethics. **The instructor** gave everyone a quiz on values in the workplace. *(You can easily infer that the course has an instructor.)*

it's specific shared knowledge: **The boss** wants to meet us in **the conference room** at 10 A.M. *(The listener and speaker share information about their office.)*

it's a familiar noun: I had to see **the doctor** after I went to **the gym**. *(Names of certain people, places and things are easily understood.)*

it's unique (there is only one):   I tripped and scraped my knee on **the ground**.
Sign your name at **the bottom** of the page.

- The definite article *the* is used when both you and the person you are speaking to (the listener) know the specific noun you are talking about. The noun is specific because you can both identify it.

- Some examples of **familiar nouns** include: *the airport, the bank, the beach, the doctor, the government, the gym, the library, the mall, the movies, the office, the police, the radio, the store.*

- Some examples of **unique nouns** include: *the earth, the environment, the sun, the top, the middle, the bottom, the beginning, the end, the remaining, the rest.* Superlatives and ordinal numbers can also make a noun unique: <u>*the biggest*</u> *problem,* <u>*the highest*</u> *salary,* <u>*the first*</u> *time,* <u>*the second*</u> *planet.*

- Some proper nouns use the definite article.
  the Philippines   the United Nations   the King of Jordan   the Indian Ocean

For the definite article with certain proper nouns, see page A-17.
For the definite article with familiar and unique nouns, see page A-17.

Listening

A. 🎧 Each sentence in the passage is incomplete. Listen to the entire passage first. Then listen again and put a caret (^) where you hear a missing word. Listen once more to fill in the missing words, and correct the punctuation.

A recent

   ^Recent study of new housing in area shows that there are many barriers to building

affordable housing. Not only is there lack of government subsidies, but there is also

limited land for new construction in region. Developers need tax credits that lower debt

on construction projects. Subsidies allow them to offer lower rents to public, and as result,

affordable housing becomes reality.

B. 🎧 Listen. Choose the best sentence to complete each conversation.

1. **a.** Did you like the chicken?
   b. Did you like chicken?

2. **a.** What kind do you want?
   b. Which one do you want?

3. **a.** Which one?
   b. How does it look?

4. **a.** Call a bank.
   b. Call the bank.

5. **a.** It's the flower.
   b. It's a flower.

6. **a.** The kitchen.
   b. A kitchen.

B2 **Using *A / An* and *The***

Match the two parts to make logical sentences. Then add *a / an* or *the*.

1. We'll be arriving on __e__
2. I'm so tired of hearing ____
3. I got ____
4. I was surprised to hear that ____
5. I've never seen ____
6. I can't finish ____
7. We saw ____
8. I usually take ____
9. Working for ____
10. You can use ____

a. ____ big raise at work.

b. ____ Atlantic Ocean.

c. ____ same popular songs on the radio.

d. ____ walk before dinner.

e. __the__ last flight from Los Angeles.

f. ____ sad movie about an orphan last night.

g. ____ government was the best job I've ever had.

h. ____ director of the program resigned today.

i. ____ Swiss army knife for a variety of purposes. Do you own one?

j. ____ rest of this sandwich. Do you want it?

B3 Reasons for Using Specific Nouns

A. Complete each sentence with *a / an* or *the*.

1. Can you answer _____ phone? I'm busy at the moment.

2. **A:** How was your first history class?

   B: _____ teacher was absent, so we had _____ substitute teacher instead.

3. I'm sorry I missed you. I was at _____ bank when you called.

4. Can you believe it? They just bought _____ new home, but already there's _____ problem with _____ plumbing.

5. I saw _____ strange object flying across _____ sky. _____ object stopped overhead for _____ couple of seconds and then continued on its journey.

B. Why did you use *the* with each of the specific nouns in part A? Write the number of a reason below next to each specific noun above. (For some items, there may be more than one possible answer.) Then discuss your answers with a partner.

1. The noun was mentioned before.
2. The speaker and listener can see, hear, or easily identify it.
3. It's general knowledge that the speaker can easily infer.
4. The speaker and listener have specific shared knowledge.
5. It's a familiar noun.
6. It's a unique noun.

B4 Using Articles in Newspapers

A. Rewrite these newspaper headlines by inserting *a / an* or *the* where necessary. You will also have to change the verb forms. Then add a second sentence to give more information.

1. Pirates Sweep Tigers in Best-of-Six Series

   The Pirates have swept the Tigers in a best-of-six series. They started badly but quickly _____
   began to score. This is the first time since 1952 that the Pirates have beaten the Tigers. _____

2. City Council Will Hold Hearings on Latest Scandal

   _____

   _____

3. Major Summer Storm Will Hit Cayman Islands

   _____

   _____

4. Popular Tourist Destination Closes After Accident

   _____

   _____

B. Now look at this news article based on one of the headlines above. Complete the story with *a / an*, *the*, or no article (Ø).

Popular Tourist Destination Closes After Accident

(1) _____ popular tourist destination was closed after (2) _____ unfortunate accident on (3) _____ Friday morning. (4) _____ Smythe Beach, (5) _____ destination for (6) _____ approximately 2,000 visitors every weekend, was shut down when (7) _____ large ship carrying (8) _____ chemicals lost some of its cargo overboard. The spill occurred at 8:00 A.M. and by (9) _____ noon the police were blocking (10) _____ main road that leads to (11) _____ beach.

(12) _____ man who spoke to us on condition of anonymity said, "They're saying (13) _____ accident is (14) _____ small one, but I don't think so. A lot of chemicals went into (15) _____ water and it's going to be (16) _____ mess to clean up."

For each weekend that (17) _____ beach is closed, (18) _____ city loses (19) _____ hundreds of thousands of dollars, so (20) _____ mayor's office is currently investigating (21) _____ situation.

B5 Contrasting Articles

A. Complete the sentences with *a*, *an*, *the*, or no article (Ø).

1. I got _____ "F" on _____ final exam in my math course.

2. You should try and speak _____ language of _____ country that you're visiting.

3. We had _____ amazing meal with _____ friends. Then we went to _____ dance club.

4. In _____ very exciting match, _____ Italy won _____ World Cup.

5. My car needs _____ tune-up. Please check _____ brakes and add _____ quart of oil.

6. I left _____ car keys in _____ bedroom. Can you get them for me?

7. He's _____ banker, and he works in _____ office building downtown.

8. She has _____ long brown hair, and she usually wears it in _____ ponytail.

9. I think _____ Paris is _____ most romantic city in _____ world.

10. You have _____ wonderful laugh.

11. Is there _____ subway station near here?

12. _____ Brazil is _____ large country full of _____ contrasts.

B. Discuss your answers with a partner. Explain your choices.

Other Determiners; Generic Nouns

Examining Meaning and Use

Read each sentence and the statements that follow it. Check (✓) the correct statement. Discuss your answers. Then read the notes to check them.

1. Do you have those photos I sent you?
   ____ **a.** The speaker is pointing to the photos.
   ____ **b.** The speaker is thinking about the photos.

2. Cell phones have become a nuisance in public places.
   ____ **a.** This refers to particular cell phones.
   ____ **b.** This refers to all cell phones in general.

3. We gave them our help.
   ____ **a.** We helped them.
   ____ **b.** They helped us.

Other Determiners with Specific Nouns

Possessives Adjectives and Nouns

It's **your / Sue's responsibility** to answer any questions.

Their / Joe and Bill's fight lasted for over two weeks.

Demonstrative Adjectives

Look at **this ad**! What a great idea! *(near)*

Can you read **that sign**? The print is too small for me. *(far)*

We'll be reviewing **these two grammar points**: count and noncount nouns. *(about to be mentioned)*

Do you still have **those client files** I gave you last month? *(mentioned much earlier)*

- **Possessive adjectives** *(my, your, his, her, our, their, its)* and **possessive nouns** *(Sue's, Joe and Bill's)* can be used to identify a noun and make it specific. They show that someone owns, possesses, or is connected to a specific noun.

- **Demonstrative adjectives** can also be used to identify a noun and make it specific. They indicate distance from something (*this* and *these* = near; *that* and *those* = far). They are often used when both the listener and speaker can see the noun being discussed.

- *This / these* can refer back to something just mentioned or to something about to be mentioned—as if it were "near." *That / those* refer to something mentioned much earlier or an old idea from the past—as if it were "far."

For possessive adjectives and pronouns, see page A-16.
For demonstrative adjectives and pronouns, see page A-16.

Ø + *Plural Count Nouns or Noncount Nouns*
(**Ø**) **Kangaroos** carry their offspring in a pouch.
It is unfortunate that (**Ø**) **crime** cannot always be prevented.

A / an + *Singular Count Nouns*
A kangaroo carries its offspring in a pouch.
An adult needs an average of seven to eight hours of sleep a night.

The + *Singular Count Nouns*
The kangaroo carries its offspring in a pouch.
Modern-day communication has been greatly impacted by **the computer**.

- Sometimes a noun is used to refer to a whole class or group of people, places, or things. This is called a generic noun. It refers to something <u>in general</u>.
- Plural count nouns and noncount nouns with no article are the most common type of nouns used generically. Singular count nouns with *a / an* are also common. Singular count nouns with *the* are less common and usually sound more formal or technical.
- *The* with a plural noun is not used generically. It refers to specific plural nouns.
  The computers that our company donated are helping public schools in the area. (SPECIFIC)

C1 Listening

Listen. Choose the best sentence to complete each conversation.

1. **a.** The eagles.
   b. The eagle.

2. **a.** Yes, she announced the resignation an hour ago.
   b. Yes, she announced her resignation an hour ago.

3. **a.** Take these books out of the attic.
   b. Take those books out of the attic.

4. **a.** The arm.
   b. My arm.

5. **a.** Owls.
   b. An owl.

6. **a.** How can you see it from so far away?
   b. Why are you standing so close to it?

Read about the explorer Ernest Shackleton and his attempt to cross the South Pole. Wherever possible, replace *the* with a possessive adjective.

> *Men Wanted: for hazardous journey. Small wages, bitter cold, long months of complete darkness, constant danger, safe return doubtful. Honor and recognition in case of success.*
>
> *--Sir Ernest Shackleton*

In 1914 Sir Ernest Shackleton placed this ad in a newspaper. He was looking for recruits for ~~the~~ *his* expedition to **the** South Pole. The crew and **the** ship, *The Endurance*, would sail to the South Pole, where they would use **the** dogs to attempt **the** world's first crossing of the Pole by foot. In the end, they never even made it to **the** Antarctic continent. **The** ship became frozen in ice in **the** Weddell Sea and **the** hull was crushed by **the** ice.

Using lifeboats, Shackleton and **the** crew sailed for seven days to Elephant Island. Later, Shackleton chose five men to sail one of **the** boats on to find help. Using primitive navigation equipment, they sailed for 17 days on **the** stormy seas and miraculously landed back where they had begun **the** journey—on **the** island of South Georgia.

But **the** story doesn't end there. Once on South Georgia Island, **the** six men hiked over glaciers and towering mountains to get help from a whaling station. They then sailed back to Elephant Island to rescue **the** remaining men. Twenty-two months had passed since they had left on **the** expedition.

The next time you are complaining because **the** airplane has been delayed for a few hours, remember that **the** inconvenience is nothing compared to what Shackleton and **the** men experienced!

C3 Using Demonstrative Adjectives to Identify Specific Nouns

A. Complete the sentences with *this, that, these,* and *those*.

1. Look at the boss's face. I can tell I'm not going to enjoy _____ meeting.

2. Do you remember _____ ugly pants you used to wear? The plaid ones? They're back in style!

3. Do you want to buy two tickets to tonight's game? Look. _____ seats are in the second row, so you'll be able to see all the action.

4. My computer has frozen again. If someone could help me solve _____ problem, I'd really appreciate it.

5. Did you find _____ book you were looking for?

6. When we get home, I need to move _____ boxes. Can you help me?

7. How was _____ play you went to last week?

8. _____ story begins when I started running in 1997. I read every book and article I could find about the sport.

B. Read about this immigration issue. Complete each sentence with *this, that, these,* or *those*. What are the two sides of the issue? Which person do you agree with?

The Situation: A large number of professionals are being hired overseas and brought to the United States to fill jobs in the high-tech industry.

1. We have many workers that are hired from overseas, and _____ foreign-born employees are good for our business. While Americans fill the majority of our jobs, the guest workers take _____ high-tech jobs that Americans are not qualified for. They work hard, and we should welcome them to _____ country with open arms.

2. Do you remember _____ strike that took place last year? It had a huge impact on _____ industry. American workers require a certain salary and union benefits, whereas _____ guest workers at Carlton will work for less money and fewer benefits. That's why the corporations like to hire them. All I can say is that _____ problem is going to worsen before it gets better. And in the meantime, many well-educated Americans can't find work in _____ field.

A. Choose the word that you think best completes the statement about a generic noun. Then write a follow-up sentence that gives specific information to support the statement.

1. Teachers are (overpaid / underpaid).

_____

_____

2. Overall, the cell phone has made our lives (better / worse).

_____

_____

3. Beauty is something that (can / can't) be bought.

_____

_____

4. Life is (usually / hardly ever) fair.

_____

_____

5. An air-conditioner (is / isn't) essential to survive the summer.

_____

_____

6. Cats are (more / less) loyal than dogs.

_____

_____

B. Write two statements for each pair of generic nouns. Then share your opinions with a partner.

1. pop-up ads on the Internet / TV commercials

   Pop-up ads on the Internet are annoying because they block your computer screen. TV commercials . . .

2. the English language / your native language

3. romantic love / arranged marriages

4. domestic travel / international travel

5. a movie star / a politician

6. good luck / bad luck

7. printed books / e-books

8. jogging / walking

A. Put the sentences in order to make a meaningful paragraph.

_____ Although <u>the factors</u> were changed, the employees' productivity appeared to increase each time a measurement was taken.

_2_ In 1927, Elton Mayo and two associates from the Harvard Business School decided to answer <u>this question</u>.

_____ The workers felt satisfaction because both the researchers and their supervisors had taken an interest in them, and because they had formed a sort of community with their co-workers during the course of the experiment.

_____ Before <u>the researchers</u> took a measurement, they changed a different physical factor in the plant that might affect productivity (such as increasing or decreasing the temperature, light, or noise level.)

_____ Mayo and <u>his colleagues</u> measured the productivity of a group of employees at the Hawthorne Works Electrical Plant in Illinois over a period of five years.

_1_ What physical conditions cause employees to be more productive?

_____ <u>This result</u>, now known as "The Hawthorne Effect," demonstrates that social factors are more important than physical factors in motivating employees.

_____ Surprised by <u>these results</u>, the researchers interviewed the workers and came to the following conclusion:

B. All of the underlined words are specific because they have been mentioned before. Explain what the underlined words refer to.

_2_ "this question" _refers to the question in sentence #1._____.

_____ "the factors" _____.

_____ "the researchers" _____.

_____ "his colleagues" _____.

_____ "this result" _____.

_____ "these results" _____.

Read each sentence and the statements that follow it. Write *T* if the statement is true and *F* if it is false. Then discuss your answers in small groups.

1. "The customer is always right" is the company policy.
   ____ **a.** "The customer" means all customers in general.
   ____ **b.** "The company" means all companies in general.

2. Mr. Jones is with a client. Can I take a message?
   ____ **a.** Mr. Jones probably has only one client.
   ____ **b.** The listener does not know which client Mr. Jones is with.

3. The interviews will be held in the conference room.
   ____ **a.** This is the first time the listener has heard about the interviews.
   ____ **b.** There is only one conference room.

4. The vice president wants to interview the candidates himself.
   ____ **a.** Every candidate will be interviewed by the vice president.
   ____ **b.** There are several vice presidents at this company.

5. A counselor recommended taking the business ethics class.
   ____ **a.** There is only one business ethics class.
   ____ **b.** The listener knows which counselor the speaker is referring to.

6. An interview can be a stressful experience for both the interviewee and the interviewer.
   ____ **a.** "An interview" is referring to a specific interview.
   ____ **b.** "An interviewee" is referring to a specific person.

C7 **Speaking**

A. Work with a partner. What are some positive and negative aspects of living and studying in a foreign country?

The custom of tipping so much is hard to get used to.

It's easy to get lost in foreign cities.

I don't like the way . . .

People are usually friendly and helpful.

A student can be really independent— there are fewer rules.

It's your responsibility to . . .

B. What advice would you give a student who is going to study in a foreign country? Make a list of four or five tips and then share your list with the class.

Writing

Editing: *Articles and Determiners*

Study the errors. Pay attention to the areas that you make mistakes in.

---

1. **Use of indefinite article**

                   a   a
   It is important to research ∧ company before applying for ∧ job there.

               Ø
   Always wear ~~an~~ ∧ appropriate clothing when applying for a job.

2. **Use of *the* before specific noun and *a / an* before nonspecific noun**

                            a
   Last year, I traveled to Egypt with ~~the~~ group of students.

                     the
   The person planning ~~a~~ ∧ trip gave us a reading list.

3. **Use of possessive adjective**

                                     your
   When you play soccer, don't touch the ball with ~~the~~ hands.

4. **Use of definite article**

                               the
   Have you ever been to the top of ∧ Empire State Building?

               the
   Welcome to ∧ city of New York. We hope you enjoy your stay here.

D1 **Editing**

Correct the errors in the passage. Be prepared to explain your answers.

                                                                 a
    Before leaving on my trip, I read *The Global Wanderer's Guide to Egypt,* ~~the~~ useful guide to visiting that country. The first part of the book gives a practical tips on traveling within Egypt. For example, travelers are told where to collect their bags at an airport and given directions on how to get to Pyramids outside city of Giza. Other tips are directed at keeping healthy and comfortable: The book recommends carrying bottle of water when touring in the heat and gives an advice on where to have tea in the afternoon. A last part of the book deals with customs. For example, it reminds people that they must take off the shoes before they enter a mosque. I highly recommend that you read this book before you plan the trip to Egypt.

Beyond the Sentence: *Simplifying Previously Mentioned Information and Inferring Knowledge*

Previously mentioned information is progressively simplified when it is referred back to. In this case, the noun phrase "a series of serious hurricanes" is introduced with the indefinite article. Then it is shortened and referred to with the definite article + a synonym: "the storms". Finally, "the storms" is replaced with the pronoun "they".

It is rare that **a series of serious hurricanes** hits the same area in the same season, but this can happen. **The storms** that hit the U.S. state of Florida in 2004 caused millions of dollars in damage and killed over 70 people. **They** were devastating to the region. The most obvious damage a hurricane does is the physical destruction, but it is often the psychological damage that does more harm.

The psychological damage caused when Hurricane Katrina hit the United States in 2005 was readily visible in newspaper headlines and photographs. When **the extent of the destruction** became clear in **the aftermath of the storm**, **the nation** suffered a collective sense of grief for **the victims**. Even now, many unanswered questions remain regarding what happened to those trapped by the storm, and how they were treated.

The definite article is used to refer to specific nouns that can be inferred from the main topic. In this case, it is easily understood that "the extent of the destruction", "the aftermath of the storm," "the nation," and "the victims" all refer to things connected to Hurricane Katrina.

D2 Using Articles and Pronouns

A. Choose the best articles to complete the sentences. Then complete the passages, first with an appropriate noun and then a pronoun.

1. (The / Ø) Republic of India is known not only for its beauty, but also for its vastness and diversity. _____*The country*_____ measures almost 1.3 million square meters, with a coastline of over 7,000 kilometers. _____*It*_____ has extremely varied geographical features ranging from scorching deserts to snowy mountains. As a result, (Ø / the) climate varies from tropical in the south to temperate in the north.

2. The city of Mumbai may seem overwhelming to (the / Ø) visitors at first. _____, located on (Ø / the) west coast, is (a / the) commercial and entertainment capital of India. _____ is also (a / the) most populous city. Recently, (the / Ø) population was reported to be more than 13 million.

3. The people of India speak many different languages. Although there are 15 official languages, _____ can speak countless other languages and dialects. For (the / Ø) national, political, and commercial communication, however, _____ usually speak English or Hindi.

4. The Taj Mahal was built in the 17th century by (an / the) Indian emperor Shah Jahan as a tomb for his beloved wife, Mumtaz Mahal. _____ was built on (the / Ø) banks of (a / the) sacred Jumna River near the medieval city of Agra. _____ was built from white marble.

B. Write a short review of a restaurant, café, or movie theater that you like. Make a list of things you like about the place and why. When you write, think about how you should introduce the nouns. Should you use a definite or indefinite article? When can you use a pronoun or a definite article + synonym?

> *The Blue Parrot is <u>a restaurant</u> located downstairs on <u>a quiet block</u> of Smith Street. <u>The restaurant</u> is famous for its homemade pasta. However, many people do not know that <u>it</u> is becoming popular for another reason: <u>it</u> now features a DJ on Friday and Saturday nights.*

D3   **Writing Tip:** *Moving from General to Specific in Your Writing*

> Moving from general to specific information is a common pattern in academic writing. It may be used in the introduction to a paper or in presenting supporting ideas. When you write about a topic, organize your information from general to specific, and from abstract to concrete.

Choose one of the topics to write a short essay of two to three paragraphs. Talk about different ways that people interact with their environment. Then, use the Writing Checklist to check your work.

- What different types of transportation do people use where you are from? Why? What determines how they travel? Think about cost, distance, speed, comfort, etc. What do you think is the most efficient and useful type of transportation?
- People use plants in many ways: as decoration, as food, as medicine, and to provide urban "green spaces." What different ways of using plants do you know about? How are different plants used in your neighborhood and community?
- How does the climate affect life in your country? What types of severe weather can impact your country? What can be learned from past weather disasters?

Writing Checklist

Reflect on your ability to use articles by answering the questions.

☐ **1.** Did you use definite articles or other determiners with specific nouns?

☐ **2.** Did you use indefinite articles for nonspecific nouns?

☐ **3.** Did you use an article or determiner with all singular count nouns?

☐ **4.** Did you use articles correctly with generic nouns?

☐ **5.** Did you use definite articles with appropriate proper nouns?

☐ **6.** Did you use the correct pronouns, possessive adjectives or nouns, and demonstratives where appropriate?

 # Beyond the Classroom

Writing

Write an essay using one of these topics.

1. Environmentalists often call attention to endangered animal species to get support for their dire situation. Choose an endangered animal you think should be protected. Research and write a detailed report about the animal you have chosen. Where does the animal live? Why has it become endangered? What has been done to help protect it?

2. Different cultures have different ways of socializing, and often people's behavior is different in different places (for example, a neighborhood café versus a formal restaurant). Choose two places where people socialize. Describe how people behave in the two places. What behavior is similar? What behavior is different? Is one way of behaving more "natural" than the other?

Searching for Authentic Examples

Find examples of English grammar in everyday life by completing the task below. Bring your examples to class, and be prepared to discuss them.

Find a passage in a textbook. Choose one or two paragraphs and analyze the author's use of *a/an*, *the*, and no article (Ø). Explain why each was used. Does the passage contain any pronouns or definite articles + synonyms that refer to previously mentioned nouns?

Quantifiers

A Improving Lives One Click at a Time

A1 Before You Read

Discuss these questions.

How many hours per week do you use the Internet?

What are your main online activities?

How has e-mail affected your use of the telephone and regular mail?

A2 Read

Read this report to find out what adult e-mail users used to say about the Internet and other forms of communication.

Improving Lives One Click at a Time

Both men and women are spending **a great deal of** time online. What exactly are they doing? You may be surprised at **some of** the information we uncovered about computer habits. A recent Gallup poll finds that **almost all** e-mail users say that **both** e-mail (97%) and the Internet (96%) have made their lives better.

How many hours a week do you spend online?

The results of the poll show a wide range in the amount of time **each** user spends online. A typical e-mail user spends 7 to 8 hours online. (**A lot of** users spend fewer than 5 hours per week on the Internet, but some spend 20 hours or more.) There are **few** differences in the amount of time spent

on the Internet by gender or age.

What are your main online activities?

A majority of e-mail users (52%) say that sending and receiving e-mail is their most common online activity. **Some** (32%) spend their time online searching the Internet for information on topics that interest them. **Very few** (4%) spend **a lot of** time making financial transactions (such as buying products, paying bills, and checking financial accounts). **Hardly any** (2%) send and receive instant messages more often than they send e-mail or search for information.

Men and women differ somewhat in their online activity. A large number of women (61%) say that sending and receiving e-mail messages is the activity they do most when online. Fewer men (44%) say that e-mail is the most common online activity for them. For men, searching the Internet for information on topics of interest to them is nearly as common as sending e-mail. In contrast, only **some of** the women surveyed (23%) say searching for information is their most frequent online activity.

How has e-mail affected your use of the telephone and the U.S. mail?

Many people say they now use the telephone and regular mail less than they used to, and about one in five indicate they use the telephone and regular mail "much less frequently." Surprisingly, **quite a few** users (about one-third) say that e-mail has not decreased their use of the telephone or regular mail.

Despite the fact that e-mail messages are frequently used as alternatives[1] to telephone calls or U.S. mail, most e-mail users don't see it as indispensable.[2] When asked which of four communication modes they would be least willing to sacrifice,[3] users first say the telephone (63%), followed by the U.S. mail service (15%), e-mail (12%), and their cell phones (10%).

Adapted from: Gallup Poll: *Almost All E-Mail Users Say Internet, E-mail Have Made Lives Better,* July 23, 2001.

---

1 alternative: something that you can use instead of something else

2 indispensable: so important that it is impossible to exist without it

3 sacrifice: to give up something that is important

A3 **After You Read**

Discuss these questions.

1. Look at the three questions in the article. What is the majority response to each question?
2. How do your answers to the questions compare with the findings of the poll? Have things changed a lot since 2001? How are they the same? How are they different?

Examining Form

A. Work in pairs. Look at the highlighted quantifiers in the reading. Write them in the correct categories. (Include the accompanying noun when used.) Then answer the questions.

Quantifiers followed by count nouns _____

Quantifiers followed by noncount nouns _____

Quantifiers not followed by a noun _____

1. Are there any quantifiers that are used with both count nouns and noncount nouns?
2. Look at the quantifiers that stand alone (not followed by a noun) in the reading. Why is there no noun with these examples?

B. Discuss your observations with the class and refer to the notes on pages 134–136 and 140–141 if you need to.

B Quantifiers

Examining Meaning and Use

Read each sentence and the statements that follow it. Check (✓) the correct statement about the underlined words. Discuss your answers. Then read the notes to check them.

1. <u>Hardly any students</u> showed up for the review session.
    a. No students came.
    b. A few students came.
2. We have <u>little time</u> for cooking, so we eat out a lot.
    a. We usually don't have enough time for cooking.
    b. We do have some time for cooking, but not very much.
3. <u>Several people</u> called me yesterday.
    a. I received few phone calls.
    b. I received a lot of phone calls.
4. <u>A lot of teenagers</u> use instant messaging more than e-mail.
    a. This refers to a large number of teenagers in general.
    b. This refers to a large number of a specific group of teenagers.

Quantifiers Before Noncount Nouns or Plural Count Nouns (1)

Before Noncount Nouns

When I was a student, I spent
{
little
a little
a great deal of
a large amount of
(too) much
}
<u>time</u> on the computer.

Before Plural Count Nouns

Few
A few
Several
Quite a few
A large number of
A majority of
Many
}
<u>people</u> say that they use text messaging.

- Quantifiers come before nouns or noun phrases and are used to talk about amounts. They answer the questions: *How much?* or *How many?*

- These quantifiers don't express an exact amount, but only indicate whether the amount is large or small. They are used before either noncount nouns or plural count nouns (but not both).

(A) little and *(A) few*

Some fish need **little** <u>oxygen</u> to survive. *(They don't need much air.)*

We saved **a little** <u>money</u>. *(We saved a small amount of money)*

Few <u>people</u> know that the Grand Canyon is in Arizona. *(Not many people know this fact.)*

Can I borrow **a few** <u>dollars</u>? *(I want to borrow a small amount of money.)*

Much and *Many*

How **much** <u>time</u> do you need?	I do**n't** waste **much** <u>time</u>.
How **many** <u>friends</u> do you have?	I do**n't** know **many** <u>people</u>.

- *Little* (= not much) has a negative meaning, whereas *a little* (= not very much, but some) has a positive meaning. *Few* (= not many) and *a few* (= not very many, but some) follow the same principle.

- *Much* is used with noncount nouns. *Many* is used with plural count nouns to ask about amounts. (They usually imply there is at least some.) In negative statements, *not much* and *not many* refer to a small amount.

- *Much* is not usually used alone in affirmative statements to indicate a large amount. *A lot of* is preferred.

    That's **a lot of** information to memorize.

    * That's much information to memorize. (INCORRECT)

Before Noncount Nouns and Plural Count Nouns

No	
Hardly any	
Some	
Plenty of	<u>mail</u> was delivered today.
A lot of / Lots of	<u>questions</u> were answered at the press conference.
Almost all	
All	

- These quantifiers—except for *no*—don't express an exact amount, but only indicate whether the quantity is large or small.

- *No* and *hardly any* are not used with negative statements. *Some* is often used with negative statements in subject position. In other positions, *any* is used instead.

    Some <u>people</u> don't like to use e-mail.   I don't have **any** new e-mail messages.

- *Plenty of* implies that you have enough of something. You don't need any more.

    We have **plenty of** <u>eggs</u>. We don't need to get **any** at the store.

- *Any* is used to ask about amounts. (*Any* can cover a wide range from none to all.) In negative statements, *not any* means "none".

Did you get **any** <u>mail</u> today?	I did**n't** get **any** <u>mail</u>.
Did he make **any** <u>remarks</u>?	He did**n't** make **any** <u>remarks</u>.

Quantifiers with Nonspecific Nouns

All kids like ice cream.
  (= kids in general)

A little cheese can be good for you.
  (= cheese in general)

A lot of <u>computers</u> have anti-spam software.

No <u>homework</u> will be assigned in this class.

Quantifiers with Specific Nouns

All (of) my kids like ice cream.
  (= a certain group of kids)

A little of the cheese was moldy.
  (= a specific piece of cheese)

A lot of <u>these</u> <u>computers</u> have anti-spam software.

None of <u>our</u> <u>homework</u> has been checked yet.

Noncount Quantifiers with Singular Count Nouns

Some of <u>the</u> <u>book</u> is interesting, but I wouldn't recommend it.

A little of <u>the</u> <u>roast</u> got burnt.

- **Quantifiers with nonspecific and specific nouns:** Most quantifiers can occur with or without *of*, but they are used with different kinds of nouns. Use quantifiers alone to talk about a nonspecific noun or a noun in general. Use quantifiers with *of* + a determiner (e.g., *the, our, these*) to talk about a specific noun.

- Some quantifiers—such as *a lot of* and *plenty of*—always occur with *of*. With this group of quantifiers, *of* is used before both nonspecific and specific nouns. The difference is the addition of the determiner.

- When talking about specific nouns, *of* is optional after *all*. *No* cannot be followed by *of*. Use *none* instead.

- Use either singular or plural verbs after *none*.

    None of the answers <u>are</u> correct.   **None** of the answers <u>is</u> correct.

- Quantifiers with *of* can also be used with pronouns to talk about specific nouns.

    All of <u>them</u> like ice cream.   **None of** <u>it</u> has been checked yet.   **Some of** <u>it</u> is interesting.

- **Noncount quantifiers with singular count nouns:** If a singular count noun is thought of as something made up of parts (or having mass), a noncount quantifier with *of* can be used to refer to a part of the whole.

<u>Some</u> <u>people</u> spend their time online searching for information, but **a large number** use the Internet for e-mail.

<u>Few of my</u> <u>students</u> like homework, but **some** do.

I've run out of <u>change</u>. Do you have **any**?

I thought that <u>help</u> would arrive soon, but **none** did.

- Quantifiers can be used as pronouns when the meaning is clear from the context. To form the pronoun, the noun following the quantifier is dropped.

- When quantifiers with *of* (e.g., *a lot of, plenty, of, a large number of*) are used as pronouns, *of* is dropped.

- *No* and *every* are not used as pronouns. Use *none* and *every one* instead.

Listening

A. Each sentence in the passage is incomplete. Listen to the entire passage first. Then listen again and put a caret (∧) where you hear a missing word. Listen once more to fill in the missing words, and correct the punctuation.

Many
∧ Internet users shop online, especially adults who have time to shop. Online shoppers

are between the ages of 30 and 49. Them appreciate the convenience and choices available

online. Seniors over age 65 shop online, although would probably benefit from the

convenience of purchasing their medications and groceries from home.

B. Listen. Choose the best answer to complete each conversation.

1. **a.** OK, so I won't buy any today.
   b. OK, so I'll need to buy some today.
2. **a.** A lot.
   b. Much.
3. **a.** Great. Let's have some tea.
   b. Too bad. We won't have time for tea.
4. **a.** None.
   b. A majority.
5. **a.** I'm glad no one failed.
   b. It's too bad a few failed.
6. **a.** Wait, here's some.
   b. Wait, here are a few.

B2 Contrasting Quantifiers

Choose the best expression to complete each sentence.

1. I'm feeling better. I'm not in (much / many) pain at the moment.
2. I'm having (few / a few) difficulties with this grammar point. Please help me.
3. You'd better make a decision. There's (few / little) time remaining.
4. (Some / Lots) of people don't have air conditioning in their homes.
5. Bring (a little / a little of) your money in cash.
6. Unlike teenagers, (many / many of) adults dislike text messaging.
7. It's hard to communicate basic ideas because I don't speak (some / any) French.
8. I didn't have (no / any) dinner last night.
9. We've already received (much / plenty of) information about the situation.
10. I like (some / any) desserts, but not all of them.

A. Read about websites that offer to help students with their homework. Insert *of* after each quantifier where necessary.

There are many _____ (1) websites on the Internet that offer to help students with their writing homework. Recently, the Pew Internet and American Life Project made a survey of some _____ (2) these sites. The specific sites chosen allow students to buy, sell, share, or download essays or term papers. The survey clearly shows that some _____ (3) sites tempt students to download papers and claim them as their own. However, to avoid legal issues, nearly all _____ (4) have disclaimers. One site sells pre-written papers for $9.85 a page, and it maintains that the papers should be used as models only. But a lot _____ (5) essay databases make little effort to hide their true aims. As a counterpoint, there are several _____ (6) online services that allow teachers to check a student's work against the thousands of essays and reports available online. Most _____ (7) these websites warn that teachers can access the stock of essays as easily as students.

All _____ (8) essay sites vary in price and in quality. While some _____ (9) the sites offer free access to their stores of essays, others want cash in return. Many _____ (10) give students free access to their databases if a student either submits a paper or adds the site's banner ad to his or her own web page. The unfortunate reality is that the quality of the papers on these websites often leaves something to be desired. Studies have proven that quite a few _____ (11) the essays for sale would receive a grade of D or F if they were submitted—hardly making cheating worth the effort!

Adapted from *The Internet and Education: Findings of the Pew Internet and American Life Project.*

B. Discuss these questions with a partner. Try to use some quantifiers in your answers.

1. Why do students cheat?

   There is a lot of pressure put on students today. Some students don't study enough and then they panic right before the exam . . .

2. Do you think cheating is ever justified?
3. If someone is caught cheating, what should happen to them?
4. Do you think there is something schools can do to reduce cheating?

Vocabulary Notes: *Comparative Quantifiers*

Certain quantifiers, called comparative quantifiers, are used to compare amounts. As with other quantifiers, they can be used with or without *of* + determiner.

> *Fewer* (+ plural count noun) and *less* (+ noncount noun) indicate a smaller amount.
>
>> This fall we experienced **fewer** <u>typhoons</u> than usual.
>>
>> I drink **less** <u>coffee</u> than you do.
>
> *More* indicates a larger amount. *Most* means "almost all." They are used with both noncount nouns and plural count nouns.
>
>> I need **more** <u>time</u> to finish this essay.
>>
>> **More** <u>office buildings</u> are being put up downtown.
>>
>> **Most** <u>paper</u> does not get recycled.
>>
>> Don't **most** <u>people</u> want peace in the world?
>
> Comparative quantifiers can also be used as pronouns when the meaning is clear from the context.
>
>> We both drink a lot of <u>coffee</u>, but I drink **less**.
>>
>> There are already a lot of <u>office buildings</u> downtown, and now **more** are being put up.

B4 · Making Comparisons with Quantifiers

A. How have people's lives changed in the past hundred years? Work with a partner. Compare how people lived then to how they live now. Complete the sentences with your own ideas.

1. In the past, fewer people lived_____.

2. There was a little _____ but not like it is today.

3. Most cities didn't have _____ like they do today.

4. People had less hope of _____. These days, people have
   more _____.

5. Today, fewer children have to _____, but they are expected
   to _____.

6. Many people worked _____. Now, most people
   _____.

7. For fun, people _____. Today, most people enjoy
   _____ in their free time.

B. Work in small groups. Take a survey of each other's daily habits using these questions. Then write sentences comparing your daily lives. Share your sentences with the class.

1. How much time do you usually spend on your homework?

   We all spend plenty of time on our homework. Maria probably spends the most time on her homework. Elle spends less time on her homework than Maria does, but more than Jun does.

2. How often do you go out to eat?

3. How many movies do you watch each week?

4. How much money do you typically spend on transportation in a month?

5. How many hours of sleep do you get every night?

C Each, Every, Either, Neither, and Both

Examining Meaning and Use

Match the examples with the description that is closest in meaning. Discuss your answers. Then read the notes to check them.

- **a.** Each member gets a ticket.
- **b.** Every member gets a ticket.
- **c.** Neither member gets a ticket.
- **d.** Both members get a ticket.

____ Two members don't get tickets at all.

____ All members get tickets.

____ An individual member gets a ticket.

____ Two members get tickets for themselves.

Each and *Every*

The doctor spent at least 20 minutes with **each** <u>patient</u>. *(= each individual patient)*

Before having surgery, **every** <u>patient</u> should get a second opinion. *(= all patients as a group)*

I see **every** <u>Hollywood movie</u> I can. *(= I try to see all Hollywood movies.)*

With Nonspecific Nouns	*With Specific Nouns*
Each <u>patient</u> is given a bathrobe.	**Each of** <u>the patients</u> is going to see the doctor for 10 minutes.
Every <u>child</u> deserves a loving home.	**Every one of** <u>them</u> deserves an award.

- *Each* and *every* are followed by singular count nouns. They mean "the entire group." *Each* is used to refer to two or more of the same thing viewed individually. *Every* refers to three or more of the same thing viewed more as a group. *Every* is closer to *all* in meaning.

- *Every* can follow *not* but *each* cannot.

    Not every computer was updated.   * Not each computer was updated. (INCORRECT)

- **With nonspecific and specific nouns:** These quantifiers can also occur with or without *of* to talk about nonspecific versus specific nouns. (*Every* cannot be followed by *of* alone. Use *every one* instead.)

- *Each of* and *every one of* are followed by plural count nouns or plural pronouns. Even though the noun is plural, verbs following these expressions typically remain in the third-person singular.

Either, Neither, and Both

With Specific Nouns

Either <u>afternoon</u> fits my schedule.	= **Either of** <u>those afternoons</u> fits my schedule.
Neither <u>answer</u> is correct.	= **Neither of** <u>your answers</u> is correct.
Both <u>parents</u> share visitation rights.	= **Both of** <u>them</u> share visitation rights.

With Conjunctions

Either <u>Wednesday afternoon</u> **or** <u>Friday afternoon</u> fits my schedule.

Neither <u>the first answer</u> **nor** <u>the third answer</u> is correct.

Both <u>her mother</u> **and** <u>her father</u> share visitation rights.

- **With specific nouns:** *Either*, *neither*, and *both* are used to talk about two of the same or similar things. *Either* means "one or the other." *Neither* means "not one and not the other." *Neither* has a negative meaning. In negative sentences, use *either* instead.

   I <u>saw</u> **neither** one.   I <u>didn't see</u> **either** one.

- *Either* and *neither* are followed by singular count nouns. *Either of* and *neither of* are followed by plural count nouns or plural pronouns. Verbs following these expressions are typically in the third-person singular.

- *Both* and *both of* + are followed by plural count nouns or plural pronouns. Verbs following these expressions are always plural. *Of* can be omitted before specific nouns, but not pronouns.

   both (of) my parents.   * **both** them. (INCORRECT)

- **With conjunctions:** *Either* and *neither* can also be followed by two nouns connected with *or/nor*. *Both* can also be followed by two nouns connected with *and*.

   Neither <u>teenagers</u> **nor** <u>senior citizens</u> shop online as much as middle-aged adults.

   Both <u>e-mail</u> **and** <u>the Internet</u> have made people's lives better.

C1 Listening

A. 🎧 Each sentence in the passage is incomplete. Listen to the entire passage first. Then listen again and put a caret (∧) where you hear a missing word. Listen once more to fill in the missing words, and correct the punctuation.

                                                      either

Purchasing a computer nowadays often involves choosing ∧ a laptop a desktop model. Models perfect for everyone's needs, and type certain shortcomings. It's important for consumer to find out the advantages the disadvantages of from the standpoint of price, quality, and need.

B. 🔊 Listen. Choose the best answer to complete each conversation.

1. **a.** How much did every pair cost?
   b. How much did each pair cost?

2. **a.** Yes, but none of them fit me.
   b. Yes, but neither of them fit me.

3. **a.** Why didn't she reserve a flight yet?
   b. Did she also rent a car?

4. **a.** How many books were there?
   b. Which one did you like best?

5. **a.** Which one did he get?
   b. Did he quit?

6. **a.** How long did you speak to each one?
   b. How long did you speak to every one?

C2 Contrasting Quantifiers

Choose the best expression to complete each sentence.

1. It wasn't surprising that (both / all) twins had the same opinion.
2. The jury decided the men were innocent. In other words, (neither / either) one was guilty of the crime.
3. Not (each / every) broadcaster reports the news accurately.
4. (All / Every) the items were sold out.
5. When I saw Emma and Tim, I asked (each / every) one to sign the petition.
6. Not (all / every) students were exempt from the exam.
7. (Each of / each) the boys is on the track team.
8. We didn't see (neither / either) warning.
9. (Neither / Either) freshmen nor sophomores qualified for the finals.
10. Are you interested in (both / both of) publications?

C3 Using *Each, Every, Both, Neither,* and *Either*

Use the words in the boxes to complete the sentences. Explain your choices. Then answer the questions with a partner.

both	each	every

1. _____ grammar and vocabulary can be hard to learn. Do you agree?

2. How is your attendance rate? Have you attended _____ single English class, or have you missed some of them?

3. Is it better to learn two languages at the same time or to study _____ one separately?

4. Even if you study hard, not _____ person can learn a foreign language. Do you agree with this statement?

either	neither

5. When I have a problem, I can go to _____ parent for advice because they're easy to talk to. Do you agree with this statement?

6. I understand English, but I speak _____ French nor German. Is this true for you?

Insert *of* after each quantifier where necessary.

1. Neither _____ us could agree on a course of action.

2. They lost both _____ games in the last 60 seconds.

3. Both _____ you need to report to work immediately.

4. We can go to the museum on Tuesday or Friday. Either _____ day is fine.

5. Students must take each _____ the core courses to be eligible for the Master's Degree.

6. Every _____ time I call her, I get her answering machine.

7. Every one _____ their ideas was rejected.

8. Neither _____ the teams showed up for the game.

9. Both _____ my grandparents are in the hospital.

10. How does this machine work? What do each _____ these parts do?

C5 **Thinking About Meaning and Use**

A. **Read the sentences. Check (✓) the second sentence if it has the same meaning as the first.**

1. There are a large number of homeless people here.

_____ There are many homeless people.

2. A majority of the students passed the test.

_____ All of the students passed the test.

3. There isn't much time left in the game.

_____ There's little time left in the game.

4. They have few new ideas.

_____ They have a lot of new ideas.

5. More than half of the voters turned out for the election.

_____ A majority of voters turned out for the election.

6. We had hardly any problems on our last trip.

_____ We had few problems on our last trip.

7. Either one of our customer service representatives can help you.

_____ Neither one of our customer service representatives can help you.

8. All of the inmates escaped.

_____ Every one of the inmates escaped.

9. Most of the workers joined the strike.

_____ Almost all of the workers joined the strike.

A. In a recent survey, 100 New Yorkers were asked to choose their biggest quality of life concern. Study the results and then write some sentences using quantifiers. Use quantifiers as pronouns when the meaning is clear.

WHAT IS YOUR BIGGEST QUALITY OF LIFE CONCERN?	
lack of parking	5
litter	0
noise	51
overdevelopment	29
pollution	2
congestion	13

A majority of people complained about noise.

B. Now take a class survey about these issues. Read through the list and vote on which is your biggest concern. Tally the votes on the board.

____ lack of parking   ____ litter

____ overdevelopment   ____ pollution

____ noise   ____ traffic congestion

C. Work in small groups. Compare the results of your survey to the one in part A. Discuss these questions.

1. How is the class the same?
   A large number of people complained about noise in New York. We don't have that problem here.
   Very few people thought noise was a big problem . . .

2. How is it different?
3. What are the causes of the two biggest quality of life concerns your class voted on?
4. What can be done about the two big concerns?

Writing

Editing: *Quantifiers*

Study the errors. Pay attention to the areas that you make mistakes in.

1. **Use of quantifiers**

   Quite a few
   ~~A great deal of~~ <u>students</u> were penalized for buying essays online.

   a lot of
   Teenagers spend ~~many~~ time doing homework.

2. **Agreement**

   program is
   <u>Neither</u> computer ~~programs are~~ available until December.

   is
   <u>Every</u> student ~~are~~ here.

3. **Use of articles/determiners in *of* phrases**

   the
   Most of ∧ people in my family would agree with me.

4. **Use of negative forms**

   uses
   Neither my roommate nor my best friend ~~doesn't use~~ e-mail.

5. **Use of *of***

   Most ~~of~~ people are right-handed.

D1 Editing

Correct the errors in the sentences. Be prepared to explain your answers. For some sentences, there may be more than one possible answer.

1. Most of adults use a computer at home, work, or school.
2. Each students registered for courses online.
3. My high school friends spent much hours text messaging.
4. You might be interested in some of articles in this magazine.
5. Either answer are correct.
6. There's a few space left in the closet for your clothes.
7. Neither of my brothers does not have children.
8. Many of my e-mail is spam.
9. Hardly any of the students didn't understand the lecture.
10. In general, most of users are happy with their e-mail providers.

Beyond the Sentence: *Referring to Quantified Noun Phrases*

Quantifiers allow writers to talk about all or some of a particular group.

> *Quantifiers can be used as pronouns when the meaning is clear from the context. Writers often use quantifiers as pronouns when they are shifting focus or contrasting one part of a group with another:* certain respondents → some → others.

E-mail was originally designed for corporate communication, but because of its efficiency, it found its way into the world in general. In a recent survey, <u>many people</u> report that their main use of e-mail is to maintain a larger network of relationships. **They** arrange social events, share information, and even meet people electronically. A few of **them** even indicate that they use e-mail for all their social communications.

At the same time, <u>certain respondents</u> expressed concern that sometimes the meaning of a written message may be lost or confused. **Some** said they compensated by including symbols such as "happy ☺" or "sad ☹" faces. **Others** indicated that they worded their messages very carefully. However, an overwhelming majority of people surveyed felt confident that their messages were understood all or most of the time.

> *Pronouns or phrases with pronouns can replace previously mentioned quantified nouns:* many people = they = (a few of) them. *A pronoun must agree with its antecedent.*

D2 Using Pronouns

A. Match each sentence in the first column with the sentence that would logically flow from the second. Then underline the pronouns or pronoun phrases in column 2 that replace the boldface words.

1. I talked to **some of my classmates** about the assignment. _c_

2. **Cell phone companies** are competing for new customers. ____

3. **Most parents** want to be able to call their children at any time of the day. ____

4. **Blogs** are changing the way people hear about and discuss world issues. ____

5. **A growing number of students** are getting involved in online gambling. ____

6. **E-mail spellings** can be very different from traditional dictionary spelling. ____

a. Therefore, many of them are buying multiple cell phones.

b. A few are even making the news.

c. <u>Several of them</u> want to work together on the project.

d. Luckily, most manage to break out of the habit with help from friends and parents.

e. None of them are acceptable for academic assignments.

f. Some are offering special promotional rates for first-time users.

B. Use pronouns and quantifiers to answer these questions in complete sentences.

1. Explain where you and your friends learn about new products and services.

   Most of us learn about new products and services from friends. Some of us research and shop online. Others prefer to browse in stores and talk to salespeople.

2. Describe the ways your friends communicate with you.

3. Describe the music preferences of your friends or classmates.

D3 **Writing Tip:** *Analyzing Information in Your Writing*

> Sorting information into categories allows you to analyze it, look for patterns, and explain your findings. When you present your analysis, it's important to explain the significance of each category.

Choose one of the topics to write a short essay of two or three paragraphs. Generate and analyze information related to your own experience and/or that of your friends. Explain the data and describe your results. Then, use the Writing Checklist to check your work.

- Think about the messages you write by e-mail. Then divide your correspondence into personal, educational, and/or professional categories. You may add other categories if you wish. Explain each category in terms of how often you correspond and how important you feel it is. Try to explain why you devote more time to one area than another.

- Talk to a few classmates to find out their preferences regarding personal communications. Think of several questions to ask. For example: *When you have a problem, do you talk about it on the telephone, through e-mail, or in person?* Explain your findings by analyzing the answers and looking for interesting patterns. For example, do women have similar preferences? Do men?

- Think about your social interactions with your closest friends, colleagues, and family members. What do you notice about degrees of formality in your interactions with them? Are there certain rules of conduct that you are expected to follow? Try to group people and look for patterns. For example: *Most of my siblings behave formally at family gatherings.*

Writing Checklist

Reflect on your ability to use quantifiers by answering the questions.

☐ **1.** Did you use quantifiers to describe count and noncount nouns?

☐ **2.** Did you use pronouns or phrases with pronouns to replace some quantified nouns?

☐ **3.** Did you use quantifiers as pronouns?

☐ **4.** Did you use comparative quantifiers?

☐ **5.** Did you check agreement, determiners, and *of* phrases?

▶ Beyond the Classroom

Writing

Write an essay using one of these topics.

1. Time management continues to be an important skill in today's multitasking society. Make a list of things you want to get done next week. Then over the next week, take notes on how you spend your time. Did you accomplish your goals? How did your time management help or delay you? Write a short paper: describe different slots of time in your day, analyze the data, and say whether or not you use time effectively.

2. Modern children seem to use technology effortlessly. In contrast, many of their parents may not be as tech-savvy. Brainstorm and research the types of technology that modern children use. Then consider how their world is different from that of their parents. Write a short paper: First describe children today and the types of technology they have access to. Then compare these children to their parents and give your opinion of these differences. What predictions can you make about the future of these children?

Searching for Authentic Examples

Find examples of English grammar in everyday life by completing the task below. Bring your examples to class, and be prepared to discuss them.

Look for six examples of quantifiers in a magazine, Internet, or newspaper article that reports the results of a poll. Do your quantifiers express exact quantities, or do they only indicate large or small amounts? Do the quantifiers occur with *of*? Does the quantifier occur with a specific noun or a more general one?

Gerunds and Infinitives

A Overwork in America

 A1 Before You Read

Discuss these questions.

Recent studies show that one in three Americans feels overworked. Why do you think more and more people feel overworked?

Do you ever feel overworked? What are some of the consequences of feeling overworked?

 A2 Read

 Read this extract from a research study about the causes of overwork in America.

OVERWORK IN AMERICA:
WHEN THE WAY WE WORK BECOMES TOO MUCH

A recent research project studied a number of factors in order to determine why people feel overworked.

How Does "The Way We Work" Today Contribute to Overwork?

Because we <u>tend</u> **to focus** mainly on "time spent on the job" as the major indicator of when we are working too much, <u>it's easy</u> **to overlook**[1] other aspects of employment that contribute to overwork.

Lack of Focus
Lack of focus refers to <u>the inability</u> **to focus on one's work** because of constant interruptions and distractions. It is also <u>a result of</u> **multitasking.**[2] (**Multitasking** is obviously <u>a very important skill</u> **to develop** in today's **economy**, but employers <u>may be asking some employees</u> **to multitask too much.**)

The study shows that 56 percent of employees say they *often* or *very often* experience one or both of the following problems during a typical workweek when they <u>try</u> **focusing on their jobs:**

WHAT HAPPENS WHEN EMPLOYEES ARE OVERWORKED?

This study found that the more overworked employees are:
- the more likely they are to make mistakes at work.
- the more likely they are to feel angry at their employers for expecting them to do so much.

- I have to work on too many tasks at the same time.
- I am interrupted repeatedly during the workday. <u>It's difficult</u> **to get my work done on time.**

The study found that employees who <u>have more difficulty</u> **focusing at work** feel highly overworked.

Low-Value Work
Some employees think the tasks they are <u>asked</u> **to do** are simply a waste of time (such as having a meeting to plan a meeting). So researchers <u>have begun</u> **asking employees how strongly they agree with this statement:**
- I <u>waste a lot of time</u> **doing tasks that aren't important.**

Overall, the study found that 29 percent of employees strongly or somewhat agree with the statement. Those who agree are more <u>likely</u> **to be highly overworked**.

Accessibility[3] Outside the Office
The study asked employees this question:
- How often do co-workers, supervisors, managers, customers, or clients <u>contact you</u>—or do you contact them—**to discuss work-related matters** outside normal working hours?

As technology and flexible work schedules <u>begin</u> **to blur[4] the lines between work time and free time**, the study showed that one in three employees (33 percent) is in contact with work once a week or more outside normal working hours, and consequently, these employees feel highly overworked (44 percent).

Based on the report, *Overwork in America*, from the Families and Work Institute; conducted 2004.

---

1 **overlook:** not to notice
2 **multitasking:** doing several things at the same time

4 **accessibility:** the ability to be reached
5 **blur:** to make something unclear

 After You Read

Discuss these questions.

1. What was the purpose of the research study?
2. Briefly summarize the three research results discussed in this extract.
3. What do you think should be done about overwork? What solutions can you think of for the specific problems raised by the study?

Examining Form

A. Work in pairs. Look at the highlighted gerunds and infinitives in the reading. Write them in the correct categories. Some items are already done.

Infinitives
In a sentence beginning with *it* *it's easy to overlook*

Directly after a verb _____

After a verb + object _____

After an adjective _____

After a noun *the inability to focus on one's work*

Gerunds
As a subject _____

Directly after a verb *try focusing on their jobs*

After a verb + object *have more difficulty focusing at work*

After a preposition _____

B. Discuss your observations with the class. Refer to pages A-17–21 if you need to.

B Gerunds and Infinitives

Examining Meaning and Use

Match the examples with the statements below them. Discuss your answers. Then read the notes to check them.

1. **a.** I plan to be making dinner when you arrive.
   b. I plan to make dinner when you arrive.

   _____ I'll begin making dinner after you arrive.
   _____ I'll begin making dinner before you arrive.

2. **a.** We appreciate him helping you.
   b. We appreciate your helping him.

   _____ You helped him.
   _____ He helped you.

Gerunds: *(not)* verb + *-ing*

Gerunds as Subjects and Subject Complements
Working teaches you responsibility and discipline. *(gerund as subject)*
Her first job was **working as a researcher**. *(gerund as subject complement)*

Gerunds as Objects of Verbs and Object Complements
I <u>avoid</u> **having disagreements at work**. *(object of verb)*
Do you really <u>enjoy</u> **working 60 hours a week**? *(object of verb)*
Don't <u>spend time</u> **worrying**. *(object complement)*
I'm <u>having difficulty</u> **focusing on my work**. *(object complement)*

Gerunds as Objects of Prepositions
He succeeded <u>by</u> **working hard for his entire life**. *(verb + preposition + gerund)*
Don't be afraid <u>of</u> **making mistakes**. *(adjective + preposition + gerund)*
Just the thought <u>of</u> **multitasking** makes me feel anxious. *(noun + preposition + gerund)*
Without saying goodbye, she left. *(preposition + gerund)*

- **Gerunds function as nouns.** All verbs, except modal auxiliaries, have gerund forms. A gerund can be one word (*working*) or part of a longer phrase (*working as a researcher*).

- **Gerunds can be subjects or subject complements:** The subject complement describes the subject of the sentence.

- **Gerunds can follow some verbs:** Many of these verbs (such as *avoid, dislike, enjoy, finish, go, practice,* and *quit*) can only be followed by gerunds—never infinitives. Gerunds can also follow the object of certain verbs (such as *have difficulty / fun / a problem; spend / waste time*) acting as object complements.

- **Gerunds can follow prepositions:** The prepositions may come after verbs, adjectives, or nouns. Infinitives never follow prepositions.

For verbs + gerund, see page A-18.
For verbs with object + gerund, see page A-18.
For verbs, adjectives, and nouns with preposition + gerund, see page A-19.

Infinitives as Objects of Verbs (Three Patterns)

I <u>hope</u> **to find a new job.** *(verb + infinitive)*

We <u>urge you</u> **to resign immediately.** *(verb + object + infinitive)*

They <u>expect me</u> **to pay the bill.** ≠ They <u>expect</u> **to pay the bill.** *(verb [+ object] + infinitive)*

Infinitives as Subjects and Subject Complements

It's impossible **to get a promotion** at that firm. *(infinitive replaced by* it *subject)*

Less common: **To get a promotion** is impossible. *(infinitive as subject)*

My goal is **to get a promotion.** *(infinitive as subject complement)*

Infinitives as Adjective and Noun Complements

Don't be <u>afraid</u> **to make mistakes.** *(adjective + infinitive)*

I can't take the <u>time</u> **to answer your question now.** *(noun + infinitive)*

- Infinitives function as nouns. All verbs, except modal auxiliaries, have infinitive forms. An infinitive can be two words *(to work)* or part of a longer phrase *(to find a new job)*.
- **Infinitives can follow some verbs:** Many of these verbs (such as *agree, decide, expect, hope, intend, plan,* and *urge*) can only be followed by infinitives—never gerunds.
- **Infinitives can be subjects or subject complements:** Although an infinitive can function as the subject of a sentence, using *it* as the subject of the sentence is more common (with no change in meaning). The pronoun *it* is followed by *be* or one of a limited group of verbs (such as *take, cost, seem*).
- **Infinitives can follow adjectives and nouns:** Infinitives are often used after adjectives to talk about people's feelings. Gerunds never follow adjectives directly. Infinitives are used after nouns to give information about the noun.
- **Other issues:** The continuous infinitive (*to be* + present participle) is used to emphasize an ongoing activity.

  I hope **to be watching TV** when they announce the winner.

- Infinitives may follow the expression *in order.* They are called purpose infinitives.

  The manufacturing division was moved overseas **(in order) to save money.**

For verbs + infinitive, see page A-20.
For adjectives + infinitive, see pages A-20 and A-21.
For nouns + infinitive, see page A-21.

Gerunds

She <u>likes</u> **taking on new responsibilities**.

After I left, I <u>remembered</u> **saying goodbye**.

(I had a memory of saying goodbye earlier.)

Infinitives

= She <u>likes</u> **to take on new responsibilities**.

≠ I <u>remembered</u> **to say goodbye**.

(I didn't forget to say goodbye at that moment.)

- Certain verbs (such as *continue, hate, like, love, prefer,* and *start*) can be followed by infinitives or gerunds with no change in meaning. A few verbs (such as *stop, remember,* and *forget*) have different meanings when followed by infinitives versus gerunds.

For verbs + infinitives or gerunds, see page A-21.

Performer of the Action with Gerunds and Infinitives

Verb + Gerund or Infinitive

<u>I</u> don't like **working late,** but I have to. / <u>I</u> don't like **to work late,** but I have to.

(I am the performer of the action.)

Verb + Object + Gerund or Infinitive

I don't like <u>John</u> / <u>him</u> **working late**. / I don't like (for) <u>John</u> / <u>him</u> **to work late.**

(John is the performer of the action.)

Possessive + Gerund

I don't like <u>John's</u> working late.

<u>His</u> working late is affecting our relationship.

* Him working late is affecting our relationship. (INCORRECT)

Infinitives with It *Subjects*

It is hard **to get up early** every day. *(In general, getting up early Is hard.)*

It is hard <u>for me</u> **to get up early** every day. *(I find it hard to get up early.)*

- **Verb + gerund or infinitive:** When a gerund or infinitive directly follows a verb, the subject of the sentence is the performer of the gerund or infinitive action.

- **Verb + object + gerund or infinitive:** When gerunds and infinitives do not directly follow the verb, the performer of the gerund or infinitive is *not* the subject of the sentence. The performer is the object.

- **Possessive + gerund:** A possessive can also be used before a gerund to show the performer of the action. (This sounds more formal.) However, when the gerund is in the subject position, a possessive must be used.

- **Infinitives with *It* subjects:** Sentences with *It* . . . + infinitive are often used to talk about an action in general, without indicating its performer. To express the performer of an infinitive action, *for* + noun / pronoun is used before the infinitive.

A. 🎧 Each sentence in the passage is incomplete. Listen to the entire passage first. Then listen again and put a caret (^) where you hear a missing word. Listen once more to fill in the missing words.

breaking

Some employees can't imagine ᴧ all ties with work, even for a short vacation.

They admit their voice mail and even e-mails during vacation. Studies show, however,

that employees need and themselves on their vacations by fully themselves from work.

Employees who can do this are much less likely stressed when they return.

B. 🎧 Listen. Choose the best sentence to complete each conversation.

1. **a.** Why do you want to become manager?
    b. Why don't you want to become manager?
2. **a.** Well, it's good he doesn't stay late often.
    b. Well, it's good you don't stay late often.
3. **a.** Yes, that's a good time to start.
    b. Yes, then we'll be familiar with the issues.
4. **a.** Yes, I read it online.
    b. Yes, here it is.
5. **a.** Why do I need to learn it?
    b. Why do you need to learn it?
6. **a.** I'm glad I could do it.
    b. I'm glad you could do it.

B2   **Contrasting Gerunds and Infinitives**

Choose the gerund or infinitive form to complete each sentence.

1. I don't mind (to study / studying) algebra. In fact, I kind of like it.
2. She's not willing (to take / taking) a cut in salary.
3. You did an excellent job of (to coordinate / coordinating) the project.
4. I can't believe that she left without (to say / saying) goodbye.
5. It will be necessary for you (to file / filing) the papers by April 1st.
6. We need four staff members (to run / running) the emergency room during the night shift.
7. I may be healthier now, but I do miss (to have / having) my coffee before breakfast.
8. Although he wasn't popular, he was determined (to win / winning) the election.
9. I'm sorry, but I don't have time (to discuss / discussing) this right now.
10. We're having trouble (to answer / answering) the first question. Can you help us?
11. Are you good at (to fix / fixing) computers?
12. His (to sing / singing) really annoys me.
13. I've asked him (to stop / stopping), but he keeps (to do / doing) it.
14. At the moment, the criminal is believed (to hide / to be hiding) in the mountains.

A. Read each pair of sentences. Complete each sentence with a gerund or infinitive, depending on the meaning of the sentence.

1. **a.** I lost 20 pounds. I was successful because I stopped _____ (eat) sugary, high-fat foods.

   b. He was in a hurry, so he stopped _____ (eat) at a fast-food restaurant.

2. **a.** Grandma called yesterday. Did you remember _____ (call) her back? You were supposed to.

   b. I must have been half asleep. I don't remember _____ (call) him at midnight, but he says I did.

3. **a.** I'll never forget _____ (see) Julia Roberts on the street. I was so surprised.

   b. I forgot _____ (see) my advisor before the end of the semester.

B. Now make up six more sentences. Use *stop*, *remember*, and *forget* followed by a gerund or an infinitive, depending on the meaning of your sentence.

B4   **Completing Sentences with Gerunds and Infinitives**

A. Complete the sentences with information about yourself. Use gerunds or infinitives.

1. Over the next 10 years, I want to . . .
2. Given the chance, I would volunteer to . . .
3. It's silly, but I can't stand . . .
4. I often need someone to remind me to . . .
5. When I'm in a bad mood, my friends recommend . . .
6. In my hometown, it's easy to . . .
7. Recently, I decided to . . .
8. I enjoy . . . on the weekends.
9. I'm afraid to . . .
10. It's important for people to . . .
11. You could never convince me to . . .
12. I'm excited about . . .
13. I have a hard time . . .

B. Choose five of the sentences to ask your partner about. Then ask follow-up questions.

A: Over the next 10 years, what do you want to do?
B: I want to get a good job and save some money for graduate school.

B5 Changing Gerunds to Infinitives

A. Read the doctor's letter. Underline the five sentences that contain gerund phrases as subjects. (The first one has been done for you.)

Dear Samantha,

<u>Having constant food cravings can be very unsettling.</u> But don't be discouraged—there is hope!

To lose weight, you'll need to change your eating habits. Changing your eating habits takes a lot of discipline. (And it won't happen overnight.) But once you do it, you'll start to slim down. And we all know that losing weight feels great!

So, what can you do? First, learning the triggers for your cravings is very helpful. Once you understand that, you'll be able to avoid situations that make you overeat. In addition, occupying your mind with other thoughts can be helpful. Distract yourself—go for a walk or pick up a good book. Finally, if you must eat something, substituting healthy foods for fatty ones is a smart move. The next time you want that big bag of potato chips, why don't you eat a bowl of berries instead?

Good luck to you!

Dr. Neil

B. Rewrite the sentences you underlined. Change them to *It ... + infinitive*.

It can be very unsettling to have constant food cravings.

B6 Verbs Followed by Object + Infinitive

What might these people say to each other? First write down two commands, instructions, or pieces of advice for each person. Then rewrite the advice using an infinitive. Use some of the verbs in the box or others of your own.

advise	ask	convince	encourage	invite	order
permit	persuade	tell	urge	want	warn

1. a female teacher to you and your classmates

   a. *Turn in your homework by Friday.* ⟶ *She told us to turn in our homework by Friday.*

   b. _____ _____

2. a boy to his dog

   a. _____ ⟶ _____

   b. _____ _____

3. a wife to her husband

   a. _____ ⟶ _____

   b. _____ _____

4. parents to their children

   a. _____ ⟶ _____

   b. _____ _____

A. Read the sentences. Rewrite them using a possessive or an object pronoun + a gerund wherever possible. Pay attention to the underlined words. (Some sentences can only use a possessive + gerund.)

1. <u>He leaves</u> early. I don't mind <u>it</u>.

   I don't mind his leaving early.   OR   *I don't mind him leaving early.*

2. <u>He speaks</u> so loudly. <u>It</u> makes me uncomfortable.

   His speaking so loudly makes me uncomfortable.

3. <u>You call</u> every day. <u>It</u> means a lot to me.

   _____

4. <u>She bosses</u> everyone around all the time. I don't like <u>it</u>.

   _____

5. <u>You play</u> music at all hours. I can't tolerate <u>it</u>.

   _____

6. <u>My parents</u> allowed me to attend the party. <u>It</u> was a lucky turn of events.

   _____

B. Read the sentences. Rewrite them using an object pronoun + an infinitive. Pay attention to the underlined words.

1. <u>He gets</u> angry. I expect <u>it</u>.

   I expect him to get angry.

2. <u>She walks</u> to work. <u>It</u> takes too much time.

   _____

3. <u>She picks up</u> the kids in the afternoon. <u>It's</u> convenient.

   _____

4. <u>He didn't go</u> on the trip. I advised <u>it</u>.

   _____

5. <u>The children told</u> the truth. I encouraged <u>it</u>.

   _____

6. <u>You're</u> friends with Kelly. <u>It's</u> not a good idea.

   _____

C. Write about family members, friends, and classmates you know using gerunds and infinitives.

I'm embarrassed by my father's singing in the shower.
I don't like my mother to tell me what to do.

C Passive and Perfect Gerunds and Infinitives

Examining Meaning and Use

Match the examples with the statements below them. Discuss your answers. Then read the notes to check them.

1. **a.** We don't like being called at night.
    b. We don't like calling at night.

    ____ We don't want to make calls.
    ____ We don't want to get calls.

2. **a.** I'm worried about leaving.
    b. I'm worried about having left.

    ____ I left.
    ____ I might leave.

3. **a.** She expects to be told the results.
    b. She expects to tell us the results.

    ____ She'll announce the results.
    ____ Someone will tell her the results.

4. **a.** I hope to have passed.
    b. I hope to pass.

    ____ The exam is tomorrow.
    ____ The exam was yesterday.

> **Passive Gerunds and Infinitives:** *being / getting* + past participle
> *to + be / get* + past participle

Passive Gerunds
I don't like **being told what to do**.

(Active version: *I don't like people telling me what to do.*)

Passive Infinitives
My friend hopes **to get promoted soon**.

(Active version: *My friend hopes they will promote her.*)

Reducing Passive Infinitives
I want him **(to be) fired immediately**.

- Like passive sentences, passive gerunds and infinitives are used to focus on the receiver of the action instead of the performer, or agent, of the action. Use the passive when you want to emphasize the receiver or when the agent is unimportant, unknown, or obvious. Passive gerunds and infinitives very often do not mention the agent at all.

- *Get* passives are often more dynamic and emotional than *be* passives and usually describe people rather than objects.

- Passive infinitives following an object can be reduced by omitting *to be / to get*.

Perfect Gerunds and Infinitives: *having* + past participle
to have + past participle

Perfect Gerunds

He denied **having taken the money**.
  (First the money disappeared. Second he denied stealing it.)

Perfect Infinitives

They are reported **to have made a large third-quarter profit**.
  (First they made money. Second it was reported.)

Perfect Form (Unnecessary; Time is Clear) vs. *Simple Form*

It was nice of you **to have called yesterday**. = It was nice of you **to call yesterday**.

After **having completed the project on time**, = After **completing the project on time**,
  I felt relieved.   I felt relieved.

- The perfect (or past) gerund and infinitive are used to show the difference in time between two events. The event in the perfect gerund or infinitive happened before the time of the main verb.
- The perfect gerund or infinitive is often unnecessary if the time is understandable from the context. In such cases, use the less formal simple form instead.

C1 Listening

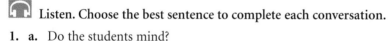 Listen. Choose the best sentence to complete each conversation.

1. **a.** Do the students mind?
   b. Does Professor Anderson mind?

2. **a.** Who are you going to call?
   b. Who's going to call you?

3. **a.** Has he received it?
   b. Have we received it?

4. **a.** When will you let them know?
   b. When will they let you know?

5. **a.** You should have gotten the e-mail reminder.
   b. You should have sent an e-mail reminder.

6. **a.** Isn't she a good employee?
   b. Isn't she a good employer?

7. **a.** OK, it'll be there at noon.
   b. OK, when will you bring it?

8. **a.** Why did you send it?
   b. Then who sent it?

A. Read the article about campus stress. Write the correct passive gerund or passive infinitive form of the verb in parentheses.

Being overworked (overwork) is quite common among university students. Students in academically demanding programs often tend _____ (challenge) to an extreme. A typical phrase you are likely to hear on campus is "I can't wait _____ (do) with this semester!"

High levels of stress are common on campus. Professors often give low grades for poor work or late assignments. Students dislike _____ (tell) that they manage their time badly, even though this is often the problem.

Some college students, especially freshmen, suffer from burnout. (Burnout is a combination of exhaustion, depression, and negative feelings about oneself.) Typically, as a first step towards recovery, an afflicted student's lifestyle needs _____ carefully _____ (evaluate). _____ (treat) by a professional is crucial in these situations. The student may then receive counseling and advice on how to alter his or her lifestyle to make it less stressful.

Universities need to develop appropriate resources to help maintain the mental health of their students. Unfortunately, unless the problem of anxiety on campus is taken seriously, it is unlikely _____ (solve) anytime soon.

B. Use an item from each column to make eight logical sentences.

I can't imagine	to be hired by a company that I like
I'm willing	being given more responsibility
I dislike	being understood when I speak English
I don't appreciate	to be corrected by my teachers
I don't have a hard time	to be taken seriously
I expect	being told what to do
I'm interested in	being stressed about schoolwork
I need	being ignored
I plan	to be left alone
I'm afraid	to be given a lot of time off

I can't imagine being stressed about schoolwork.

A. Read excerpts from news articles about the theft of a painting from a major museum. Complete the sentences with a perfect gerund or infinitive.

1. The painting was reported stolen on Thursday night. It seems
   _____ (disappear) sometime between 10:00 P.M. and midnight.

2. The police have arrested a man named Daniel Green. He denies _____ (take)
   the painting.

3. Under police questioning, he has given little information. However, he does remember
   _____ (see) the painting in the museum.

4. He claims _____ (leave) the museum with a friend around 8:00 P.M.

5. Two nights ago, the police arrested another man named Greg White. At first, he pretended
   _____ (not / understand) their questions. Finally, he confessed to the crime.

6. Mr. White appears _____ (commit) the crime with the help of two
   accomplices.

7. The police were happy _____ (catch) Mr. White, and now are actively
   searching for the other two men.

8. After _____ (conduct) a thorough examination of the museum, they will
   move on to search some of the surrounding buildings.

9. Clues found at the scene seem _____ (indicate) that Mr. White's accomplices
   escaped through a window.

10. They are thought _____ (carry) weapons but it is not yet clear what types of
    weapons.

B. Which sentences in part A can be rewritten using the simple form without changing the
meaning? Rewrite those sentences.

1. *can't rewrite* _____

2. *He denies taking the painting.* _____

3. _____

4. _____

5. _____

6. _____

7. _____

8. _____

9. _____

10. _____

Read the sentences. Check *Same* if the sentences have the same meaning. Check *Different* if their meanings are different.

		SAME	DIFFERENT
1.	It was unnecessary for you to have worried so much about the presentation. Your worrying about the presentation was unnecessary.	✓	☐
2.	I always love his coming to work late with some wild story. He loves coming to work late and telling wild stories.	☐	☐
3.	It's easy to learn a second language. Learning a second language isn't hard.	☐	☐
4.	After working in the London office, I was transferred to Tokyo. After having worked in the London office, I was transferred to Tokyo.	☐	☐
5.	I stopped to visit my family. I stopped visiting my family.	☐	☐
6.	I expect to be taken to the airport by my sister. I expect to take my sister to the airport.	☐	☐
7.	I don't appreciate being fired by him. I don't appreciate him firing me.	☐	☐
8.	When I turned the key again, the motor started running. When I turned the key again, the motor started to run.	☐	☐
9.	Are you afraid to make mistakes when you speak English? Are you afraid of making mistakes when you speak English?	☐	☐
10.	It's fun for her to learn new things. It's fun to learn new things.	☐	☐

A. What is something you would like to accomplish, but just can't seem to do?

learn to drive, speak French, juggle, make sushi

B. Make some notes about your personal goal by answering these questions. In your notes, use some of the words below (and others of your own) with gerunds and infinitives.

- Why do you want to be able to do it?
- Why do you have trouble accomplishing it?
- How do you feel about doing it?
- How do you plan to accomplish your goal in the future?

Verbs: decide, hope, intend, need, plan, want, would like
Adjectives: afraid, anxious, hesitant, interested, reluctant
Nouns: plan, trouble, time

C. Work with a partner. Tell your partner about your goal, your obstacles in reaching it, and how you will achieve it. Listen to your partner and give some advice.

A: I want to get a promotion at work. I need to be able to give presentations in English. The problem is that I'm afraid of speaking in public.
B: You should try . . .

D Writing

Editing: *Gerunds and Infinitives*

Study the errors. Pay attention to the areas that you make mistakes in.

1. **Subject-verb agreement**

   are
   Knitting and listening to music ~~is~~ very relaxing.

2. **Parallel structure (two gerunds or infinitives)**

   dancing
   Lily loves doing yoga and ~~to dance~~ in her free time.

3. **Parallel structure (with auxiliaries)**

   turned
   They expect to have signed the papers and ~~to turn~~ over the keys by Thursday.

   be
   He hopes to walk off the plane and ~~was~~ greeted by his family.

4. **Use of negative forms**

   not being given
   She resents ~~being not given~~ a bonus this year.

D1 Editing

Correct the errors in the passage. Be prepared to explain your answers.

Work-centric people focus almost exclusively on their work life. Dual-centric people, on

to focus
the other hand, tend ~~focusing~~ on both their families and their work. They enjoy working with

colleagues as well as to stay at home with their families. Most "dual-centrics" say they want to

work hard, play hard, and enjoy life.

The big question is how do dual-centric people manage to balance their lives so well? Setting

a strict boundary between home life and office life are obviously one strategy. They do this by

taking not phone calls from the office while they are at home. They also take time off. When

they decide go on vacation, they take it—no matter what.

Interestingly, although dual-centric people usually work fewer hours, they don't have fewer

responsibilities on the job. They are just as productive as other workers, but they have decided

to set and keeping boundaries between work life and home life.

Although competition can be motivating, many newer management models focus on collaboration. One success story comes from a nonprofit organization. Employees had started <u>complaining about co-workers, ignoring e-mails and phone calls, even refusing to attend meetings</u>. **The situation** got so bad that many employees were thinking of quitting.

Nouns referring to actions or states are often used to summarize and replace longer gerund or infinitive phrases. These nouns help keep writing short and succinct.

A consultant was brought in to help people better understand themselves as team members. The administration's purpose in sponsoring the workshop was to help people become better at collaborating. "<u>Knowing their own personality type</u> seemed to help employees understand their own role in the drama that was being played out," said the manager. "**It** helped them find humor in the situation, and from humor they were able to renew relationships."

Subject or object pronouns can follow and replace a gerund or infinitive phrase.

D2 **Referring to Gerunds and Infinitives**

A. Match each sentence in the first column with the correct sentence from the second. Then underline the pronoun or summarizing noun phrase and the gerund or infinitive it refers to.

1. I expect <u>to be transferred overseas</u>. __c__

2. Walking to work takes a lot of time. ____

3. Hiring smart people and giving them a large budget and complete freedom was popular a few years ago. ____

4. I plan to travel around the world next year. ____

5. To achieve my goal of finishing a marathon, I trained for a year. ____

6. Choosing a suitable career is an important task for college students. ____

a. Unfortunately, this business model didn't work for a variety of reasons.

b. Unless I start saving money now, it may not happen, though.

c. <u>The move</u> will give me a chance to see a new culture.

d. However, it also gives me time to plan my day.

e. Many students cannot decide on a major until they face this challenge.

f. The experience taught me to face my fears and doubts.

B. Complete each sentence with your own ideas. Use a pronoun or a summarizing noun to replace the gerund or infinitive.

1. I need to read magazine articles, search the Internet, and talk to colleagues.
   This preparation will help me when I begin my job search.

2. Raising children changes people over time because . . .

3. I tried studying alone in the library, and then I tried working with classmates, but . . .

4. Owning your own business can be rewarding. However, . . .

5. Many people expect to earn a lot of money in their first professional job. Unfortunately, . . .

Vocabulary Notes: *Passive Verbs + Infinitive*

In more formal or academic writing, when mental activity and communication verbs are used in the passive, they are usually followed by an infinitive. This infinitive often refers to a state or condition rather than an action.

Mental activity verbs: *believe, consider, expect, know, think*
   The treatment **is believed / considered to be effective**.
   (People believe the treatment is effective.)

Communication verbs: *claim, estimate, say, report*
   The treatments **are said / reported to cost a great deal**.
   (People say that the treatments cost a great deal.)

D3 Reporting Opinions and Ideas

A. Rewrite the sentences with a passive verb followed by an infinitive.

1. Some journalists report that the housing market is a good investment.
   The housing market is reported to be a good investment.

2. Some people estimate that the average commute takes 45 minutes.

3. Some people believe that the number seven is lucky.

4. Some consumers expect that prices will rise dramatically.

5. Some people think that spiders and other insects are helpful.

6. Some people say that parents are too permissive these days.

B. What stress reduction practices are popular today? Make a list. Use your list to write sentences with a passive verb followed by an infinitive.

Yoga is said to be good for back pain and headaches.

One form of research is a survey. The steps involved in conducting and reporting on a survey are as follows:

1. Think about an assumption or hypothesis that you have and write a statement. For example, "Most people prefer bosses who are formal rather than friendly."
2. Create a set of questions that will help you check your statement. (In surveys, *Wh-* questions are often stronger than *yes/no* questions.) For example, "Who has been your favorite boss? Why?"
3. Decide if you will interview people orally or ask them to write their answers.
4. Conduct your interviews. Be sure to tell them how you will use the results of the survey and whether or not their names will be included.
5. Study your results and draw conclusions.

Choose one of the topics below. Follow the procedure above to gather information for a three-paragraph essay. Then write your paper. In the first paragraph, state your hypothesis and describe your survey. In the next paragraph, share your answers, giving evidence from your survey where possible. In the final paragraph, explain whether your hypothesis was correct.

Alternatively, write a paper that describes your own beliefs about one of the topics. Then, use the Writing Checklist to check your work.

- Do most students feel that they live a balanced life? Conduct a survey that explores the feelings, behaviors, and/or experiences of students to learn whether or not they are generally satisfied or dissatisfied with their lifestyles.
- How confident do people feel about their future happiness? Conduct a survey that examines people's hopes and expectations. Find out whether they are generally optimistic or pessimistic and why.
- How have people experienced family life in the past 20 years? Conduct a survey to investigate reported changes in traditional family structure.

Writing Checklist

Reflect on your ability to use gerunds and infinitives by answering the questions.

- [ ] 1. Did you use gerunds and infinitives to talk about actions and states?
- [ ] 2. Did you use pronouns to replace gerund or infinitive phrases?
- [ ] 3. Did you use summarizing nouns to replace gerund or infinitive phrases?
- [ ] 4. Did you use any passive or perfect gerunds or infinitives?
- [ ] 5. Did you use any verbs in the passive followed by an infinitive?
- [ ] 6. Did you check your sentences for correct form?

▶ Beyond the Classroom

Writing

Write an essay using one of these topics.

1. Owning a business is a goal for many individuals. What sort of business would you like to own? Write a paper describing a business you are interested in and the steps that you would take in order to make it successful. In the final paragraph, summarize the reasons why you think your business would be successful.

2. In your opinion, how important is the connection between health and lifestyle? Write a short comparative essay. First describe the lifestyle habits of a typical healthy person. Then describe the lifestyle of an unhealthy person. Finally, explain any connections you see between lifestyle and health. Make recommendations for how companies and governments can foster better health.

3. Some people say that a person's life is incomplete without children. Others disagree, saying that for career-minded people, being a parent is not necessary. Consider the activities and challenges of each option. Then write a paper explaining your views on this issue. First state your opinion. Then support your opinion by describing how having or not having children might affect the different stages of adult life.

Searching for Authentic Examples

Find examples of English grammar in everyday life by completing the task below. Bring your examples to class, and be prepared to discuss them.

Look for examples of simple, perfect, and passive gerunds and infinitives in letters from banks, insurance companies, phone companies, credit card companies, etc. Can you change the perfect forms to simple forms? What happens to the meaning? Why do you think the passive forms were used?

Relative Clauses and Adjective Phrases

A All About Einstein

A1 Before You Read

Discuss these questions.

What do you know about Albert Einstein, the famous physicist?

Do you think geniuses such as Einstein have difficult personal lives? Do you think they sometimes have trouble relating to people?

A2 Read

  Read this article to learn some lesser-known facts about Einstein.

ALL ABOUT EINSTEIN

Many people would argue that Albert Einstein was the greatest thinker of the 20th century. However, it was not only Einstein's incredible intellect **that captured the public's imagination**, but also his simple, engaging manner. Even more than 50 years after his death, he remains a popular historical figure—proven by the hundreds of books about him that are currently in print, **which include several published in the past year alone**.

Most of us know about Einstein's important contributions[1] to science, but as with any significant historical figure, there were many sides to this outwardly simple, yet complex, man. Here are some details about his life **that you may not know**.

As a child, Einstein spoke slowly and hesitantly, and his parents worried that he was not very intelligent. Some experts have suggested that he may have spoken slowly because he had a mild personality disorder[2] or a learning disability **which affected his speech**. We will never know for sure.

Einstein is probably known to most people for his mathematical equation about the nature of energy, $E = MC^2$

He is remembered as a child **whose interests included playing the violin and listening to classical music**—a passion which continued into his adult life. He said, "I often think about music. I daydream about music. I see my life in the form of music."

As an adolescent in Munich, Einstein disliked his school, **where success was determined by one's ability to memorize facts.** He excelled in mathematics, and in Latin, **which he respected because of its emphasis on logic.** Einstein eventually quit school at the age of 15.

Einstein was a man whose unsettled[3] private life differed greatly from his focused and balanced consideration of the problems of the universe. He could be a playful man **who was easy to talk to** and,

at the same time, a cool and aloof father.

Einstein was married twice. His first marriage ended in a bitter divorce, and he began seeing his cousin Elsa, **whom he eventually married.** He had two sons from his first marriage: Hans Albert, the elder, became a professor, while Eduard, **who excelled in the arts**, died in a psychiatric hospital in Switzerland.

Einstein may have been a man of science, but he was also deeply spiritual. He said, "What I see in Nature is a magnificent structure that we can comprehend only very imperfectly, and that must fill a thinking person with a feeling of humility."

---

1 **contribution:** actions made to help something succeed
2 **personality disorder:** a mental illness characterized by abnormal thoughts or behavior

3 **unsettled:** changeable; not peaceful

A3 After You Read

Discuss these questions.

1. What is the purpose of the article?
2. Which of these words would you use to describe Einstein: a dreamer, consistent, a cooperative student, a quick learner, or curious? Find sentences in the article that support your answers.
3. What is the most surprising thing you learned about Einstein?

A4 Examining Form

A. **Work in pairs. Look at the highlighted relative clauses in the reading. Complete the tasks and answer the questions.**

1. Circle the nouns or noun phrases that the clauses modify.
2. The words that begin relative clauses are called relative pronouns. What are the different relative pronouns in these clauses?
3. Write the clauses under the correct categories on a separate piece of paper.

Relative pronoun + verb	Relative pronoun + subject + verb
that captured the public's imagination	

B. **Discuss your observations with the class. Refer to the notes on pages 172–173 if you need to.**

B Relative Clauses

Examining Meaning and Use

Match the examples with the statements below them. Discuss your answers. Then read the notes to check them.

1. **a.** Point to the one which is on the list.
    b. Point to the one who is on the list.

    ____ This sentence is about a person.

    ____ This sentence is about a book.

2. **a.** These are the students you need to call.
    b. These are the students who need to call you.

    ____ You have to make some calls.

    ____ Some students have to make some calls.

3. **a.** Our TV, which is broken, is in the family room.
    b. Our TV which is broken is in the family room.

    ____ We have one TV.

    ____ We have more than one TV.

Subject and Object Relative Clauses

Subject Relative Clauses

J. K. Rowling is <u>the author</u>. <u>She</u> wrote the Harry Potter books. ⟶
J. K. Rowling is the author **who wrote the Harry Potter books**.

Object Relative Clauses

She is <u>the author</u>. I have interviewed <u>her</u>. ⟶
She is the author **that I have interviewed**.

Object Relative Clauses with Prepositions

She is <u>the author</u>. The committee gave an award <u>to her</u>. ⟶
She is the author **that the committee gave an award to**.
She is the author **to whom the committee gave an award**. *(more formal)*

Continued

- Relative clauses are also called adjective clauses. Like adjectives, relative clauses modify nouns. These clauses identify, define, or comment on the noun that they follow.
- Relative clauses are dependent clauses; they cannot stand alone as independent sentences.
- Relative clauses usually begin with a relative pronoun (e.g., *who, that*). The relative pronoun and the modified noun refer to the same thing (e.g., *who, that = the author*).
- Sentences with relative clauses can be thought of as a combination of two sentences, i.e., as a shorter way of saying the same thing.
- **Subject relative clauses:** The relative pronoun takes the place of the subject of the clause (e.g., *she*). It is followed by a verb. The verb agrees with the noun that the clause modifies.
- **Object relative clauses:** The relative pronoun takes the place of the object of the clause (e.g., *her*). It is followed by a subject + a verb. The verb agrees with the subject.
- **Object relative clauses with prepositions:** The relative pronoun takes the place of the object of a preposition (e.g., *her*). It is followed by a subject + a verb. The verb agrees with the subject. The preposition usually appears at the end of the clause, but can also be put before the relative pronouns *which* or *whom*.

Relative Pronouns

Subject
The students <u>who/that</u> **live next door** make too much noise.
There are numerous viruses <u>that/which</u> **cause the common cold**.

Object
Last year, someone <u>that/who</u> **I know** had a book published.
The beach <u>that/which</u> **we visited last week** has been closed for the summer.

Object with Preposition
The man <u>that/who</u> **I spoke to** had a thick accent.
This is a problem <u>that/which</u> **we know nothing about**.

- The relative pronoun *who* can be used to refer to people and the relative pronoun *which* can be used to refer to things. *That* can refer to either people or things.
- In **subject relative clauses**, *who* is more commonly used to refer to people than *that*. In all other subject or object relative clauses, *that* is more common. *Which* and *who* usually sound more formal, but are often used in writing.
- In **object relative clauses**, *whom* can be used instead of *who* to convey a more formal tone.
    Ladies and gentlemen, it is my pleasure to introduce a woman **whom** I greatly admire.
- Object relative clauses with prepositions follow the same rules as object relative clauses. However, when the preposition is placed before the relative pronoun to create a more formal tone, *whom* or *which* must be used.
    The woman **to whom** the award was given is a great humanitarian.

Object Relative Clauses

These are the documents **(that) you need to enter the country**.

You can ask anyone **(that) I spoke to**.

Kate is the woman **(who) I told you about that I met on vacation**. (2 relative clauses)

- In object relative clauses, the relative pronoun can be omitted with no change in meaning. This is also true in object relative clauses ending with prepositions. This is common in everyday speech.
- When there are two object relative clauses in a row, the first relative pronoun is usually omitted but the second one cannot be omitted.
- You cannot drop the relative pronoun in subject relative clauses.
  * The lecture was given by a professor lived in Tibet for 20 years. (INCORRECT)

Restrictive vs. Nonrestrictive Relative Clauses

Restrictive Relative Clauses

My sister **who lives in New York** works for Donald Trump. *(Which sister? The one in New York.)*

The car **that I think changed the world** was the Model T. *(Sentence is meaningless without relative clause)*

Nonrestrictive Relative Clauses

My sister, **who lives in New York,** works for Donald Trump. *(Implies that I have only one sister and she lives in New York)*

The Model T, **which Ford produced from 1908 to 1927,** was the first affordable car. *(Sentence is still meaningful even if clause is omitted)*

- The preceding charts have addressed the most common kind of relative clause, called a **restrictive** (or defining) **relative clause**. This kind of clause answers the question: *Which one?* It is used to identify one noun and distinguish it from other similar nouns. The information in the restrictive relative clause is necessary to make the meaning of the sentence clear.
- There is another kind of relative clause called a **nonrestrictive** (or nondefining) **relative clause.** This kind of clause adds extra information to the noun you are talking about. The information in the clause is not necessary—it can be omitted and the meaning of the sentence is still understandable. These kinds of clauses are less frequently used and occur mainly in writing.
- Nonrestrictive relative clauses are used after proper nouns and other specific or unique nouns.
  <u>My mother</u>, **who lives in Texas,** ...
  <u>The Model T</u>, **which Ford produced from 1908 to 1927,** ...
- Nonrestrictive relative clauses are always offset by commas. They can only be used with the pronouns *who, whom,* or *which.* You cannot use *that* or omit the relative pronoun.
  * My mother, that lives in Texas, sells real estate. (INCORRECT)
  * The Model T, Ford produced from 1908 to 1927, was the first affordable car. (INCORRECT)

Restrictive Relative Clauses

She is the <u>author</u> **whose books have won many awards.**

It was a <u>time</u> **when I didn't have any money.** *(= a time during which . . .)*

I often pass by the <u>street</u> **where you used to live.** *(= a street on which . . .)*

I know the <u>reason</u> **why the workers went on strike.** *(= the reason that . . .)*

Nonrestrictive Relative Clauses

<u>J. K. Rowling</u>, **whose books are all bestsellers,** donates a lot of money to charity.

I can't pay rent until <u>next week</u>, **when I get my paycheck in the mail.**

When I visit <u>Taipei</u>, **where I used to live,** I make sure to buy some of my favorite tea.

- Some object relative clauses can begin with other relative pronouns, (e.g., *whose, when, where, why*).
- **Restrictive relative clauses:** *Whose* shows a possessive relationship between the nouns before and after it. *When* can be used as a relative pronoun when it follows words like *time, month,* or *year. Where* follows words like *place, street, city,* and *situation.* You can use *why* after the noun *reason.*
- **Nonrestrictive relative clauses:** *Whose, when,* and *where* can also be used in these clauses. Unlike their use in restrictive relative clauses, *when* and *where* can follow specific times (e.g., *last summer*) or place names (e.g., *Taipei*).

B1 ## Listening

A. 🎧 Each sentence in the passage is incomplete. Listen to the entire passage first. Then listen again and put a caret (∧) where you hear a missing word. Listen once more to fill in the missing words.

In both ancient and modern times, the idea of dreams has been something *that*∧ captures peoples' imaginations. A dream is a series of images, events, and feelings occur in your mind while you are asleep. In ancient times, dreams were believed to be messages the gods sent to warn people about the future. In 1900, Sigmund Freud, is considered the father of modern psychology, published a famous book is called *The Interpretation of Dreams.* Today, people still believe they have dreams information about the future is revealed. Moreover, there are numerous reports of artists and inventors dreams inspire them, and many actually keep notebooks they record their dreams.

B. 🎧 **Listen. Choose the best sentence to complete each conversation.**

1. **a.** How many brothers do you have?
   b. I didn't know that you only have one brother.

2. **a.** The one who you liked.
   b. The one that was on sale.

3. **a.** What did you write?
   b. Who did you write to?

4. **a.** To my house, which is on the corner.
   b. To my house which is on the corner.

5. **a.** The one I ate.
   b. The one I ate at.

6. **a.** I'm sorry. I didn't know who it was.
   b. I'm sorry. I didn't know whose it was.

B2 Contrasting Subject and Object Relative Clauses   *what is describe*

Choose the correct word(s) to complete each sentence.

1. The company was looking for people who (were / they were) bilingual in Chinese and English.
   describe object
2. There are certain rules of conduct which (are / you are) expected to follow.   *(object / relative)*
3. You have to take this money back to the person that (got / you got) it from.
4. I waste a lot of time doing tasks that (aren't / they aren't) important.
5. Have you read the article that (were / we were) talking about yet?   *object relative*
6. Most people prefer bosses who (are / they are) formal rather than friendly.
7. I need to find the guy that (bought / I bought) this computer from.   *describe / which guy*
8. Do you remember the strike that (happened / it happened) last year?   *that + it*
9. It was a show that (was / I am) not likely to forget.   *S do action*
10. I got to see some people that (hadn't / I hadn't) seen in a long time.   *which people*

B3 Combining Sentences

A. Combine each pair of sentences. Use a subject or object relative clause with *who* or *which*.

1. The computers were given to public schools in the area. Our company donated them.

   The computers which our company donated were given to public schools in the area.

2. Free speech is a freedom. Many people in the United States take it for granted.

   Free speech is a freedom which many " " take for grt

3. A storm caused millions of dollars in damage. It hit the U.S. state of Florida in 2004.

   A storm which hit the U.S state of florida in 2004 caused millions dol.

4. The job was given to another man. He had been at the company for only one year.

   The " " " who " , " " "

5. They are a really good group of workers. We appreciate and respect them a lot.

   They are " " " who we " " "

6. The city built a lightrail system. It connects the suburbs and downtown.

   " " " which " " " "

B. Which sentences can be rewritten using *that* as a relative pronoun?

B4 Writing Definitions with Relative Clauses

A. Write your own definitions for these people, places, and things. Use a relative clause with *who*, *which*, or *that*. Then compare your ideas with a partner.

1. A generous person is someone . . . *who helps other people.*
2. A best friend is a person . . . *who shares happiness & sorrow*
3. A good job is one . *which you like most*
4. A classic book is one *that gives you lesson*
5. A home is a place . *where you feel comfortable*
6. A good teacher is a person . *who teaches well*
7. A museum is a place *where you can see antique/historical things*
8. A holiday is a time . *when you go outside*

B. Work with a partner. Choose five nouns from the dictionary that you don't know. Write a true definition and a false definition for each word. Use a relative clause with *who*, *which*, or *that*.

A carnivore is an animal that only eats meat.

A carnivore is a person who works at a carnival.

C. Join another pair and take turns. One pair reads the true and false definition for one of their words. The other pair guesses which definition is correct.

A: Is a carnivore an animal that only eats meat, or is it a person who works at a carnival?

B: I think a carnivore is an animal that only eats meat.

B5 Other Relative Pronouns

A. Complete the sentences with information about yourself. Use object relative clauses with *where*, *when*, or *why*.

1. I remember the day . *when my son was born*
2. I know a great restaurant . *where you can enjoy delicious food*
3. *2007* was the year *when I came to Canada*
4. Someday I'd like to live in a place . *where I'm friend*
5. I don't know the reason . *why I cannot improve my English*
6. *Karachi* is a city . *where you can enjoy*

B. Choose one sentence from part A and develop it into a short paragraph.

I remember the day when I received my job offer. I was so happy. I had been filling out applications for weeks and . . .

B6 Object Relative Clauses with Prepositions

A. Match each sentence in the first column with the correct sentence from the second. Then combine each pair of sentences using a relative clause with *who, which,* or *that.* Put the preposition at the end of the sentence.

1. Immigration is an issue. ___e___

   Immigration is an issue that I'm very concerned about.

2. Einstein is a famous person from history. ___a___
3. Physics is an academic subject. _____
4. Rio de Janeiro is a city. _____
5. Acting and writing are two jobs. _____
6. My birthday is an event. _____

a. I would like to have a conversation with him.
b. I always get excited about it.
c. I'm well suited for them.
d. I would like to live in it someday.
e. I'm very concerned about it.
f. I excel in it.

B. Rewrite your sentences from part A. Make them more formal by moving the preposition to the beginning of the relative clause.

Immigration is an issue about which I'm very concerned.

C. Now choose three of these questions to discuss with a partner. Ask follow-up questions to get more information.

1. What current political or social issues are you interested in?
2. Who is a famous person from history you would like to talk to?
3. What academic subject are you good at?
4. What's a city that you would like to move to someday?
5. What are two jobs that you are qualified for?
6. What upcoming events are you looking forward to?

B7 Omitting Relative Pronouns

Read the sentences about inventors and their inventions. Can you omit the relative pronouns in any of the sentences? Cross out the relative pronouns where possible.

1. Television is an invention **that** we cannot credit to a single inventor.
2. The ideas **that** many inventors come up with can appear strange to people **that** aren't inventors.
3. The person **who** invented the ballpoint pen was a Hungarian journalist.
4. There's a new book about Thomas Edison **which** I've read **that** I highly recommend.
5. Guglielmo Marconi was the inventor **who** I think invented the radio.
6. Elias Howe was the inventor **who** created the sewing machine and the zipper.
7. Many men and women **who** we think of as our greatest inventors were considered strange by their colleagues.
8. The light bulb and the phonograph are the inventions **that** Thomas Edison is most famous for.

178   Chapter 10 • Form, Meaning, and Use 1

Contrasting Relative Pronouns

Choose all the correct relative pronouns in each sentence. (More than one pronoun is often possible.)

1. The girl (that / who / which) I sat next to in math class always knew the answers.
2. I was surprised to see the log house (where / in which / Ø) my father grew up.
3. My grandmother, (who / which / whose) maiden name was Faust, grew up in Germany.
4. It's a situation (that / which / to which) I'd rather not think about.
5. I saw a former professor of mine (that / whose / whom) name I can never remember.
6. I was not expecting the present, (that / which / Ø) was much too expensive to accept.
7. Nelson Mandela is a politician (who / whom / Ø) I respect a lot.
8. It's ten miles from the town (when / where / Ø) I grew up.
9. My twin brother, (that / who / Ø) lives next door, calls me every day.
10. Anyone (who / whom / Ø) enjoyed *Pirates of the Caribbean* will love this movie, too.
11. I didn't see the face of the man (who / whom / to whom) I gave the money.
12. I have fond memories of the day (that / when / Ø) I met my wife.

important   essential   non-important information   which, Ø
Equal defining clause

B9 **Restrictive and Nonrestrictive Relative Clauses**

A. Combine each pair of sentences where marked with the (^) symbol. Use relative clauses. Add commas where necessary. (You will use either restrictive or nonrestrictive relative clauses in your answers.)

1. My parents ^ had four children. They emigrated to this country thirty years ago.

   My parents, who emigrated to this country thirty years ago, had four children.

2. I have one older brother ^. He lives in Los Angeles.

   I have one older brother, who lives in Los Angeles.

3. He is an actor ^. You may have seen him in several TV commercials.

   whom

4. My sister ^ is only ten months older than me. Her family recently moved to Dallas.

   whose family recently moved to Dallas, is only 10 months older than me

5. She lives in a housing development ^. Almost everyone there works for the same company.

   where

6. My twin brother, Marcus, is the one ^. I'm the closest to ~~him~~.

   whom

7. My neighbor has an old van ^. It always breaks down.

   that / which

8. Our family reunion ^ is always a lot of fun. It happens every other year.

   which happens every other year, is always lots of fun

B. **Choose four or five friends or family members. Write two simple statements about each of them. Answer two of these questions to write about them.**

1. How old are they?
2. Where do they live?
3. What do they do or where do they work?
4. What do they like to do?
5. What else can you say about them?

My mother is 50 years old. She likes to draw.
My brother Julio lives in Mexico City. He attends graduate school there.

C. **Now combine your statements about each person using nonrestrictive relative clauses.**

My mother, who is 50 years old, likes to draw.
My brother Julio lives in Mexico City, where he attends graduate school.

Usage Note: *Using* Which *to Modify a Clause*

Nonrestrictive relative clauses beginning with *which* are sometimes used to modify the entire main clause rather than just a single noun or noun phrase. This occurs most often in conversation and informal writing.

It's starting to rain, **which means the picnic will have to be postponed.**

B10 Modifying Clauses

A. **Add a relative clause with *which* to each sentence. Use the sentences from the box.**

That proves she's not very responsible.   That's going to make it hard for me to
That's exactly what I hoped she would do.   finish my work.
That's what I wanted to do in the first place.   That means I won't be home until late.
That isn't very convenient for me.

1. I told my mother I'd go shopping with her today, *which means I won't be home until late* .

2. My computer isn't working, _____.

3. The board meets the first Tuesday of every month, _____.

4. My sister forgot to pick me up again today, _____.

5. We're going to go to dinner instead of a movie, _____.

6. The professor is giving us an extra week to finish our papers, _____.

B. **Add *which* clauses to modify these sentences. Use your own ideas.**

1. I lost my cell phone this morning, _____.

2. I have to catch up on my homework, _____.

3. The weather is supposed to be terrible today, _____.

4. The movie doesn't end until midnight, _____.

Adjective Phrases

Examining Meaning and Use

Read each sentence and the statements that follow it. Check (✓) the correct statement. Discuss your answers. Then read the notes to check them.

1. The guy talking to the receptionist was rude.

   ____ The guy was rude.

   ____ The receptionist was rude.

2. Go speak to Tom Gray, chairman of the committee.

   ____ You should speak to one person.

   ____ You should speak to two people.

3. I'm wearing a necklace made in Brazil.

   ____ I am from Brazil.

   ____ My necklace is from Brazil.

Adjective Phrases from Clauses with *Be*

Only people ~~who are~~ **on the guest list** will be allowed to enter. *(prepositional phrase)*

The therapist treated my muscles, ~~which were~~ **stiff from lack of use**. *(adjective phrase)*

This computer is perfect for someone ~~that is~~ **working at home**. *(continuous verb)*

The thief used a credit card ~~that was~~ **found on the street**. *(passive verb)*

Alan Tam, ~~who is~~ **the CEO of Dynamix**, is a billionaire. *(noun [phrase]* = appositive*)*

- Subject relative clauses with *who, which,* or *that* can sometimes be reduced to adjective phrases in order to make the language less wordy and more concise. You cannot reduce object relative clauses to adjective phrases.

  * That's the guy telling you about. (INCORRECT)

- Adjective phrases are most commonly reduced from clauses with a form of the verb *be* + a prepositional phrase, adjective phrase, continuous verb, passive verb, or a noun (phrase). To reduce these clauses, omit the relative pronoun and *be*.

- You cannot reduce a clause with *be* followed by a single adjective:

  * The therapist treated my muscles, <u>stiff</u>. (INCORRECT)

- When *be* is followed by a noun phrase, it can only be reduced in nonrestrictive clauses. The reduced form is called **an appositive**.

  Nonrestrictive: John, **a relative of a staff member**, can use the facilities for free.

  Restrictive: * Anyone a relative of a staff member can use the facilities for free. (INCORRECT)

Anyone ~~who arrives~~ **arriving** late will be denied entrance.

There was a sign ~~that warned~~ **warning** us to leave the area.

A meteor ~~that weighs~~ **weighing** over 440 tons could hit the Earth in 2120.

My grandparents, ~~who knew~~ **knowing** the Nazis would soon find them, fled to America.

- Some relative clauses not containing forms of *be* can be reduced to adjective phrases. To reduce these clauses, omit the relative pronoun and change the verb to the present participle: verb + -*ing*.
- You cannot reduce a relative clause if it would change the meaning of the sentence. This often happens when the meaning of the adjective phrase is different from the meaning of the relative clause in the original sentence.

  The man who jogs by your house is my uncle. *(habitual activity)*

  The man jogging by your house is my uncle. *(happening now — different meaning)*

C1 Listening

A. Each sentence in the passage is incomplete. Listen to the entire passage first. Then listen again and put a caret (^) where you hear a missing word. Listen once more to fill in the missing words.

called

Personal data assistants, ^ PDAs, are handheld electronic devices to help busy working people. These small devices, now essential by many in the business world, have become extremely versatile. The models by all leading manufacturers help users perform many tasks browsing the Internet, sending and receiving e-mail, playing computer games, and even making phone calls. A person a PDA, therefore, may have a dozen electronic tools at the same time.

B. Listen. Circle the best answer to complete each conversation.

1. **a.** Where is it located now?
   b. Where is she located now?

2. **a.** When was it written?
   b. I'll look for a newer one.

3. **a.** Yes, it is.
   b. Yes, I was sick.

4. **a.** Did he report it to the police?
   b. Do they know who owned the car?

5. **a.** John's
   b. John is.

6. **a.** You must miss him a lot.
   b. You must miss them a lot.

C2 Adding Information with Appositives

A. Add an appositive phrase from the box to modify each underlined noun or noun phrase. Add commas where necessary.

a machine for transmitting written information by wire	an event featuring action sports
the naturalist who proposed the theory of natural selection	the period from the mid-1300s to about 1600
an international organization founded in 1945	the scientific study of human language

1. The Renaissance followed the Middle Ages.
   The Renaissance, the period from the mid-1300s to about 1600, followed the Middle Ages.
2. The telegraph sends messages using a coded series of dots and dashes.
3. One of the foundations of modern biology is the work of Charles Darwin.
4. Linguistics was first recognized as an academic discipline in the early 1800s.
5. Unlike the Olympics, the X Games are held every year.
6. The United Nations aims to facilitate cooperation between countries.

B. Complete the list with your favorite things. Then write sentences with appositives about these people and things. Tell a partner about them.

One of my favorite . . .

books: _____ actors: _____ foods: _____

movies: _____ songs: _____ places to visit: _____

Noodles with tamarind sauce, a dish from Thailand, is made with coconut milk.

C3 Using Adjective Phrases

Read the excerpt about skyscrapers. Pay attention to the underlined relative clauses. Which ones can be reduced? Reduce the clauses wherever possible.

Anyone who looks at that symbol of the modern age, which is the skyscraper, can easily tell that it wasn't the idea of a single person. Rather, the skyscraper is the result of a series of technical innovations that were made in many fields over the course of many decades. First, in the mid-19th century, a process that allowed steel to be produced inexpensively was developed by William Kelly, who was an American, and Henry Bessemer, who was an Englishman. Cheap steel made it possible to build structures higher than had been done with traditional materials. Reinforced concrete, which uses steel bars to strengthen the material, was also used. Moreover, since most people find it difficult to climb more than six stories of stairs, the development of the elevator was another innovation that was essential for the building of skyscrapers.

The engineering that was required to build skyscrapers was in place by the middle of the 1880s, when the Home Insurance Building in Chicago, which was the world's first skyscraper, was built. Initially, the architectural styles that were used in the design of these tall buildings imitated past eras, such as the Renaissance. However, in the 20th century, a style developed that many people most strongly associate with the skyscraper—art deco. This style, which reached the height of its popularity in the 1920s–1930s, represented a forceful modern belief in the promise of the future. The Chrysler Building and Empire State Building, which are two of the most famous skyscrapers in New York, were built in the art deco style.

A new type of building which belongs to the "skyscraper family" is the next step in skyscraper development. Called "superscrapers," these buildings are even taller and are being constructed using the latest technological advances. One example of a superscraper is the Burj Dubai building in Dubai.

C4 Combining Sentences

A. **Combine each set of sentences. Use adjective phrases. Add commas where necessary. (There is more than one way to combine some sentences.)**

1. The construction company plans to build town houses. It is purchasing the property.

   The construction company purchasing the property plans to build town houses. OR

   The construction company planning to build town houses is purchasing the property.

2. Many runners collapsed before they reached the finish line. They were exhausted from their efforts.

   _____

3. The meeting was held in secret. It determined the winner.

   _____

4. I saw a strange object. It was flying across the sky.

   _____

5. The runner up was very disappointed. She hoped to win the contest.

   _____

6. We think the plan is good. It was suggested by the group leader.

   _____

7. You can get help at the Writing Center. It is located on the lower level of the library.

   _____

8. My boss is an avid car collector. He just bought an original Model T. It was built in 1908.

   _____

Read each sentence and the statements that follow it. Choose the statement that best explains the meaning of the sentence.

1. My brother who lives in Philadelphia is an attorney.
   a. I have one brother.
   b. I have more than one brother.

2. Stan is the kind of guy people like to have at a party.
   a. People like to invite Stan to their parties.
   b. Stan likes to invite a lot of people to his parties.

3. Last week I finally met my friend's mother, whose book has won an award for literature.
   a. My friend is an author.
   b. My friend's mother is an author.

4. The man my friend Ted works with is from Boston.
   a. The man is from Boston.
   b. Ted is from Boston.

5. My next door neighbor, to whom I have stopped speaking, was extremely insulting.
   a. My neighbor stopped speaking to me because I insulted him.
   b. I stopped speaking to my neighbor because he insulted me.

6. The woman near the door talking to the tall man teaches in the chemistry department.
   a. The man teaches in the chemistry department.
   b. The woman teaches in the chemistry department.

7. I didn't receive a call from my sister, which was very upsetting.
   a. I feel upset.
   b. My sister feels upset.

C6 **Speaking**

A. Think about your dating habits now or at a time when you used to date. Take this dating questionnaire. Write *True* or *False* for each statement.

1. _____ I'm the kind of person who likes to be in charge.

2. _____ On a first date, I always look for a place where the prices are affordable.

3. _____ I'm someone that feels comfortable meeting new people.

4. _____ I'm a good listener.

5. _____ I think it's difficult to find time to meet new people.

6. _____ I can always find something to talk about on a date.

7. _____ I don't think people on dates behave like themselves.

8. _____ I've never been on a date that I didn't enjoy.

B. Work in small groups. Discuss your answers to the questionnaire. Do you think you're good at dating? Does the group agree with you?

I'm definitely the kind of person who likes to be in charge. I don't like surprises. That probably isn't a good quality for a person who is trying to date and meet new people.

D | Writing

Editing: *Relative Clauses*

Study the errors. Pay attention to the areas that you make mistakes in.

> **1. Subject-verb agreement**
>
>   are
> He's the writer whose books ~~is~~ on all the best-seller lists.
>
> **2. Use of commas**
>
> This is the friend ~~,~~ that I told you about. *(restrictive clause)*
>
>   ,
> The book is at the college bookstore ∧ which is on Bank Street. *(nonrestrictive clause)*
>
> **3. Use of subject/object**
>
> The author who ~~she~~ wrote the novel is having a book signing.
>
> The book that you recommended ~~it~~ is out of print.
>
> **4. Use of prepositions**
>
>   for
> The invention which Edison is most famous ∧ is the phonograph.
>
> **5. Use of adjective phrases**
>
>   who eats
> My father, ~~eating~~ eggs, doesn't eat meat or fish.
>
> **6. Use of relative pronouns**
>
>   who
> I met an inventor ∧ is very famous.
>
>   which
> My friend climbed Mt. Fuji, ~~that~~ is in Japan.

D1 | Editing

Correct the errors in the sentences. Be prepared to explain your answers. (There may be more than one correction.)

                                 are

1. There are several people in my class who ~~is~~ planning to major in English.

2. Last year, I visited the Grand Canyon, that I found awe-inspiring.

3. Radium is the discovery which Marie Curie is famous.

4. The hardware store did have the tools that I needed them to repair my bicycle.

5. My friend, you met yesterday told me about a new restaurant.

6. Architects use space creatively are always in great demand.

Beyond the Sentence: *Defining Nouns and Adding Information*

Writers use relative clauses to avoid repetition and make information flow smoothly. Relative clauses provide a concise way of defining nouns and adding information without starting a new sentence.

> *A relative clause is often used early in a paragraph to introduce and define a new noun.*

> *A relative clause is also commonly used after a specific noun to define the noun or remind the reader of the identity of the noun.*

> *Nonrestrictive relative clauses or those reduced to adjective phrases are a concise way to add background information.*

There are many ways to define a good leader. A good leader doesn't have to be famous. A leader can simply be <u>someone</u> **that people admire and whose guidance they respect**. My best friend, who I have known for years, is a quiet and determined activist. In <u>the community</u> **where he lives,** he has earned a reputation for being fair-minded and level-headed on a variety of issues such as traffic congestion and property taxes. This is why many people seek his advice, and he is considered a leader.

Some local leaders do become famous, though. <u>Mohammed Yunus</u>, **the economist who won the Nobel Peace Prize in 2006**, became renowned for his work in the area of <u>microfinance</u>, **which is the practice of lending small amounts of money to poor people so they can start businesses**. Yunus felt that these small loans were the key to helping millions overcome poverty. Today <u>the Grameen Bank</u>, **which he founded in 1976**, makes loans to almost seven million people and provides services to more than 72,000 villages in Bangladesh.

D2 **Introducing Paragraphs**

A. Complete the sentences with relative clauses or adjective phrases.

1. A true friend is someone *who will help you with any kind of problem*   .

2. The United Nations is an organization _____.

3. The Louvre, _____, is the best museum I know.

4. Living in a foreign country is an experience _____.

5. Nature preservation areas are places _____.

B. Choose one sentence from part A and use it to introduce a short paragraph. Try to use at least one more relative clause in the paragraph that you write.

> *A true friend is someone who will help you with any kind of problem, regardless of the circumstances. My best friend Dyogo, who I have known my whole life, is that kind of friend . . .*

> Good writers provide specific details. These details allow the reader to create a mental picture. Relative clauses help writers express complex details more precisely.

Choose one of the topics to write a short essay of two or three paragraphs. Be sure to provide specific details to describe the people and things you are writing about. Then, use the Writing Checklist to check your work.

• In your opinion, what makes a good leader? Think of the people you feel are strong leaders. What qualities do or did they have? Why are or were they successful?

• There is a well-known expression: "Beauty is in the eye of the beholder." In your opinion, what makes something beautiful? Is visual beauty the only type of beauty? In what other ways can something be beautiful? How do we decide what is beautiful?

Writing Checklist

Reflect on your ability to use relative clauses and adjective phrases by answering the questions.

☐ **1.** Did you use subject and object relative clauses to introduce, define, or identify nouns?

☐ **2.** Did you use nonrestrictive relative clauses to add background information?

☐ **3.** Did you use relative clauses with other relative pronouns *(whose, when, where)*?

☐ **4.** Did you use any adjective phrases?

☐ **5.** Did you check your sentences for correct form?

 # Beyond the Classroom

Writing

Write an essay using one of these topics.

1. Life is full of "firsts." Some moments may be trivial—such as the first time you tried a new food. Other moments may have had a serious impact on defining our lives—such as a marriage, a graduation, or a career decision. Choose a first from your life. Describe in detail why that moment was important, and how it influenced your life.

2. For many countries, tourism is a multi-million dollar industry. Every country has its famous tourist destinations. Many of these places have become so well-visited, that they are now known as "tourist traps." Choose one tourist attraction that you have visited and explain why, despite its popularity, you still consider it a "must see."

Searching for Authentic Examples

Find examples of English grammar in everyday life by completing the task below. Bring your examples to class, and be prepared to discuss them.

Find a newspaper or magazine article. Look for three examples of relative clauses. Try to find ones with different relative pronouns. Look for three examples of adjective phrases. Can you paraphrase them using full relative clauses instead?

Coordinating Conjunctions and Transitions

A   Kiss and Make Up

A1   Before You Read

Discuss these questions.

What does "conflict resolution" mean?

How do you learn how to settle an argument? Is it something that is taught, or is it simply learned through experience?

A2   Read

 Read this article about how and why conflicts are resolved in animal groups.

KISS AND MAKE UP[1]

Why can't we be more forgiving? Ongoing violence worldwide is incredibly destructive, **yet** we humans find it very difficult to stop fighting. It seems that we are not good at conflict resolution, and it makes you wonder: What about other animals? How and when do they resolve their disagreements? **Most importantly**, is there anything that we can learn about conflict resolution from the animal kingdom?

Let's look at the spotted hyena, **for instance**. They are highly sociable, but similar to other animals that live in close-knit social groups, they don't always get along. The interesting thing, **however**, is that they don't hold a grudge.[2] Within about five minutes of fighting, combatants[3] can often be seen playing together. **Like** hyenas, many other animals engage in conflict resolution as well: Bottlenose dolphins, goats, and most primates generally prefer to "settle their differences" rather than stay angry.

Furthermore, conflict resolution seems to be a necessity in many animal groups. If the loser of a fight left the group every time an altercation[4] occurred, the group would quickly shrink and eventually die out. The

size of the group needs to be maintained for it to continue functioning, **so** animals have learned this behavior in order to survive.

When there is a fight, the loser often initiates[5] the process of forgiveness, **but** sometimes the winner approaches the loser to make up. This is because without some kind of resolution, the winner will worry that a fight will flare up[6] again. That worry can lead to further anxiety and raised levels of stress. In the long run, it pays to patch things up[7] and keep everyone loyal to the group. Reconciliation[8] is so beneficial to a group of chimps, **in fact**, that if neither opponent will initiate it, another chimp may step in to settle the fight.

Nevertheless, not all disputes are created equal, **and** some are not likely to end in resolution. Researchers have found that in primates, reconciliation almost never occurs when individuals fight over food. This is because a fight over food will naturally end when the food is gone. However, fights that are more vague in origin need resolution because they have the potential to happen again unless there is closure.

The question becomes: Can conflict resolution be learned? Researchers think so. They studied rhesus and stumptail monkeys. Rhesus monkeys are aggressive and rarely choose reconciliation; **on the other hand**, stumptails have a talent for making up. Researchers wanted to see what would happen if they raised these two species together from a young age. They discovered that the stumptails had a positive influence on the rhesus monkeys, whose behavior toward other group members gradually became gentler. The idea that natural conflict resolution can be taught by observation means there is some hope for us humans!

Adapted from *Why Don't We Just Kiss and Make Up?* by Lee Dugatkin, *New Scientist*, May 7, 2005.

1 **make up:** to become friendly again after a disagreement
2 **hold a grudge:** have angry feelings toward someone for a long time
3 **combatants:** fighters
4 **altercation:** a noisy disagreement
5 **initiate:** to begin
6 **flare up:** to start suddenly or unexpectedly
7 **patch things up:** to settle an argument
8 **reconciliation:** the act of ending a disagreement

 A3 **After You Read**

Discuss these questions.

1. Why is conflict resolution in animal groups sometimes necessary?
2. Which individuals may initiate the resolution of a conflict?
3. What did researchers find out when they studied rhesus and stumptail monkeys?
4. When you have an argument with a close friend or family member, do you try to make up afterward or do you just act as if nothing happened? What are the advantages and disadvantages of each approach?

A4 Examining Form

A. Work in pairs. Look at the highlighted words and expressions in the reading. Which connect ideas in a single sentence? Which connect ideas between sentences or paragraphs? Write them in the correct categories.

Connect ideas in a single sentence:

yet _____

_____

Connect ideas between sentences or paragraphs:

most importantly _____

_____

B. Discuss your observations with the class. Refer to pages A-21–23 if you need to.

FORM, MEANING, AND USE 1

B Coordinating Conjunctions

Examining Meaning and Use

Match the examples with the statements below them. Discuss your answers. Then read the notes to check them.

a. Some people resolve conflicts themselves, or they seek outside help.

b. Dolphins are sociable, so it's not surprising that they resolve their conflicts easily.

c. Many animals fight with each other, yet they make up almost immediately.

d. Making up is crucial in the animal kingdom, for animals do not thrive under stress.

____ The second sentence is a bit surprising or unexpected.

____ The two sentences show choices.

____ The second sentence tells why the first sentence is true.

____ The second sentence is a result of the first.

Showing Additional Ideas

She spent a summer abroad in China, **and** she plans to perfect her Mandarin in college.

She didn't ask me why I was late, **and** I didn't tell her.

She didn't ask me why I was late, **nor** <u>did I</u> tell her.

Showing a Contrast Between Ideas

I usually read every night, **but** I haven't had time lately.

Many people say they want to help, **but / yet** they never do anything. *(concession)*

Showing Alternative Ideas

He may have been lying to you, **or** he may just have been exaggerating.

Do you think you lost your wallet, **or** was it stolen?

Showing a Result

People are getting married when they are older, **so** they can't have as many children.

Showing the Cause or Reasons

The speaker is well-known among academics, **for** she has published numerous books.

- Coordinating conjunctions can join independent clauses to form a compound sentence. They are called coordinating because the two clauses have equally important ideas. You can join clauses with the same subject or with different subjects. The conjunction shows how the clauses are related.

- A comma is used before the conjunction. The comma can be omitted if both clauses are short.

   Fish can swim **and** birds can fly.

- **Showing additional ideas:** We usually use *and* to show additional ideas. *Nor* can only connect two negative ideas; it is used in more formal situations. After *nor*, the subject and auxiliary or form of *be* are inverted.

- **Showing a contrast between ideas:** We usually use *but* to show a contrast between ideas. *Yet* or *but* are sometimes used to emphasize a more unexpected contrast and convey the idea, "This is true, but . . ." This is called a concession.

- **Showing alternative ideas:** We most often use *or* to join alternatives in questions or in sentences with modals of possibility (e.g., *may* and *might*). *Or* is more commonly used to join words or phrases rather than whole clauses (see Omitting Words in the Second Clause on page 194).

- **Showing a result:** *So* shows that the second idea is the result of the first idea.

- **Showing the cause or reason:** *For* connects two ideas like other conjunctions, but the clause with *for* is not considered equally important; the reason is more of an afterthought. *For* is more formal and not common in conversation.

Showing Additional Ideas

She spent a summer abroad in China **and** ~~she~~ plans to perfect her Mandarin in college.

He was driving up the mountain **and** ~~he was~~ listening to the radio.

Showing Alternative Ideas

He may have been lying to you **or** ~~he may~~ just ~~have been~~ exaggerating.

You can purchase your tickets online **or** ~~you can~~ go to the box office.

- When two clauses with the same subject are joined by *and* or *or,* the subject does not need to be repeated in the second clause. No comma is used in this case.
- If any auxiliary verbs are the same in the two clauses, they are usually also omitted.
- The sentence may also be considered as having a single subject performing two actions.

    He <u>was driving up the mountain</u> **and** <u>listening to the radio</u>.

- More than two verbs or verb phrases may be connected using *and* and *or.* Separate the verbs or phrases with commas and use the conjunction before the last one.

    He was driving up the mountain**,** listening to music**, and** singing along.

    He may have been lying, exaggerating**, or** just trying to impress you.

- In writing, sentences with *but* and *yet* may occasionally omit subjects. This makes them sound informal. With *nor, so,* and *for,* subjects and auxiliaries cannot usually be omitted.

    I usually read every night **but** haven't had time lately. (INFORMAL)

    * People are getting married when they are older so can't have as many children. (INCORRECT)

B1   Listening

A.   Each sentence in the passage is incomplete. Listen to the entire passage first. Then listen again and put a caret (∧) where you hear a missing word. Listen once more to fill in the missing words, and correct the punctuation.

A day at the zoo may be a treat for you ∧*, but* is it really paradise for the animals? This is a controversial issue let's look at the some of the most important pros and cons. Zoos provide food and shelter for animals they protect endangered species. These may sound like good ideas in theory what actually happens at many zoos is another matter. Are the animals being protected are they being kept from their natural environment? There is no simple answer a simple solution. We're just asking you to think about it. For more information, contact your local animal rights advocacy group.

B. 🎧 Listen. Choose the best sentence to complete each conversation.

1. **a.** Which one did you do?
   b. You must be exhausted.

2. **a.** I know. Like you, I was very surprised.
   b. I know. Like you, I wasn't surprised at all.

3. **a.** So we can meet an hour later. I don't mind.
   b. And we can meet an hour later. I don't mind.

4. **a.** Which is better?
   b. I don't want both.

5. **a.** So you didn't need the key.
   b. So you needed the key.

6. **a.** Or I will. No problem.
   b. Nor will I. No problem.

B2 Contrasting Conjunctions

Choose the best conjunction to complete each sentence.

1. You need to respect both your friends (and / or) your enemies.
2. He didn't study for the exam, (but / nor) he still got an A.
3. I didn't receive a telephone call, (and / nor) did I receive a confirmation by e-mail.
4. I know that I should lose weight, (so / yet) I can't give up dessert.
5. You can have cake (and / or) ice cream for dessert, (but / so) you can't have both.
6. It's late (so / but) I think I should go home.
7. I know that I should recycle, (so / yet) I always forget to do it.
8. You don't have an account here, (or / so) you can't cash this check.
9. He has to be at the meeting by 10, (but / so) he's got to take a taxi.
10. Sore throats are usually caused by viruses, (but / so) strep throat is caused by bacteria (and / so) can be treated with antibiotics.
11. If you are sick (and / yet) the symptoms don't go away after a few days, you should see your doctor, (so / for) it could be something serious.
12. The guard wouldn't let me in, (but / nor) would he let me use the telephone.

B3 Connecting Ideas

A. Complete each sentence in three different ways. Use the conjunctions in parentheses and your own ideas.

1. Skydiving is dangerous, (and, but, so)
   Skydiving is dangerous and it's expensive.
2. I want to quit smoking, (for it, or, so)
3. When he got to the airport, he didn't have his ticket, (nor, yet, so)
4. If you see an accident, you could call 911, (or, but, and)

B. Complete these sentences with your own ideas.

1. I don't like to eat _____, but _____.

   I don't like to eat _____, nor _____.

2. In my free time, I enjoy _____, and _____.

   In my free time, I enjoy _____, but _____.

3. I think it's important to _____, for it_____.

   I think it's important to _____, yet _____.

4. In the next year, I might _____, so _____.

   In the next year, I might _____, or_____.

B4 Omitting Words after Conjunctions

Cross out any unnecessary repeated words and commas.

My best friend and I decided to take a vacation together. At first, we couldn't decide what to do: spend time at the beach or spend time in the mountains. After much discussion, we settled on a cruise through the Virgin Islands. The plan was to fly to St. Thomas, and to do some quick sightseeing, and to board the cruise ship.

The night before our departure, I washed my clothes, and I packed my clothes. My brother called me at around midnight, and he wished me a safe journey.

On the day of our flight, my friend and I were very excited. However, when we got to the airport, we found out that our flight was overbooked, and the next one didn't leave for 48 hours. Taking the later flight would mean that we'd miss our ship's departure from St. Thomas.

Although I'm usually a patient person, this time I lost my temper. After all, it wasn't our fault. We hadn't checked in late nor had we forgotten our tickets or passports. We'd gotten our tickets months in advance, and we had confirmed our seats on the flight. After much discussion, we decided to buy tickets on a different airline so we could get to St. Thomas in time. The new tickets were not cheap!

Now it's three months later, yet we're still arguing with the airline. They have apologized, and they have offered to give us a $50 travel voucher or to give us a rental car coupon, but we want a complete refund. We haven't yet been reimbursed for our unused tickets, but we still hope that it will happen. The vacation was wonderful, but it was also very expensive!

C Transitions

Examining Meaning and Use

Match the examples to an idea below. Discuss your answers. Then read the notes to check them.

a. Dogs are close descendants of wolves. Like wolves, they are essentially pack animals.

b. Owning exotic pets is cruel to animals. Indeed, most exotic pet owners cannot meet the true physical and social needs of a wild animal.

c. Goats and chimps may seem to have little in common. They do, nevertheless, share certain conflict resolution behaviors.

d. Many dog owners don't understand their pets very well. Consequently, they are unable to train their dogs adequately.

e. The animal shelter was closed because of damage from the storm. In the meantime, a temporary shelter was opened.

The second sentence shows . . .

____ a contrasting idea.   ____ a similarity.   ____ more detailed information.

____ a time relationship.   ____ a result.

Overview: Transitions

Chimps can be taught to understand human language. **In addition,** they can master computer skills.

People are getting married when they are older. They don't, **as a result,** have as many children.

Hyenas look and act a lot like dogs. They aren't closely related to dogs at all, **however**.

- Transitions are words or phrases that connect ideas between separate sentences. Transitions express very specific meanings and show how sentences are related. They are used more often in writing.

- Most transitions can occur at the beginning of the second sentence, but many can also occur in the middle or at the end of the sentence. Transitions are usually offset by commas.

- Transitions are placed at the beginning of the second sentence to emphasize the transition. A transition placed in the middle may not be as emphatic. A transition placed at the end is the least emphatic.

- Transitions can also join two sentences into a single sentence using a semicolon.

    Hyenas look and act a lot like dogs; **however,** they aren't closely related to dogs at all.

    For a list of common transitions, see page A-22.
    For more on placement of transitions, see page A-23.

Chimps can be taught to understand human languages. **In addition,** they can master computer skills.

Chimps can be taught to understand human languages, <u>and</u> they can master computer skills. **Moreover,** they can use complex reasoning.

Chimps and humans differ by only 1 percent of their DNA. There are, **for example,** notable similarities in the composition of their blood and their immune systems.

Chimps and humans differ by only 1 percent of their DNA. **In fact,** chimps are biologically more closely related to humans than they are to gorillas.

- Transitions that add ideas have different meanings and uses:

  In addition is used simply to add information to the previous sentence.

  Moreover often follows another addition. It sounds more formal.

  For example gives a specific example of the previous sentence.

  In fact adds more detailed information to support the previous sentence.

- Transitions used to show additional ideas include:

  Simple addition: *in addition, additionally, also, plus*

  Addition following another addition: *moreover, furthermore*

  Addition of a specific example: *for example, for instance*

  Addition of more detailed information: *in fact, actually, as a matter of fact, indeed* (more formal)

Chameleons change color to blend in with their surroundings. **Similarly,** the Arctic fox changes color with the seasons for camouflage.

Chameleons change color to blend in with their surroundings. **Similar to** <u>chameleons</u>, the Arctic fox changes color with the seasons for camouflage.

Managers often use conflict resolution techniques to keep peace in the office. **Likewise,** parents use these techniques to keep peace at home.

Managers often use conflict resolution techniques to keep peace in the office. Parents, **like** <u>managers</u>, use these techniques to keep peace at home.

- Transitions that show a similarity between two ideas have different meanings and uses:

  Similarly indicates that the ideas in the two sentences are comparable.

  Likewise indicates a stronger similarity or parallel between the two sentences.

  Similar to and *like* have the same uses as *similarly* and *likewise,* but they repeat the noun in the first sentence.

- Transitions used to show similar ideas include:

  Similarity: *similarly, similar to* + noun

  Stronger similarity or parallel: *likewise, in the same way, like* + noun, *in the same way as* + noun

Since 1930, Pluto has been considered the ninth planet. In 2006, **however**, it was reclassified as a "dwarf planet."

Most historical landmarks in Europe are already preserved and protected. **In contrast**, people in the United States often struggle to safeguard their landmarks.

The black bear is not an endangered species in Canada. **On the contrary**, the population has increased by 6 to 24 percent in the past decade.

Real estate prices are growing at an enormous rate in urban areas. **Despite this** (fact), people continue to move to cities.

- Transitions that show a contrast between two ideas have different meanings and uses:

  However is used to add information that contrasts with the previous sentence.

  In contrast indicates a more direct opposition between the ideas in the two sentences

  On the contrary is used to add or reinforce an idea that is different from what is commonly expected or thought.

  Despite this is used to add a concession or qualify the previous sentence. (*Despite this* can be followed by a noun—such as *fact*—that refers back to the idea in the first sentence.)

- Transitions that show a contrast between two or more ideas include:

  Contrast: *however, though* (more informal)

  Contrast of more directly opposite ideas: *in contrast, on the other hand*

  Contrast that is different from what is expected: *on the contrary, actually, rather*

  Concession: *despite this / that* (+ noun), *even so, however, nevertheless, in spite of this / that* (+ noun), *on the other hand*

People are getting married when they are older. They don't, **as a result,** have as many children.

Many hospital emergency rooms are overcrowded. **Because of this** (problem), patient safety and health are being endangered.

- Transitions such as *as a result* and *because of this* are used to add information that shows a result or outcome. The information in the previous sentence shows the reason or cause. (*Because of this* can be followed by a noun—such as *problem*—that refers back to the cause in the first sentence.)

- Transitions that show results include: *because of this / that* (+ noun), *consequently, as a result (of this / that* + noun), *therefore.*

You will be informed about your acceptance into the program next week. **At the same time,** you will be told if you have been awarded a scholarship.

On Tuesday, we visit another site in Peru—Chan Chan. **Afterward,** we return to Huaraz, where we spend our last night.

The UN is sending aid to the region. **Meanwhile,** the local government is struggling to restore order.

- Transitions that show time relationships between two events or ideas include: *at the same time, before (this), after (this), afterward, later, soon, for now, in the meantime, meanwhile.*

Several steps taken by the government contributed to the return of the bald eagle from near extinction. **First,** eagles were declared a protected species in 1967. **Next,** most uses of DDT, a chemical which had devastated eagle populations, were banned in 1972. **After this,** various efforts to protect eagle habitats were . . .

There are several ways to protect endangered species. **First,** reserves can be set aside to provide safe homes for rare animals. **Second,** zoos that house rare species can . . .

There are a few things to keep in mind as you prepare to enter the job market. **Most importantly,** choosing a career is a difficult process, so you should give it the time it deserves . . . . **To summarize,** many people think they know how to pick an occupation, but they often wind up choosing a career that is unsatisfying.

These transitions are usually used to connect ideas in paragraphs.

- Transitions that are used to list a sequence of events or ideas include: *first, second, third, then, next, after (this / that),* and *finally.*

- We use *to begin* to introduce a set of ideas. *Most importantly* is used to show the most important idea. Transitions such as *in conclusion, to conclude,* and *to summarize* are used to end a set of ideas.

Listening

A. 🎧 Each sentence in the passage is incomplete. Listen to the entire passage first. Then listen again and put a caret (^) where you hear a missing word. Listen once more to fill in the missing words, and correct the punctuation.

Like any
^~~Any~~ close-knit group in the animal kingdom, people who work together don't always get along. A majority of managers cite employee conflicts as a major problem. Training employees in conflict resolution has become a big business itself. One Seattle conflict resolution center reports that business has tripled over the last five years. "It's not that employees are fighting more," says director Mark Mason. "They're just more aware that something can and should be done about workplace conflicts."

B. 🎧 Listen. Choose the best sentence to complete each conversation.

1. a. Unfortunately, they don't have the funding for it.
   b. Likewise, they don't have the funding for it.
2. a. Good. We shouldn't have any more trouble, therefore.
   b. Good. We shouldn't have any more trouble, however.
3. a. Furthermore, we shouldn't miss this opportunity.
   b. Nevertheless, we shouldn't miss this opportunity.
4. a. It's nice that he followed her example.
   b. What does his mother do?
5. a. In conclusion, I'd say they need our help immediately.
   b. On the contrary, I'd say they need our help immediately.
6. a. That's quite amazing, isn't it?
   b. That's a shame, isn't it?

Contrasting Transition Words

Choose the correct transitions to complete the passage.

The Gulf of Guinea, off the west coast of Africa, is rich in marine wildlife. [1](In addition / However), threats to this diverse ecosystem are great, since the area is becoming more important for supplying the world's growing demand for many natural resources. [2](For example / Meanwhile), industrial fishing in this area has greatly increased recently, and much of it is conducted in illegal zones. [3](On the other hand / Most importantly), the fishing ships are not required to use devices to prevent sea turtles from becoming caught in the ships' immense nets.

more informed

⁴(As a result / For instance), dead sea turtles and other marine life have washed ashore in record numbers over the past few years. ⁵(Moreover / Even so), local fishermen report smaller fishing catches. ⁶(At the same time / Because of this situation), many local people are being forced to go into the forests to find meat from wild animals, including many endangered species. *(Problem)*

⁷(Similarly / In contrast), off-shore oil drilling is causing damage to the marine life. Even the most careful methods of drilling result in some contamination of the water, which can have a devastating effect on wildlife. There are, ⁸(in fact / as a result), many reports of local spills in Central Africa. ⁹(Despite this / To summarize), careful monitoring, which could help prevent these spills, has been inconsistent and difficult to do.

Indeed (emphasize , more strongly

Even that

Despite the _____ Noun

even thows

C3 Connecting Ideas

Complete each sentence in two different ways. Use your own ideas.

1. If you eat fast food every day, you'll gain weight.

    In fact, *you may be endangering your overall health.* _____

    Similarly, _____

2. In my job, I have to work 75 hours a week.

    As a result, _____

    Despite this, _____

3. If you work out regularly with weights, you can gain muscle mass.

    At the same time, _____

    Most importantly, _____

4. Since acupuncturists treat patients with needles, some people think it must be a painful treatment.

    On the contrary, _____

    Because of this, _____

5. Many large corporations have struggled to adapt to the changing global economy.

    Likewise, _____

    However, _____

6. There are several things you can do to lower your stress level.

    First, _____

    For example, _____

7. I've presented some ideas on how to prepare for a job interview.

    Moreover, _____

    In conclusion, _____

A. **Put the sentences in order to make a meaningful text.**

__7__ First, elephants are known to be very compassionate.

__3__ Also, dolphins, like humans and chimpanzees, have demonstrated this ability to a limited degree.

__6__ Recently, scientists decided to begin work with elephants. "Why elephants?" you may ask.

__10__ Next, they put Happy in front of a mirror, where she began to touch the tip of her trunk to the X mark on her face.

__1__ We all know that human beings can recognize themselves in a mirror.

__13__ However, some scientists remain skeptical of the research and its results, saying that it is too simplistic.

__4__ Scientists are always looking for other mammals to study that demonstrate self-awareness. The problem is that most animals are obviously not intelligent enough to recognize themselves in a mirror.

__11__ Furthermore, Happy seemed to be following her own movements in the mirror as if she was mesmerized. She was recognizing the image in the mirror as her own.

__2__ Similarly, chimpanzees have been shown to exhibit the same level of self-awareness.

__14__ Despite this negativity, the researchers who worked with Happy remain optimistic and have pledged to do further testing with the elephants.

__9__ To begin the tests, scientists gave an elephant named Happy a "mark test." They painted a white X on her right cheek. The mark would be visible to her only when she looked in a mirror.

__8__ In addition, their large brains make them intelligent candidates for this kind of test.

__5__ Dogs, for example, will bark at their own image in a mirror—thinking it's another dog. They have no sense of self-recognition.

__12__ This research about the self-awareness and recognition of Happy and other elephants has generated a great deal of attention in the press and the scientific world.

B. **Work with a partner. Read through the sentences again. Decide where the different paragraphs should end and begin. Write the sentence numbers.**

Paragraph 1: _1, 2, 3, 4, 5_

Paragraph 2: _6, 7, 8_

Paragraph 3: _9, 10, 11_

Paragraph 4: _12, 13, 14_

Choose the best way to complete each sentence.

1. She finished the marathon, but _a_   Contrast
   a. she wasn't satisfied with her time.
   b. she received a certificate of achievement.

2. I believe in always telling the truth, so _b_   (Result)
   a. honesty is the best policy.
   b. sometimes I offend people.

3. Many small town hospitals may be closing, or _a_   (Parallel Structure)
   a. they might be forced to cut staff.
   b. they should consider cutting staff.

4. I've had many other opportunities to travel abroad, yet _b_   (Surprising result)
   a. I'm fairly sensitive to other cultures.
   b. my favorite experience is still the Peace Corps.

5. Computer access is available throughout the college campus. In addition, _a_
   a. there is a separate room for the exclusive use of graduate students.
   b. students must limit themselves to 20 hours of use per week.

6. We don't want to cause undue alarm because the disease is rare. On the other hand, _a_   Contrast
   a. we need to give people the facts.
   b. there have been only 10 cases reported in the past year.

7. He passed the mid-term exam. Moreover, _b_
   a. he failed the final exam.
   b. he got the top grade in his class.

8. Private entrepreneurs have poured funding into the city schools. As a result, _a_
   a. the facilities have greatly improved.
   b. they donated over $100,000.

9. I called my parents over the Internet. At the same time, _b_
   a. they were very surprised.
   b. I could see them on my computer screen.

10. My mother spent a great deal of time abroad as a young woman. Similarly, _b_
    a. she has not had the chance to travel much in her later life.
    b. I have chosen a profession which allows me to travel extensively.

Usage Note: *Beginning Sentences with Conjunctions*

> In academic writing, it is not usually acceptable to begin a sentence with a conjunction. However, conjunctions are often used to begin sentences in conversation and more informal writing. This often happens with ideas that show additions, contrasts, or results.

More Formal Written Language	*Conversational Language*
Anyone who knows my father will say he is very generous. **In addition**, he is known as an extremely kind person.	"Anyone who knows my father will say he's really generous. **And** he's extremely kind."
Anyone who knows my father will say he is very generous. **On the other hand**, his brother, who my family is not close to, is very stingy.	"Anyone who knows my father will say he's really generous. **But** his brother is pretty stingy. My family isn't very close to him."
My father is almost too generous with his time and money. **As a result**, he sometimes takes on more than he can handle.	"My father is almost too generous with his time and money. **So** he sometimes takes on more than he can handle."

C6 Speaking vs. Writing

A. Write answers to these questions. Use transition words to connect the ideas in each answer.

1. What are two things you like about the community you live in?
   (Use a transition to show an addition.)

   I like the shopping that is available in my neighborhood. Additionally, there are many excellent restaurants in the area.

2. What is one other thing you like and one thing you dislike about the community you live in?
   (Use a transition to show a contrast.)

3. What are one or two things that have been changing in your community? How have they been changing over time?
   (Use transitions to show a time relationship.)

4. What will be the result of these changes?
   (Use a transition to show a result.)

B. Work in small groups. Talk about the questions in part A. Share your ideas. Make them more conversational by using conjunctions and making other changes where possible. Ask follow-up questions.

   A: What do you like about the community you live in?
   B: The shopping in my neighborhood is great. And there are a lot of really good restaurants.

Writing

Editing: *Conjunctions and Transitions*

Study the errors. Pay attention to the areas that you make mistakes in.

> **1. Placement of transition**
>
>   however, to say
> Pack animals tend to have more sophisticated systems of communication; ~~to, however, say~~
> that they use language is an exaggeration.
>
> **2. Choice of transition**
>
>   Likewise,
> "Time outs" are a common form of discipline in human society. ~~Like,~~ wild horses will also
> isolate a disobedient colt from the herd for a short period of time.
>
> **3. Use of conjunction + transition**
>
> Collaboration is highly valued in human society, but it is sometimes in conflict with our sense
> of independence~~, however~~.
>
> **4. Punctuation**
>
>   ;
> Wolf families usually include extended family members~~,~~ for example, a mother, a father and
> an uncle may share in raising wolf cubs.
>
> **5. Parallel structure**
>
> He might have found a new job and ~~might have~~ changed his e-mail address.

D1 Editing

Correct the errors in the sentences. Be prepared to explain your answers. (There may be more than one way to correct some errors.)

1. Scientists have studied and have demonstrated the great capacity of the chimpanzee for both learning and teaching.

2. Humans pass down knowledge and traditions from parents to children; chimpanzees train, likewise, their offspring in particular behaviors. To show this, researchers examined problem-solving in two control groups.

3. Researchers presented the same problems to two groups of chimps. The first group found one set of solutions to the problems, meanwhile, the second group devised completely different solutions. Both groups passed on their unique solutions to their offspring.

4. Previous studies suggested that chimps simply conform to the behaviors of the group, but new research conflicts with that idea, however.

5. "It's quite meaningful," said Dr. Feagan, a lead researcher. "Chimps can learn and can transmit knowledge over many years. This helps us gain a deeper understanding of early human history."

6. Chimpanzee culture is quite sophisticated; in addition, other primates do not share such complex social organization.

7. Chimpanzees have a complicated communication system. Scientists can learn, therefore, a great deal from observing them in the wild.

Beyond the Sentence: *Showing Relationships Between Supporting Ideas*

Conjunctions and transitions are used to add supporting ideas to paragraphs. They act as signposts, indicating where one idea finishes and a new idea begins.

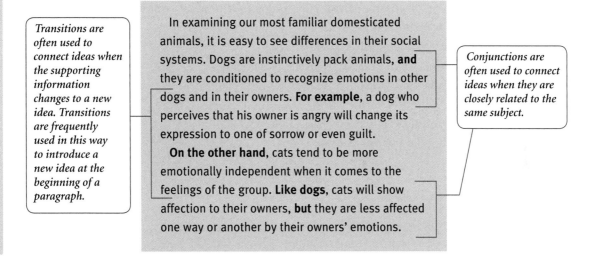

Transitions are often used to connect ideas when the supporting information changes to a new idea. Transitions are frequently used in this way to introduce a new idea at the beginning of a paragraph.

In examining our most familiar domesticated animals, it is easy to see differences in their social systems. Dogs are instinctively pack animals, **and** they are conditioned to recognize emotions in other dogs and in their owners. **For example**, a dog who perceives that his owner is angry will change its expression to one of sorrow or even guilt.

On the other hand, cats tend to be more emotionally independent when it comes to the feelings of the group. **Like dogs**, cats will show affection to their owners, **but** they are less affected one way or another by their owners' emotions.

Conjunctions are often used to connect ideas when they are closely related to the same subject.

Rewrite each set of sentences as a paragraph. Use conjunctions and transitions to connect and introduce the ideas. Make any additional changes necessary.

1. In the 1980s, business managers began recognizing that competition was hurting productivity.
   They sought ways to encourage collaboration.
   Personality testing was introduced to help employees understand themselves and each other.
   Workshops on conflict resolution also became popular in large companies and organizations.
   In the 1980s, business managers began recognizing that competition was hurting productivity, so they sought ways to encourage collaboration. Personality testing . . .

2. Dogs are territorial creatures.
   Dogs will fiercely defend their territory against other animals.
   Dogs usually behave differently when they are in neutral territory.
   Dogs typically get along well with other dogs when they meet in public.

3. It is true that children can be taught ways to work out their differences.
   Young children can be quite immature.
   Experts suggest teaching conflict resolution only after a child can speak well.

4. When experts examined the brains of birds, they did not see physical signs of intelligence.
   They assumed birds were not intelligent.
   New technology offers much improved brain imaging.
   Recent research shows that birds are smarter than was previously thought.

5. Professor Logan became a celebrity after his appearances on a television talk show.
   He has always been a serious scholar.
   He has earned three research grants and published several articles just in the past two years.
   He is well qualified to head the committee.

Vocabulary Notes: *Point of View*

Indicating opinion or viewpoint: You can use adverbs as transitions to show your opinion or reaction, and to qualify what you are saying. These words express various degrees of negative or positive reactions or opinions about the sentences they introduce.

clearly	coincidentally	fortunately	incredibly
ironically	strangely	unexpectedly	

See page A-22 for a list of point of view transitions.

Complete the sentences with words from the box. More than one answer may be possible.
(Look up any words you do not know in your dictionary.)

1. Oil prices are rising. _____, people are continuing to buy large vehicles.

2. My computer had a virus that wiped out my files. _____, I had a back up.

3. The decoding of the human genome is expected to contribute greatly to our understanding of
    disease. _____, the research is widely available due to a government oversight.

4. Exercise has always been known to provide many health benefits. _____, it also
    seems to provide mental health benefits.

5. England and the United States share a common language, but _____, many
    American employees find it difficult to communicate effectively with their British colleagues.

6. The space shuttle was scheduled to launch, but _____, a flu spread among the
    crew, which delayed departure.

D4 **Writing Tip:** *Organizing and Clarifying Your Ideas*

> It is important to give examples and evidence in your writing and it is equally important to organize
> these ideas and present them in a way the reader will understand. Using conjunctions and
> transitions can help you organize your ideas, avoid redundancy, and make your intentions clear.

Choose one of the topics to write a short essay of two to three paragraphs. Compare different
ideas, opinions, and attitudes about your topic. Give examples from your experience. Then, use
the Writing Checklist to check your work.

• What are the advantages and disadvantages of living alone? How can living alone or living
  with other people affect your mood or behavior? Is living alone something that is appropriate
  for you? Why or why not?

• Humans have a complex relationship with meat. What are two or three different attitudes
  toward meat consumption that you know of? Why do some people choose not to eat meat?
  What are the consequences or effects of eating or not eating meat?

• Evaluate several pets and their characteristics. What are their positive and negative features?
  What sort of pet would be the most appropriate for you? How would it fit with your lifestyle
  and personality?

Beyond the Classroom

Writing

Write an essay using one of these topics.

1. People resolve conflicts in different ways. Some avoid conflict by backing down, some consistently try to win, and a third group strives to create a win-win situation that is acceptable to all. In a three-paragraph essay, try to think of examples of each of these types of people and describe how they might handle a difficult situation.

2. Hunting is a popular sport. Hunting advocates claim that hunters replace natural predators and, in some cases, help maintain the health of an animal population, such as deer. Yet, hunting is seen by animal rights' activists as contributing to the extinction of certain species. Write an essay. In the first paragraph, describe the point of view of the hunters or the activists. In the second and third paragraphs, give reasons why you agree or disagree with this position.

3. Does your physical environment affect your interactions with others? Does it affect your creativity or ability to solve problems? Write a short essay. In the first paragraph, describe a physical environment where you were happy and productive. In the second paragraph, describe a physical environment where you were uncomfortable or perhaps unable to work productively. In the third paragraph, identify two or three features that support healthy environments.

Searching for Authentic Examples

Find examples of English grammar in everyday life by completing the task below. Bring your examples to class and be prepared to discuss them.

Find a short article in a textbook about a topic that interests you. Look for four different examples of conjunctions and five different examples of transitions. What is the relationship between the two ideas connected by the conjunction or transition? Can you find a transition that is used to connect ideas in two paragraphs?

Adverb Clauses and Adverb Phrases

A Exam Superstitions

A1 Before You Read

Discuss these questions.

What do you do to prepare for an exam? Which methods have been most helpful in preparing for an exam?

Do you have any superstitions about exams? Are there any special things you do before an exam?

A2 Read

 Read this excerpt from a popular magazine to find out about exam superstitions.

EXAM SUPERSTITIONS

It's exam day. Daisuke's mother is urging him to hurry or he'll be late for school. **Before he leaves home, his mother pushes a carefully-crafted, boxed lunch into his hands**—just as she does every school day. Today, however, there is one difference: his mother has made certain that his lunch menu includes *katsu*, a meat cutlet that is fried in breadcrumbs. In Japanese, **although the words for *meat cutlet* and *to win* are written differently, they are pronounced the same way: *katsu*.** A traditional exam superstition states that eating *katsu* on the day of a test will make one "victorious" over the exam.

A newer pre-exam ritual[1] in Japan revolves around chocolate. Around exam time, a certain candy bar manufacturer can barely keep up with the demand for its product. Students who eat the candy bar swear[2] that it helps them on their exams. **While there is no proof that the chocolate bars do anything, that doesn't stop**

students from gobbling them down.[3]
Wherever there are students being tested, there are exam superstitions. Exeter University student Alice Biederman makes sure to use brand new pencils when she takes an exam. **She considers new pencils to be "pure" because they have never been used to write or erase any mistakes.** On the other hand, Alice's best

friend Ian uses hand-me-down[4] pencils that come from someone who has already been successful at passing the test. **Ian borrows the special pencils so that he can harness[5] their "lucky power" on his exam.**

Some rituals are even gender-specific.[6] For example, some men at the University of Illinois won't shave for the entire week of their final exams. At the same school, **some women wear a new perfume while they are studying for their finals. Once they arrive at the exam hall, they apply the same perfume**—hoping that the lucky scent will help them easily to recall what they've studied.

So can pre-exam rituals really help? Dr. Patrick Foley, a psychology professor, thinks that they can. "Having seen many students engage in[7] these rituals over the years, I think they do serve a purpose. They can put students in a relaxed and positive frame of mind[8]—and that's the right attitude to have when you're walking in to take a test."

However, **although exam superstitions can be fun and even beneficial, they could be distracting us from some serious issues surrounding testing.** Dr. Kay Lewis, a testing expert, explains, "Because of the severe pressure, students are suffering and will do almost anything to relieve that distress. We must look at the underlying problem of pre-exam anxiety and analyze ways to make the testing system less pressurized. Students shouldn't feel that the world is ending if they fail an exam. No matter what the outcome, life goes on."

---

1 **ritual:** an action repeated in the same way and done under certain circumstances
2 **swear:** to believe something deeply
3 **gobble down:** to eat quickly (informal)
4 **hand-me-down:** a possession that is passed on to a younger person

5 **harness:** to control and use the power of something
6 **gender-specific:** particular to male or female (behavior)
7 **engage in:** participate in
8 **frame of mind:** mood

A3 After You Read

Discuss these questions.

1. What are three of the pre-exam rituals mentioned in the article?
2. What is Dr. Foley's main point? What is Dr. Lewis's main point? Briefly explain each in your own words.
3. What are some other possible advantages or disadvantages of engaging in pre-exam rituals?
4. Do you agree with Dr. Lewis's final statement: "Students shouldn't feel that the world is ending if they fail an exam. No matter what the outcome, life goes on." Why or why not?

A4 Examining Form

A. Work in pairs. Look at the highlighted sentences in the reading. Each sentence consists of an independent main clause and a dependent adverb clause. Circle the adverb clause in each sentence.

B. Discuss your observations with the class. Refer to the notes on page 214 if you need to.

B Adverb Clauses

Examining Meaning and Use

Read each sentence and the statements that follow it. Check (✓) the correct statement. Discuss your answers. Then read the notes to check them.

1. Although there was traffic, I got to the meeting on time.
   __ **a.** I didn't expect to get to the meeting on time.
   __ **b.** This tells why I got to the meeting on time.

2. Let's send the application early so that it'll arrive before the deadline.
   __ **a.** This explains why I want to send the application early.
   __ **b.** This shows a surprising or unexpected contrast.

3. I'm moving this plant to a new location since it needs more sunlight.
   __ **a.** This explains a time relationship.
   __ **b.** This explains the cause and the effect.

Overview: Adverb Clauses

Main Clause	*Adverb Clause*
We'll have finished the meeting . . .	**by the time** he gets here. *(when)*
We celebrated all night . . .	**because** we met our deadline. *(why)*
Hockey has become a popular sport . . .	**wherever** there are ice-skating rinks. *(where)*

- Adverb clauses modify independent main clauses. They tell *when, where, how,* or *why.*
- Adverb clauses are dependent clauses; they cannot stand alone as independent sentences. All adverb clauses contain a subject and a verb.
- Subordinators (such as *by the time, because,* and *wherever*) are used at the beginning of adverb clauses. The subordinator shows how the main clause and adverb clause are related.
- Most adverb clauses can come before or after the main clause. When the adverb clause comes first, it is usually followed by a comma.
  By the time he gets here, we'll have finished the meeting.
- See Chapter 13 for information on real and unreal conditional adverb clauses.

For subordinates introducing adverb clauses, see p. 88.

<u>Once</u> **you've finished your test**, you may leave.

I tripped and fell <u>as</u> **I was running for the bus**.

He struggled for years <u>until</u> **he found the job of his dreams**.

<u>Since</u> **he's stopped eating sugary, high-fat foods,** he's lost 20 pounds.

<u>While</u> **you're meeting with clients,** I'm going to be making some phone calls.

We'll have finished the meeting <u>**by the time**</u> **he gets here**.

- Adverb clauses showing time tell <u>when</u> the action or state in the main clause occurs. Subordinators that introduce time relationships include *when, while, as, once, as soon as, until, before, after, since,* and *by the time*.

- Remember that in sentences expressing future time, the adverb clause usually uses a present form. The main clause uses a future form. Do not use the future form in both clauses.

  * While you're going to be meeting clients, I'm going to be making phone calls. (INCORRECT)

- Refer back to Chapters 1, 2, and 3 for more information on various time clauses and how they are used with different tenses.

We celebrated all night <u>**because**</u> **we had met our deadline**.
<u>Since</u> **he doesn't have a lawyer,** he will probably lose his case.
I was surprised to meet Joe, <u>as</u> **I thought I knew everyone in the neighborhood**. *(more formal)*
Rainbows exist <u>**due to the fact that**</u> **raindrops scatter light**.

- Clauses used to give reasons tell <u>why</u> the action or state in the main clause occurs.

  They express cause and effect. Subordinators that introduce reasons include *because* and *since*.

- *As* sounds more formal and is not often used to give reasons. When it is used to give a reason, instead of expressing time, the clause is usually offset by commas whether it is placed at the beginning or the end of the sentence.

- *Due to the fact that* can give a reason, but it is often considered too wordy. Nevertheless, it is common in sentences expressing factual information.

He wants to compete in the race **even though** **he is ill**.

Though **he wasn't popular,** he was determined to win the election. *(more informal)*

Statistics have shown that many athletes end up earning more money than their peers **despite the fact that** **they have low test scores in school.**

Fred's math skills were poor, **while** **John always did well in math.** *(more direct contrast)*

- Clauses used to show a concession <u>emphasize unexpected contrasts</u> to the idea in the main clause. They convey the idea, "That's true, but . . ." Subordinators that introduce concessions include *even though* and *although. Though* is more informal.

- *Despite the fact that* and *in spite of the fact that* can show concession, but they are often considered too wordy. Nevertheless, they are common in sentences expressing factual information.

- *While* is used to show <u>a contrast or a more direct opposition</u> to the idea in the main clause. This use of *while* is much less common than its use as a time subordinator. When it is used to show a contrast, the clause is usually offset by commas whether it is placed at the beginning or the end of the sentence.

Hockey has become a popular sport **wherever** **there are ice-skating rinks**.

- Clauses used to show place tell <u>where</u> the action or state in the main clause occurs. Subordinators that introduce place include *where, anywhere, everywhere,* and *wherever.*

Runners use their arms **so (that)** **they can maintain a smoother stride.**

You should learn how to reduce your anxiety **in order that** **it doesn't interfere with your life**.

- Clauses used to give purpose tell <u>the reason for</u> the action or state in the main clause. Subordinators that introduce purpose include *so that* and *in order that. That* is often omitted after *so,* especially in conversation. *In order that* is not used very often.

- Purpose clauses usually appear after the main clause. They are often used with modal verbs (e.g., *can, could, be able to, would*) or negative verbs.

- When the subject of the two clauses is the same, purpose is more commonly shown with *to* or *in order (not) to.* A verb follows the expression, not a noun.

  Runners use their arms **to / in order to** <u>maintain</u> a smoother stride.

  You should learn how to reduce your anxiety **in order not to** <u>let</u> it interfere with your life.

B1 Listening

A. 🎧 Each sentence in the passage is incomplete. Listen to the entire passage first. Then listen again and put a caret (^) where you hear a missing word. Listen once more to fill in the missing words, and correct the punctuation.

Even though my

^^M̶y̶ brother denies it, he's really quite superstitious. For example, he always puts a lucky charm in his pocket he leaves for an exam. A soccer tournament begins, he won't shave. He stays home on Friday the Thirteenth he can avoid bad luck. And of course, he won't walk under a ladder he's sure that's asking for trouble. He's asked about this behavior, he says he's just being careful, not superstitious!

B. 🎧 Listen. Circle the best answer to complete each conversation.

1. **a.** I'm surprised you tried it only once.
   b. I'm surprised you didn't try it sooner.
2. **a.** What were you doing when he called?
   b. Did you wake you up when he called?
3. **a.** When is he coming to our district?
   b. Has he gone anywhere yet?
4. **a.** Why did you close them?
   b. When did you close them?
5. **a.** Oh, so that's the purpose.
   b. Oh, so that's the reason.
6. **a.** That's odd.
   b. That's why.

B2 Contrasting Subordinators

Read this excerpt from an article about dizziness. Choose the best answer to complete the sentences.

Balance is controlled mainly by two things: information received through our eyes and the chambers in the inner ear. Dizziness can often be a described as confusion between what the eyes see and what the inner ear feels. For example, ¹(because / when) you spin your body around, the fluid in the inner ear begins to spin as well. ²(Even though / By the time) you stop spinning, the fluid will continue to move. The inner ear is telling the brain that the body is still moving, ³(while / as) the eyes are indicating that the body has stopped. These contradicting signals cause the feeling of dizziness.

We can look to the world of dance for a way to control this. ⁴(Since / Though) spinning is such an essential part of classical dance, the dancers learn a special technique called spotting

⁵(so that / despite the fact that) they don't get dizzy. ⁶(Wherever / As) they spin, they focus their eyes on one point as long as possible— ⁷(once / until) their turning body snaps their head around to catch up. In this way, the fluid in the inner ear remains fairly still.

Some people may experience dizziness for other reasons. For example, some people feel dizzy ⁸(since / when) they stand up or sit down. Some individuals may even need to close their eyes and take a few deep breaths ⁹(in order that / in order to) stop the feeling. ¹⁰(Though / As) this sensation is unsettling, it isn't a serious issue. This sort of dizziness often occurs ¹¹(as soon as / because) an individual has low blood pressure.

B3 Showing Time

A. Complete the sentences with the correct form of the verb in parentheses. Pay attention to the time in the main clause. (More than one answer is sometimes possible.)

1. Once I began to pay for things myself, I _____ (learn) how to manage my money.

2. I'll fold the letters while you _____ (stuff) the envelopes.

3. Just as she _____ (say) Mark's name, he walked through the door.

4. I'm not putting this book down until I _____ (read) every last page of it.

5. As soon as a storm _____ (hit), you should move to a lower elevation.

6. My children aren't allowed to leave the table until they _____ (finish) everything.

7. My French _____ (improve) dramatically once I studied abroad in Paris.

8. I'm going to be heating the water while you _____ (chop) the vegetables.

9. I had already taken several college courses before I _____ (enter) the university.

10. By the time the ceremony starts, everyone should _____ (be) in their seats.

11. After the report is finished, it _____ (send) to the marketing offices worldwide.

12. As you _____ (come) to the top of you hill, there's a driveway on your left.

B. Check (✓) the sentences that are true for you. Rewrite the sentences that are not true with your own information. Then compare your ideas with a partner.

_____ 1. When I was a kid, I used to get in trouble a lot.
   When I was a kid, I was really well-behaved.

_____ 2. I've lived in three different apartments since I moved here.

_____ 3. As soon as I finish classes this semester, I'm going on vacation.

_____ 4. Before I traveled abroad, I didn't appreciate other cultures as much.

_____ 5. I don't want to work until I finish graduate school.

_____ 6. After I graduate, I'm going to use English in my job.

_____ 7. By the time I turn thirty, I want to be married.

_____ 8. Once my parents retire, I want them to live with me.

A. Write at least two responses to each question—one with a clause of reason, and one with a clause of concession or contrast. Use the words in the box.

although	even though	while
because	since	

1. Would you consider changing your name?

   Even though I don't like my name that much, I probably wouldn't ever change it.

   I probably wouldn't consider changing my name since I'm named after my father—it's a family tradition.

2. Would you lie to keep a friend from being expelled from school?
3. Would you ever date somebody ten years older than you?
4. Would you ever consider working 80 hours a week if they paid you a lot of money?
5. Would you rather be rich and unhappy, or poor and happy?

B. Work in small groups. Share your ideas.

B5 **Combining Sentences**

Match the two sentences. Decide which one should be the adverb clause. Then use a subordinating conjunction in the box to combine the sentences into one.

even though	since	so that	while
~~since~~	so that	wherever	while

1. He's gained 10 pounds. _d_

   He's gained 10 pounds since he lost his job last month.

2. Joe is about five foot six. _b_
3. I took the day off from work. _g_
4. You can see the stage clearly. _h_
5. You're walking there at night. _a_
6. She passed the test. _f_
7. I want to buy a personal computer. _c_
8. I was coming to work today. _e_

a. You shouldn't go alone.
b. His brother Josh is over six feet tall.
c. I can work from home.
d. He lost his job last month.
e. I saw a horrible accident.
f. She had a fever.
g. I could see my son's piano recital.
h. You sit in the theatre.

So that model

Vocabulary Notes: *Prepositional Phrases*

Sometimes a prepositional phrase (preposition + a noun) can express the same meaning as an adverb clause. We choose the prepositional phrase because it is more concise.

Showing time: *during, after, before*

      I was daydreaming **during the meeting**. *(= . . . while I was in the meeting.)*

      After the rain, the race continued.

      I need to get some coffee **before class**.

Giving reasons: *because of, as a result of*

      Because of the weather, the event was canceled. *(= Because the weather was bad, . . .)*

      He lost his scholarship **as a result of his bad grades**.

Showing concession: *despite, in spite of*

      In spite of his illness, he wants to compete in the race. *(= Even though he's ill, . . .)*

      He was determined to win the election **despite his unpopularity**.

B6   Replacing Adverb Clauses with Prepositional Phrases

Rewrite the sentences. Change each adverb clause to a prepositional phrase.

    1. I have to finish this report before I go to lunch.

       I have to finish this report before lunch.

    2. Because he has a knee injury, he can't go dancing anymore.

    3. We're going to dinner after we go to the movie.

    4. I got extremely thirsty while I was in the marathon.

    5. Even though she works hard, she did not receive the promotion.

    6. The after-school program has been canceled because there was a cut in funding.

B7   Completing Sentences with Adverb Clauses

A. Complete the sentences with your own ideas.

    1. Everywhere I went on my last vacation, . . .

    2. I went to college to study _____ so that I could . . .

    3. Although I don't like it when people _____, . . .

    4. Because I made a resolution to _____, . . .

    5. Wherever you go in _____, you can find . . .

    6. You should study harder in order that . . .

B. Share your sentences with a partner. Ask follow-up questions to get more information.

    A: Everywhere I went on my last vacation, I met friendly people.

    B: Really? Where did you go?

Read about something called the "Mozart effect." Then answer the questions. Use the words in parentheses in your answers.

The Mozart Effect

Researchers in the early 1990s conducted an experiment that measured the effect of listening to Mozart on the IQ of college students. Their research found that the music had a slight positive impact on IQ, though this increase was temporary.

Subsequently, a man named Don Campbell wrote a book stating that listening to Mozart would make children smarter. Some argue that the ideas presented in his book overstated the original researchers' findings. Even so, the media widely reported on the book's claims and called it the "Mozart effect."

When people learned about the Mozart effect, many things happened: some hospitals started giving the parents of newborns a free classical music CD, and some preschools were required to play classical music every day.

A few scientists support the idea that listening to music can have an impact on one's IQ, but others are skeptical. They say that hearing Mozart while you work may improve your performance on specific tasks, but only if you enjoy the music. Other researchers have claimed that listening to the music may actually *decrease* performance. Even so, you'll still hear of parents who plan to expose their babies to classical music as they grow.

Listening to classical music may not improve one's intelligence in a significant way for the long-term, but everyone can agree that it helps you to relax. One thing is certain: more research is needed to find out the truth about the Mozart effect.

1. In the original research, why did the college students' IQ increase? (because)

   The college students' IQ increased because they listened to Mozart. .

2. What did the media do when Don Campbell's book came out? (after)

   _____ .

3. What did some hospitals do, and what did some schools do? (while)

   _____ .

4. Why was every newborn given a CD in some hospitals? (so that)

   _____ .

5. Do all scientists support the research? (although)

   _____ .

6. Do any parents believe in the Mozart effect? (despite the fact)

   _____ .

7. When will we know the truth about the Mozart effect? (until)

   _____ .

C **Adverb Phrases**

Examining Meaning and Use

Read each sentence and the statements that follow it. Check (✓) the correct statement. Discuss your answers. Then read the notes to check them.

1. Ken called home upon hearing the news.
   ____ **a.** This tells where Ken called from.
   ____ **b.** This tells when Ken called home.

2. Feeling upset after the exam, he sent me an e-mail.
   ____ **a.** I was upset.
   ____ **b.** He was upset.

3. Having eaten lunch, I went shopping.
   ____ **a.** I ate lunch after I went shopping.
   ____ **b.** I ate lunch before I went shopping.

4. Though cold, it was sunny outside.
   ____ **a.** It was sunny but cold.
   ____ **b.** It was cold inside and sunny outside.

Overview: Adverb Phrases

Adverb Phrases Showing Time
He became sick **while trekking in the Himalayas.**
  (= He became sick <u>while he was trekking in the Himalayas.</u>)

Adverb Phrases Used to Give Reasons
Not having a lawyer, he will probably lose his case.
  (= <u>Since he doesn't have a lawyer,</u> he will probably lose his case.)

Adverb Phrases Used to Show Concession
Though still recovering from an injury, she's actively training for a triathlon.
  (= <u>Though she is still recovering from an injury,</u> she's actively training for a triathlon.)

- Adverb clauses of time, concession, and reason can be reduced to adverb phrases. An adverb clause can be reduced only when the subject of the two clauses is the same.
  * While ~~you're~~ sleeping, I'm going to be working. (INCORRECT).
- Adverb phrases are typically used in writing to make language more concise and tie ideas together. You should only use an adverb phrase if the meaning remains clear and the sentence sounds natural.
- Adverb phrases of reason and concession typically come before the main clause.

Present

When ~~he isn't~~ **not helping the elderly**, he's tutoring needy children.

Before ~~she jogs~~ **jogging**, she warms up thoroughly.

Past

He became sick **while** ~~he was~~ **trekking in the Himalayas**.

After ~~I got~~ **getting home,** I realized I'd left my keys at work.

Since ~~I learned~~ **learning about the problem,** I have done everything I can to help.

Future

While ~~they are~~ **waiting for the results,** they will be given a questionnaire to complete.

Before ~~we visit~~ **visiting Pompeii,** we will go on to Rome.

I'll to be able to speak fluently **after** ~~I complete~~ **completing the course**.

- Adverb phrases showing time can occur in past, present, or future time, but most frequently occur in past and future sentences.
- To reduce a time clause, omit the subject and any auxiliary. Then change the main verb to the present participle: verb + *-ing*. (With continuous forms, the main verb will already be in the correct form.) If the clause is negative, leave *not* before the participle.
- Clauses with *before, after, while,* and *since* are most commonly reduced. Clauses with *when* (expressing simultaneous events) are also commonly reduced.
  When ~~I was~~ **living in Seattle,** I worked for Boeing. *(= During the time I was living, . . .)*
- Clauses with *when* (expressing events in sequence) can be reduced, but in these sentences we typically replace *when* with *upon* or *on.*
  ~~When she heard~~ **Upon hearing the news,** she cried. *(= She heard the news and then cried.)*

Omitting Subordinators in Adverb Phrases of Past Time

Past

~~While he was~~ **Traveling through the Canadian wilderness,** he became sick.

~~After I got~~ **Having gotten home from work,** I realized I'd left my keys at the office.
(having + past participle)

- In affirmative adverb phrases showing past time, *while* and *when* (expressing simultaneous events) can be omitted along with the subject and any auxiliary.
- Time subordinators cannot be omitted in adverb phrases of present or future time.
    * Cooking, I listen to music. (INCORRECT)
- *After* and *since* can be omitted, but they are replaced with *having* + past participle. *Having* makes it clear that the action in the adverb phrase happened before the action in the main clause.
- Time clauses with *as* can also be reduced. Unlike *after* and *while, as* is always omitted.
    ~~As I was running~~ **Running for the bus,** I tripped and fell.

C1   Listening

A.   Each sentence in the passage is incomplete. Listen to the entire passage first. Then listen again and put a caret (∧) where you hear a missing word. Listen once more to fill in the missing words, and correct the punctuation.

Having just

∧ ~~Just~~ picked up our new car, my father parked outside our house. I stood there in awe, every

inch of it. Then without warning, a shower of salt landed on the car. I looked around my

mother's hand was returning to her pocket for more salt. "Stop," yelled my father, to her

side how the salt would damage the paint. My mother insisted that bad luck could damage

it more. Not to challenge this superstition, my father permitted her to throw more salt; my

father's reaction, I was glad that our new car would be "protected!"

B. 🎧 Listen. Circle the best answer to complete the conversation.

1. **a.** While jogging.
   b. So we could jog.

2. **a.** Now I understand why he studied.
   b. Now I understand why he didn't meet us.

3. **a.** Good then let's go.
   b. Good then let's not go.

4. **a.** Did you get a response yet?
   b. Why did you eat first?

5. **a.** How can you do two things at once?
   b. Have you spoken to Anna yet?

6. **a.** So that we can miss the traffic.
   b. In order not to miss the traffic.

C2 Reducing Adverb Clauses

Check (✓) the sentence if the adverb clause can be reduced. Write the reduced version. Then look at the sentences you did not check. Why can't they be reduced?

Showing Time

✓ **1.** Before I leave the house every day, I make sure I have my cell phone.

   Before leaving the house every day, I make sure I have my cell phone.

___ **2.** While Mark was looking for Gina, his brother drove around the block.

_____

___ **3.** Since they won the World Cup, the team has given many interviews.

_____

___ **4.** When she isn't winning Olympic medals, she's busy volunteering at her favorite charity.

_____

___ **5.** We can expect a full recovery from him after he rests.

_____

___ **6.** When they reached the top of the mountain, the hikers drank a lot of water.

_____

Giving Reasons

___ **7.** As she was injured, she had to forfeit the match.

_____

___ **8.** Because his job requires him to travel, he's gone from home nearly two months a year.

_____

___ **9.** Since he has never given a speech before, he's very nervous.

_____

___ **10.** Because they knew that I liked sweets, they gave me a box of chocolate.

_____

___ **11.** Since I forgot her birthday, my sister won't speak to me.

_____

_____ **12.** While Lisa is doing well this semester, her sister is failing two of her classes.

_____.

_____ **13.** Though they were planning a trip to Italy, they hadn't begun to save money for it.

_____.

_____ **14.** Though I'm not dating anyone special, I have gone out a couple of times recently.

_____.

_____ **15.** Although he isn't trying to make me angry, he's managed to offend me twice!

_____.

_____ **16.** Although it is difficult, swimming is wonderful aerobic exercise.

_____.

_____ **17.** Even though she worked very hard, she did not receive the promotion.

_____.

C3 Omitting Subordinators in Adverb Phrases Showing Time

Check (✓) the box if the subordinator can be omitted. Rewrite the sentence without the subordinator.

_____ **1.** After finishing his final exams, he went home for the summer.

       Having finished his final exams, he went home for the summer.

_____ **2.** While getting into a taxi, Eliza dropped her cell phone in the street.

_____

_____ **3.** Before getting a job here, he worked at one of our competitors.

_____

_____ **4.** After exercising at the gym on my lunch break, I went back to the office.

_____

_____ **5.** After taking a break, we're going to discuss the latest sales figures.

_____

_____ **6.** Since learning English, she has had better job opportunities.

_____

_____ **7.** As he was leaving the hotel, he was stopped by a security guard.

_____

_____ **8.** When looking through some old papers, I found a photo of my mother as a girl.

_____

Read this story about Mike Pierce. Reduce the underlined adverb clauses. Try to omit the subordinator where possible.

while studying the history of the area

Mike Pierce was interested in the Antarctic. Years ago, ~~while he was studying the history of the area~~, he became interested in the daring exploits of the early explorers to the South Pole. <u>After he read the exciting stories about their trips to the South Pole</u>, he decided he wanted to have his own adventure in that cold wasteland. That desire led him to participate in a marathon run that was held in Antarctica last year. <u>When he finished the run and he returned from his trip</u>, he knew that he wanted to go back. When it was announced that there would be another race this year, he jumped at the opportunity to participate.

This year's race will be longer: It's a double marathon (100 kilometers). Mike is one of only two runners from the previous year's race who will be returning to the Antarctic to compete. <u>Because he has completed a marathon there before</u>, he knows how challenging it can be. He's taking four layers of clothing, which he will wear at all times during the race. <u>Although Mike is excited about the physical challenge</u>, he is not returning to the South Pole simply because of the race. He's going back because he's fallen in love with the place.

It's not going to be easy, though. While he's running across the snow and ice, the environment will provide many challenges. It will be windy, lonely, and of course, cold. However, the one thing he won't he won't have to worry about is sunlight. There will be plenty of it, as the sun never sets this far south.

Training for the upcoming race has proven to be a challenge. <u>Since Mike doesn't have anywhere cold enough to train for his run</u>, he has had to think creatively. To address this problem, he called up businesses, asking if he could rent space in their walk-in freezers for training purposes. <u>Because they thought he was a prank caller</u>, most of the people he called hung up on him. However, one person listened to his story and then agreed to let him do it.

Mike will be leaving soon to head down south. <u>Before he departs</u>, he will undoubtedly be thinking about his next adventure. Rumor has it that he'd like to cross the entire Antarctic sometime in the near future. <u>Because we know the degree of his determination and drive</u>, we won't be surprised if he reaches that goal!

Usage Note: *Dangling Participles*

> Remember, an adverb phrase can be used only when it has the same subject as the main clause. When the subject is not the same, the sentence sounds illogical. In the sentence on the left, the participle *(running)* is called "dangling" because it is not clear what the subject is. Dangling participles are often a problem in adverb phrases that do not include subordinators.
>
> *Illogical sentence (dangling participle)*:
>
> * Running down the stairs, the telephone rang. (INCORRECT)
>
> *(This implies that the telephone was running down the stairs.)*
>
> *Logical sentences:*
>
> **As I was** running down the stairs, the telephone rang.
>
> Running down the stairs, **I heard** the telephone ring.

C5 Correcting Dangling Participles

Work with a partner. Discuss why each sentence is illogical. Then suggest a way to correct it.

1. Running toward the finish line, the crowd's cheers grew louder.

   As I was running toward the finish line, the crowd's cheers grew louder.

   OR *Running toward the finish line, I heard the crowd's cheers grow louder.*

2. Not paying attention, the ball hit me in the face.

   _____

   _____

3. Having taken a break, the meeting continued.

   _____

   _____

4. Being in a horrible condition, I needed to do a lot of work on the house.

   _____

   _____

5. Though not looking for a job, my old company made a generous offer to me.

   _____

   _____

6. Walking back home yesterday, a car nearly hit me.

   _____

   _____

A. Read the sentences. Check (✓) the second sentence if it has the same meaning as the first.

1. Wanting to get plenty of sleep, I went to bed early.

    ____ I went to bed extra early in order to get plenty of sleep.

2. Once you've passed through the security area, you can proceed to your gate.

    ____ As you've passed through the security area, you can proceed to your gate.

3. He couldn't go up to the top of the tower because he was afraid of heights.

    ____ Despite his fear of heights, he went up to the top of the tower.

4. Because I wanted to make some extra money, I worked overtime for the past three weeks.

    ____ I've worked overtime for the past three weeks so that I could make some extra money.

5. I was going to buy an MP3 player until I found out it was $200.

    ____ I was going to buy an MP3 player because I found out it was $200.

6. Because he wasn't paying attention to his driving, he didn't see the truck until it was almost too late.

    ____ Even though he was paying attention to his driving, he didn't see the truck until it was almost too late.

7. Since he was injured, the athlete was not selected for the Olympic team.

    ____ The athlete was not selected for the Olympic team because of his injury.

8. Having won eight points for the team, the player regained the team's respect.

    ____ The player regained the team's respect after he won eight points for the team.

9. Having practiced his routine repeatedly before the competition, the gymnast scored an 8.0.

    ____ Although he practiced his routine repeatedly before the competition, the gymnast scored an 8.0.

10. When he graduated from college, he went to work for a large corporation.

    ____ Upon graduating from college, he went to work for a large corporation.

A. Write answers to the questions. Use adverb clauses and phrases as indicated.

1. Where is the best place to go on vacation and why do you think so? Give at least three reasons. *(Use adverb clauses to give reasons.)*

   I've visited Hawaii three times. It's the best place to vacation because . . .

   _____

   _____

   _____

2. What is most memorable about the place?
   (Use an adverb clause of place.)

   _____

   _____

   _____

3. What is a drawback to visiting that place?
   (Use an adverb clause to show concession or contrast.)

   _____

   _____

   _____

4. What would you do to prepare for your trip? What tips would you have for someone who is travelling to this place? How about after arriving?
   (Use adverb clauses and phrases of time.)

   _____

   _____

   _____

B. Work in small groups. Talk about the questions in part A. Share your ideas. Ask follow-up questions.

A: Hawaii is the best place to vacation because the climate is so good.

B: So you like the sun! What are your favorite activities when you're on vacation there?

D WRITING

Editing: *Adverb Clauses and Phrases*

Study the errors. Pay attention to the areas that you make mistakes in.

---

1. **Fragments**

   because
   The plan to develop a section of downtown is moving forward. ~~Because~~ the city council
     approved the plan.

2. **Punctuation**

                                              ,
   When the telephone rings late at night ∧ I always start to worry.
   I always start to worry ⌐, when the telephone rings late at night.

3. **Choice of subordinator**

   While
   ~~As~~ the article about Canada is interesting, it is not very helpful for tourists.

4. **Use of subordinator + conjunction**

   Although he wasn't popular, ~~but~~ he was determined to win the election

5. **Incorrect reduction**

     Having won
   ~~Because winning~~ the game, the team qualified for the next round.

D1 ## Editing

Correct the errors in the passage. Be prepared to explain your answers. (There may be more than one way to correct some errors.)

                                             ,
Even though rock climbing is dangerous ∧ more and more people are taking up the sport.
When you are rock climbing you are trying to get from the bottom to the top of a rock.
Although this description sounds quite simple, but there is a lot more to it. One of the main
tasks for a climber is to stay out of danger. Because it is quite easy to fall and injure yourself.

Near the ground, most rocks have many handholds—cracks and outcrops—so even an
amateur can usually climb smaller rocks easily. However, after climbed for a while, you usually
find the rock face becoming smoother, and the handholds getting farther apart and smaller.

At this point, you are not only higher but also in a more dangerous position. Because the terrain becomes challenging, so you must take safety measures—primarily by using safety ropes.

Though you are climbing, you should try to do most of the work with your legs. Ideally, you should keep your body centered over your feet so that you stay balanced. By keeping your feet directly beneath your body, you can use the strength of your legs to push upwards. In certain cases, you must spend a great deal of energy in order to you can move just a few inches, but most climbers say that it is worth it. As reaching the top of a difficult rock, a climber often feels a sense of euphoria.

Beyond the Sentence: *Showing Relationships Between Ideas*

Adverb clauses provide a concise way of adding supporting ideas to main clauses. The subordinator explains the relationship between the ideas.

Although many people think they know how to get a good deal when purchasing something, this confidence may actually work against them. When most people buy a big ticket item, such as a car, they usually read up on the anticipated purchase to find out about prices, resale value, and other similar issues. **After doing this research,** many customers feel they are informed enough to engage in negotiations with the sales staff.

However, **because of the collective skill and experience of the sales team,** most car buyers are ill-prepared to endure the lengthy process of negotiating prices. In most cases, the buyer is worn down by a sophisticated system of offers and counter-offers. Eventually, the exhausted customer gives in.

Adverb clauses of concession and contrast are often used to acknowledge other opinions, especially at the beginning of a paragraph.

Adverb phrases can be used concisely to restate an idea already introduced in the text.

Adverb clauses and phrases can be used to provide background information in order to understand the main clause.

Use your own ideas to complete the adverb clauses or phrases. Connect the idea from the first sentence to the idea in the second.

Acknowledging Other Opinions

1. Technology has changed the way graphic designers work—from pen and paper to computer software.

    While some designers _____, most modern designers have welcomed the change.

2. Meditation has recently gained popularity in both Europe and the United States.

    Although some people argue that _____, most people who meditate regularly report positive results, such as stress relief and an improvement in overall health.

Restating an Idea Already Introduced

3. Marathon runners all follow similar guidelines to prepare for a race.

    Before _____, they drink plenty of water, but they do not eat any solid food.

4. Academic writing has strict rules for including the work of other writers.

    When _____, students must reference all material from other sources.

Giving Background Information

5. Cable television has changed the way major networks design and market their shows.

    Because _____, TV networks must be very creative in order to attract viewers.

6. Most college graduates do not have a lot of experience working as part of a team.

    However, although teamwork _____, it's something most employers value highly.

Vocabulary Notes: *Avoiding Wordy Expressions*

Some writers think that using more words will make them sound more academic. However, concise sentence structure is valued in academic writing. The chart below shows how to avoid wordy expressions.

INSTEAD OF	USE . . .
for the reason that due to the fact that in light of the fact that	• because / since
despite the fact that regardless of the fact that	• although / even though / while
in a situation in which under circumstances in which	• when
prior to	• before
in anticipation of subsequent to	• after
at the same time as	• as

D3 **Using Concise Language**

Circle four phrases that make the sentences in the following paragraph too wordy. Rewrite the wordy sentences to make them more concise.

In light of the fact that rabies is both deadly and agonizing, many people believe that more should be done to prevent it from spreading. Rabies is a disease spread through the saliva of certain animals and sometimes rodents. In a situation in which someone is bitten by a rabid animal, he or she must seek immediate treatment. About 72 hours subsequent to being bitten, the symptoms begin to take hold and they cannot easily be reversed. Symptoms begin with flu-like feelings which then lead to disorientation and a loss of mental control. Despite the fact that a lot of money has gone into researching rabies, scientists still know very little about the disease.

1. _____

2. _____

3. _____

4. _____

When writing about your opinions on an issue, it is important to make strong arguments that will persuade your audience to agree with you. Adverb clauses can help make your arguments strong. They can be used to help explain background information, acknowledge other opinions, give reasons for your opinions, and add other supporting ideas.

Choose one of the topics to write a short essay of two to three paragraphs. Before you write, develop a pro and con list of arguments. Give background information. Then explain both your opinions and other opinions. Give reasons why your opinions are stronger. Use the Writing Checklist to check your work.

- Some countries provide college scholarships to students who have achieved a high academic standard. People who favor this policy want to offer opportunities to their best and brightest citizens. Others believe that tax revenue should only be used to help individuals with financial need, so that the neediest people receive the help. Who do you think should benefit from public money for education?

- Recent studies have shown that more attractive people tend to have more opportunities: in dating, education, employment, and so forth. On the other hand, there is a movement against "lookism"—discrimination towards people based on appearance. What do you think? How important are looks? How important do you think they should be? What other qualities might be more valuable?

- There is much debate over what should be allowed on the Internet. Some people feel that content should be censored to meet moral guidelines. Others say that the Internet should be free of censorship. What do you think? Should content be censored on the Internet? Who would decide what is appropriate? Or should individuals be left to make that decision for themselves?

Writing Checklist

Reflect on your ability to use adverb clauses and adverb phrases by answering the questions.

- ☐ **1.** Did you check to make sure your subordinators express the relationship that you intend?
- ☐ **2.** Did you use adverb clauses to give background information?
- ☐ **3.** Did you use adverb clauses to acknowledge other opinions?
- ☐ **4.** Did you use adverb clauses to give reasons for your opinion?
- ☐ **5.** Did you use adverb phrases to make your writing more concise?
- ☐ **6.** Did you check your sentences for correct punctuation?

▶ Beyond the Classroom

Writing

Write an essay using one of these topics.

1. Elections are a cornerstone of democracy, yet in many countries, large numbers of people do not vote. Write a short essay. First, describe people who typically vote and give reasons why they vote. Second, describe people who do not vote and explain why they do not. In the conclusion, summarize the position that you agree with. You may also choose to make a prediction or give a warning about the future.

2. Many people develop strategies and skills to cope with the challenges of daily life. Choose an area where you have used strategies to be more efficient or successful at work or at school. Write a short essay. First, describe what is most challenging about your school or work life. Second, describe two or three strategies that you use and why they are helpful. Finally, comment on other skills that you would like to develop.

3. What is your favorite source of information: Is it a television show, a newspaper or magazine, or an Internet website? Write a short essay. First, describe the type of information that you like to follow. Second, describe your source and why it works best for you. Finally, say why you feel the source you use is better than the others.

Searching for Authentic Examples

Find examples of English grammar in everyday life by completing the task below. Bring your examples to class, and be prepared to discuss them.

Find a newspaper or magazine article describing an event. Look for at least one example each of adverb clauses of reason, concession, and time. Can you change any of these adverb clauses to prepositional phrases with approximately the same meaning? Look for three examples of adverb phrases. Did you find any with omitted subordinators? Change the three adverb phrases to full adverb clauses.

Conditionals

Ask an Astronomer

A1 Before You Read

Read the information. Then discuss the questions.

> Astronomy is one of the oldest sciences. Throughout history, people have been fascinated by observing the night sky and recording the movements of the heavens.

Historically, why did people study the stars and other astronomical phenomena? How were their studies useful?

What is the value of studying astronomy now?

What questions are astronomers trying to answer?

A2 Read

 Read this excerpt from a university-sponsored website about astronomy.

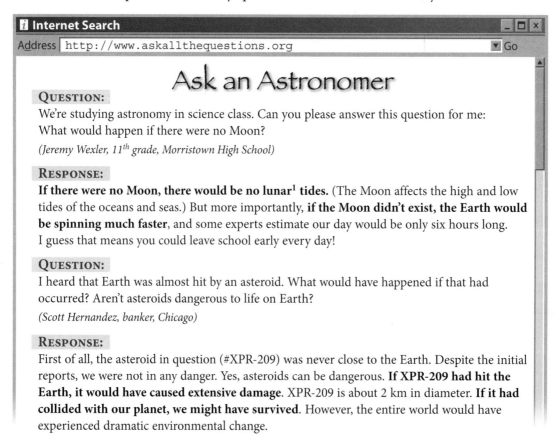

Internet Search

Address `http://www.askallthequestions.org` ▼ Go

Ask an Astronomer

QUESTION:
We're studying astronomy in science class. Can you please answer this question for me: What would happen if there were no Moon?

(Jeremy Wexler, 11ᵗʰ grade, Morristown High School)

RESPONSE:
If there were no Moon, there would be no lunar[1] tides. (The Moon affects the high and low tides of the oceans and seas.) But more importantly, **if the Moon didn't exist, the Earth would be spinning much faster**, and some experts estimate our day would be only six hours long. I guess that means you could leave school early every day!

QUESTION:
I heard that Earth was almost hit by an asteroid. What would have happened if that had occurred? Aren't asteroids dangerous to life on Earth?

(Scott Hernandez, banker, Chicago)

RESPONSE:
First of all, the asteroid in question (#XPR-209) was never close to the Earth. Despite the initial reports, we were not in any danger. Yes, asteroids can be dangerous. **If XPR-209 had hit the Earth, it would have caused extensive damage**. XPR-209 is about 2 km in diameter. **If it had collided with our planet, we might have survived**. However, the entire world would have experienced dramatic environmental change.

I was recently teaching the song "Twinkle, Twinkle Little Star" to my students and got to thinking: Why do stars twinkle? And why don't planets seem to twinkle?

(Susan Kato, teacher, Toronto)

Stars don't actually twinkle. Rather, the light from a star doesn't reach your eye steadily. There are many layers of air in the Earth's atmosphere, and these layers are in constant motion. When we look at a faraway star, we see it as a single point of light. This point of light is "bent" as it passes through these shifting layers (the scientific word is *refracted*[3]), and we see this as twinkling. **If you see an object in the sky that isn't twinkling, that probably means it's a planet, not a star**. A planet is much closer to us than a star, so it doesn't appear as a single point of light. It looks like a disc (made up of many points of light). When these many points of light are refracted through the atmosphere, some of them reach your eye steadily, so the planet doesn't seem to twinkle.

If you have questions about planets, stars, or anything else above, you can write to us at: The Gazer's Gazette, 100 Planetary Way, Loisville, FL 20022

Excerpts adapted from the website "Curious About Astronomy? Ask an Astronomer," copyright © 2007 The Curious Team (http://curious.astro.cornell.edu/)

1 **lunar:** related to the moon
2 **twinkle:** to shine with an unsteady light
3 **refract:** to change the direction of a ray of light

A3 After You Read

Discuss these questions.

1. What three topics are the readers asking about?
2. Did you learn anything new? If so, what?
3. What question(s) would you want to ask an astronomer?

A4 Examining Form

A. Work in pairs. Look at the highlighted conditional sentences in the reading. Write each clause in the correct category on a separate piece of paper.

Present *if* clause / Present in main clause

Past *if* clause / Modal in main clause

Past perfect *if* clause / Past modal in main clause

B. Discuss your observations with the class. Refer to the form charts on page A-5 if you need to.

B # Real Conditionals

Examining Meaning and Use

Read each sentence and the statements that follow it. Check (✓) the correct statement. Discuss your answers. Then read the notes to check them.

1. If I take Bus #3, I get to work early.

    _____ **a.** This is a general statement about a habitual activity.
    _____ **b.** This is a specific statement about the present moment.

2. If you like fiction, you might like this story.

    _____ **a.** I'm certain that you'll like it.
    _____ **b.** I'm not certain that you'll like it.

3. They'll cancel the meeting if it snows.

    _____ **a.** I'm certain about the result.
    _____ **b.** The result is just a possibility.

4. Whenever Joe had an appointment, he marked it on his calendar.

    _____ **a.** This is about one moment in the past.
    _____ **b.** This is about habitual past actions.

Overview: Real Conditionals

If *Clause*		Main (Result) Clause
If he takes the train,	(then)	he gets to work by 9:00. *(present)*
If it's snowing tomorrow,	(then)	they'll probably cancel the game. *(future)*
If the weather was nice,	(then)	why didn't you go to the park? *(past)*

- Real conditional sentences are used to talk about possible situations and their results.
- Conditional sentences have an *if* clause and a main clause. The *if* clause introduces a condition or event, and the main clause expresses a result of the condition.
- *If* clauses are dependent clauses; they cannot stand alone. All *if* clauses contain a subject and a verb.
- The *if* clause usually comes first, and it is followed by a comma. *Then* is usually omitted, but it is always implied. When the main clause comes first, there is no comma and *then* is not used.

    He gets to work by 9:00 if he takes the train.

Present Real Conditionals, Timeless: *if / when* + present, *(then)* + present
if / when + present, *(then)* + future

If/When/Whenever he **takes** the train, he **gets** to work by 9:00.
If/When/Whenever the sky **is** cloudy, you **can't see** the moon clearly.
If/When I'**m working** really hard, I <u>sometimes</u> **lose** track of the time.

- Like simple present sentences, present conditional sentences can express general, timeless statements and habitual activities. They indicate that something always happens as a result of a certain condition.
- Both clauses often use simple present verb forms. The *if* clause can also use continuous forms. The main clause may also use *can/can't* (for ability). Main clauses may include adverbs of frequency (e.g., *sometimes, usually*) to qualify the statement, although only certain adverbs can occur in the same sentence as *whenever* (e.g., *always, usually*).
- Since these sentences are timeless, *when* and *whenever* can be used in place of *if* with no change in meaning.
- Timeless conditionals can also use *will* in the main clause.

    If/When/Whenever the sky is cloudy, you **won't see** the moon clearly.

Present Real Conditionals, Possibilities: *if* + present, *(then)* + present

If he **doesn't like** to cook, he <u>probably</u> **buys** a lot of takeout.
If he **enjoys** skiing, he **might like** snowboarding, too.
If the cost of housing **is decreasing**, why **can't** we **find** an affordable apartment?
If she **hasn't done** anything wrong, she **shouldn't have** anything to worry about.

- Present conditional sentences can also express <u>possible</u> events and situations and their results. The *if* clause suggests a possible condition, and the main clause suggests a possible result. Unlike timeless conditionals, these sentences do <u>not</u> express something that always happens.
- Conditional sentences that express possible events use a much greater variety of verb forms, including present perfect, continuous, and modal verb forms.
- Modals of possibility *(could, might, may, should, must)* are often used in the main clause to show different levels of certainty. Adverbs such as *maybe, probably,* and *definitely* may also be used.
- Since these sentence are not timeless, *when/whenever* cannot be used in place of *if*.

    * When/Whenever he enjoys skiing, he might like snowboarding, too. (INCORRECT)

Predictions About Future Activities or States
If it**'s snowing** tomorrow, they**'ll** probably **cancel** the game.
If she**'s not** here yet, she **must not be coming**.

Planned Future Activities
If I **have** time, I**'m** probably **going to visit** some friends in Turkey next year.
I **might take** a dance class **if** I **can find** a friend to go with me.

- Future conditional sentences express possible future results of present or future conditions. The *if* clause usually uses a present form. The main clause uses a future form, including modals of possibility *(could, might, may, should, must)* to show different levels of certainty.

Advice, Requests, and Commands: *if* **+ present, *(then)* + present/future**

If you**'re having** constant headaches, you**'ve got to see** a doctor. *(advice)*
If you **have** time, **could** you **help** me decorate for the party tomorrow? *(request)*
If you**'re finished** with your test, **pass** it to the front of the room. *(command)*

- Social modals (e.g., for advice and requests) and imperatives are also used after present *if* clauses expressing present and future meaning.

Mixed Time Real Conditionals: *if* **+ past, *(then)* + present/future**

Past Affects Present
If he **didn't smile** at you, he probably **doesn't remember** you. *(He didn't smile at you, so . . .)*

Past Affects Future
If he **injured** his ankle, he **won't be playing** in the game on Friday. *(He injured his ankle, so . . .)*

- Sometimes real conditional sentences do not follow the regular patterns. Instead, past time may be mixed with present or future time.

As long as I'm not interrupted, <u>I'll finish</u> most of the work by the end of the day.

Unless I can find a friend to go with me, I <u>won't take</u> that dance class.

Even if it's snowing tomorrow, they <u>won't cancel</u> the game.

- Other expressions can be used to introduce real conditionals:
  - *As long as, only if,* and *providing / provided that* (more formal) emphasize a <u>single</u> condition that will cause a result.
  - *Unless* emphasizes a <u>single negative</u> condition that will cause a result. It means *if . . . not.*
  - *Even if* and *whether or not* mean that the condition doesn't matter—the result will always be the same. The clause is offset by commas whether it is placed at the beginning or the end of the sentence.
    They won't cancel the game, **even if** it's snowing tomorrow.
- These expressions occur most often when *will* or *won't* are in the main clause. One clause is usually negative and one clause is usually affirmative.
- When *only if* begins a sentence, the subject and auxiliary in the main clause are inverted: auxiliary + subject + verb.
  Only if I'm not interrupted <u>will I finish</u> the work. *(Formal)*

Timeless

If/When the plane **left** New York at 5:30 P.M., it usually **arrived** in Prague at 7:30 A.M.

If/When the sky **was** clear, he **was able to see** for miles.

If/When she **was having** a bad day, she **used to turn off** the phone and **take** a bath.

Not Timeless

If the weather **was** nice, why **didn't** you **go** to the park?

If he **was acting** strangely, something **might have been bothering** him.

- Past conditional sentences can express timeless situations in the past or possible (not timeless) situations in the past. Both clauses use past forms. Past real conditional sentences are not used as often as the other types of conditional sentences.

Listening

A. 🎧 Each sentence in the passage is incomplete. Listen to the entire passage first. Then listen again and put a caret (∧) where you hear a missing word. Listen once more to fill in the missing words, and correct the punctuation.

If you
∧ ~~You~~ drive a hybrid car, you better gas mileage and you create less carbon dioxide and other pollution. You can't afford a hybrid, however, there still things that every car owner can do. First, if you regular tune-ups, then better gas mileage and you'll pollute the air less. Second, also get better mileage you your tires properly inflated. Finally, drive at a medium speed you can. Your engine works harder than necessary, it more gas and more emissions.

B. 🎧 Listen. Choose the best answer to complete each conversation.

1. a. Does this happen often?
   b. He talks a lot, doesn't he?

2. a. So you might not be able to come.
   b. So you definitely can't come.

3. a. OK, I'll pick you up if it clears up soon.
   b. Why not? We'll have so much fun if it clears up.

4. a. When did you stop?
   b. Did you ever ask him any questions?

5. a. That's a reasonable request.
   b. That's good advice.

6. a. If you don't know, I'm not going to tell you.
   b. As long as you know, I'm not going to tell you.

B2 **Using Present Real Conditional: Timeless**

A. Match the phrases. Decide which clause will be the *if* clause and which will be the main clause. Then write timeless general statements using present real conditionals.

1. it takes seven years to digest __g__
   If you swallow a piece of gum, it takes seven years to digest.

2. you are orbiting above the Earth ____

3. you cross the International Date Line ____

4. a tsunami can occur ____

5. it's called a solar eclipse ____

6. you eat late at night ____

7. you tap the top of a soda can ____

a. the Moon temporarily blocks the Sun in the sky

b. the food in your stomach immediately turns into fat

c. it stops the contents from foaming

d. the Great Wall of China is the only visible manmade structure

e. you lose or gain a day

f. an earthquake causes a violent shift on the ocean floor

g. you swallow a piece of gum

B. Four of the statements in part A are false. Do you know which ones? Can you explain why?

B3 Using Future Real Conditionals

A. Match the verb phrases to form conditional sentences. Decide which phrase will be in the *if* clause and which will be in the main clause. Then write sentences about changes you can make in your daily behavior to help save the environment.

1. help prevent the destruction of forests worldwide _e_

   If you use recycled paper, you'll help prevent the destruction of forests worldwide.

2. unplug electronic devices that you're not using ____

3. reduce your need for air conditioning ____

4. buy food from local farmers ____

5. help cut down on air pollution ____

6. take fewer showers ____

a. keep money in your community

b. save on your utility bill

c. lower your water consumption

d. form a carpool with coworkers

e. use recycled paper

f. plant shade trees around your home

B. Work with a partner. Write two more tips for helping the environment. Explain the positive results of making changes in your life.

If you walk instead of driving to school, you'll feel better. You'll also save money and not pollute the air.

B4 Using Conditionals with Modal Forms

A. Read each statement. Then write a present or future real conditional sentence to express possibility or advice. Use a phrase in the box with a modal in the main clause.

help me make breakfast	be stuck in traffic somewhere	have a virus
be off the hook ✓	look for a new one	take a break
do it later	not be able to eat at all	

Possibility

1. "The line is still busy."

   <u>*If the line is still busy, the phone could be off the hook.*</u>

2. "Nancy's late for the meeting."

   _____

3. "Joe has to work through lunch."

   _____

4. "Tina's computer keeps crashing."

   _____

Advice

5. "I can't finish my homework now."

   _____

6. "I'm exhausted."

_____

7. "I'm unhappy in my current job."

_____

8. "I might wake up early tomorrow."

_____

B. Work with a partner. Take turns sharing three or four minor problems you are having. (Think about problems at home, at work, at school, with friends, or with family.) Give your partner advice. Use _if_ clauses.

A: Somehow I've got to do my laundry in the next few days, even though I don't have enough time.
B: If you don't have enough time, maybe you could drop it off at a laundromat.

B5 **Using Mixed Time Real Conditionals**

Combine ideas from the box together. Write sentences using mixed time conditionals.

He's going to love Prague. ✓	He was off last week.
He probably doesn't feel very well today.	He wasn't at school yesterday.
He'll have to work a double shift next week.	He committed the crime.
He's probably pretty tired today.	He may be out of town.
He ate something spoiled.	He was out late last night.
He enjoyed Paris. ✓	He'll be convicted.

If he enjoyed Paris, he's going to love Prague. _____

_____

_____

_____

_____

_____

A. Study the course listing. Write sentences using the words given.

Course title	Department	Prerequisite
Advanced Algebra	Mathematics	Must have completed Intermediate Algebra
Biomedical Ethics	Philosophy	Must have completed Introduction to Critical Thinking
Brain, Mind, and Behavior	Psychology	Three credits in psychology or biology
Intermediate Algebra	Mathematics	Strong mathematics background required
Introduction to Critical Thinking	Philosophy	No philosophy background necessary
Principles of Psychology	Psychology	For first-year students only
World Religions	Religious Studies	Appropriate for all religious studies majors

1. Advanced Algebra / as long as *You can take Advanced Algebra as long as you've completed Intermediate Algebra.*

2. Biomedical Ethics / unless _____

3. Brain, Mind, and Behavior / only if _____

4. Intermediate Algebra / providing that _____

5. Introduction to Critical Thinking / even if _____

6. Principles of Psychology / unless _____

7. World Religions / as long as _____

B. Write a few sentences of advice for each situation using the expressions in parentheses. Give reasons for your advice.

1. get married in high school (*even if*)
   You shouldn't get married in high school, even if you're in love. At that age, you're too young to make such a serious decision.

2. buy an expensive home (*unless*)

3. get a large dog (*providing that*)

4. go back to school for a second degree (*only if*)

5. skip class (*even if*)

6. give money to charity (*as long as*)

C. Join a partner. Take turns sharing your ideas about each situation in part B. How are your opinions different?

Unreal Conditionals

Examining Meaning and Use

Read each sentence and the statements that follow it. Check (✓) the correct statement. Discuss your answers. Then read the notes to check them.

1. She acts as though she didn't care. She's a terrible liar.
   _____ **a.** She probably does care.
   _____ **b.** She definitely doesn't care.

2. If I had been offered the job, I would have taken it.
   _____ **a.** I took the job.
   _____ **b.** I wasn't offered the job.

3. There wouldn't be any snow if the temperature were a bit higher.
   _____ **a.** This is about the present.
   _____ **b.** This is about the past.

Present/Future Unreal Conditionals:
if + past, *(then)* + *would / could / might* + verb

If I **lost** my passport while I was abroad, I **would contact** the U.S. embassy.
(I have <u>not</u> lost my passport. The condition is untrue now, but it's possible in the future.)

If your dog **could talk**, what **would** he **say**?
(The dog <u>cannot</u> talk. The condition is untrue and impossible.)

If a large meteor <u>**were**</u> **coming** toward the Earth, we **couldn't do** anything about it.

A: I really want to buy that leather jacket.

B: **If** I <u>**were**</u> you, I **might** wait until it goes on sale.

- Unreal conditionals function similarly to real conditionals, but they express imaginary conditions and results. They are used to show different levels of certainty or give advice about imaginary situations.

- Present/future unreal conditional sentences are used to consider imaginary events and situations. The sentences are not true in the present. However, in some cases they could be true in the future.

- In the *if* clause, the use of the past does not indicate past time; it indicates that the situation is unreal. The *if* clause uses the simple past, past continuous, or *could/couldn't* (for past ability).

continued

- In the main clause, the use of *would* expresses a prediction (it is a more certain imaginary result). *Could* and *might* express possible or less certain results.

    If I had more time, I **would** definitely do some volunteer work.

    If I had more time, I **could** exercise after work.

    If I had more time, I **might** take a cooking class.

- *Were* is used as the form of *be* for all subjects in the *if* clause. However, in conversation *was* is sometimes used with *I* and *he/she/it*.

Past Unreal Conditionals:
if + past perfect, (then) + would / could / might + have + past participle

If I **had invested** in my brother's business, I **might have made** a lot of money.
(In reality, I <u>did not</u> invest, so I <u>did not</u> make a lot of money.)

If you **had been trying** harder, you **could have won** the contest.
(In reality, you <u>were not</u> trying hard enough, so you <u>did not</u> win the contest.)

If I **hadn't gotten** lost in Paris, I **wouldn't have met** my husband.
(In reality, I <u>did</u> get lost in Paris, so I <u>did</u> meet my husband.)

- Past unreal conditional sentences are used to consider alternative outcomes to past events and situations. They express how things could have happened differently. Because these sentences are about completed past situations, they cannot ever occur.

- In the *if* clause, the past perfect or past perfect continuous introduces the unreal past situation. In the main clause, the use of *would have* expresses a more certain imaginary result. *Could have* and *might have* express a possible or less certain imaginary result.

Mixed Time Unreal Conditionals: *if + present, (then) + past*
if + past, (then) + present

Unreal Present Affects Unreal Past

If I **could sing**, I **would have auditioned** for the musical.
(I <u>cannot</u> sing in general, so I <u>did not</u> audition in the past.)

Unreal Past Affects Unreal Present

If you **hadn't worked** the late shift last night, you **wouldn't feel** so exhausted today.
(I <u>did</u> work the late shift in the past, so I <u>do</u> feel exhausted in the present.)

- Sometimes unreal conditionals do not follow the regular patterns. Instead, present time and past time may be mixed.

As if and As though

I don't know why <u>he acts</u> **as though he has/had all the answers.**
(The condition is untrue. He <u>doesn't</u> have all the answers.)

<u>It looks</u> **as if they're going to let him graduate after all.**
(The condition may be true. He <u>may</u> be graduating.)

- Clauses with *as if* and *as though* are used to suggest a condition that appears to be true. In some cases, the speaker knows the condition isn't true. In other cases, the speaker isn't certain if it is true.
- The past tense (including *were* for all forms of *be*) may be used to emphasize the unreal meaning.
- In conversation, *like* is often used instead of *as if* or *as though*.
  I don't know why he acts <u>like</u> he has/had all the answers. *(Informal)*

C1 **Listening**

A. 🎧 Each sentence in the passage is incomplete. Listen to the entire passage first. Then listen again and put a caret (^) where you hear a missing word. Listen once more to fill in the missing words, and correct the punctuation.

would have

Do you ever wonder what ^^ happened you had acted differently at some important

point in your life? Your whole life different? What your life like now? You the chance, you go

back and make changes? Many people think they the same mistakes again. They act they all

the right answers now. Well, I'm not so sure.

B. 🎧 Listen. Choose the best sentence to complete each conversation.

1. **a.** It's too bad you didn't take the time to read it.
   b. It's good you took the time to read it.

2. **a.** I'll call you, of course.
   b. I'd have called you, of course.

3. **a.** Why did you eat them?
   b. That could be serious.

4. **a.** Why are you suggesting that?
   b. Why are you promising that?

5. **a.** Good. Let's go to the gate.
   b. Really. I wonder why it isn't.

6. **a.** When did you have a dog?
   b. Would you like to have a dog?

C2 Present/Future Unreal Conditionals

A. Read about each person's problem. Give a piece of advice for each one using *If I were you, . . .* and modals *would, might,* or *could.*

1. "I don't get along with my new boss. He's close-minded and doesn't listen."
   If I were you, I'd look for another job.
2. "I have a big exam next month, but I can't get motivated to study for it."
3. "My parents are upset with me because my grades haven't been so good recently."
4. "I love my job, but it doesn't pay well."
5. "A co-worker has asked me out on a date. I haven't told the person I'm thinking about it."
6. "My car is 10 years old. It's starting to fall apart."

B. Work with a partner. Compare your ideas from part A. What do you think your partner's answers tell you about his or her personality?

Usage Note: *Omitting the If Clause*

In conversation, after a condition is established with an *if* clause, it does not need to be repeated. Later sentences can include the result clause alone. The condition is implied.

A: *If you could take back something you once said or did, what **would** it **be**?*
B: *It **would be** something I once told my brother. I said that . . .*

C3 Omitting *If* Clauses

A. Work in small groups. Take turns asking and answering the questions. Remember to omit the *if* clause once it is established. Give reasons for your answers. Ask follow-up questions to get more information.

1. If you could take back something you once said or did, what would it be?
   I wouldn't have told my friend that I didn't like her cooking.
2. If you could make just one final visit somewhere in the world, where would you go for this last trip?
3. If you weren't afraid of anything, what are three things that you would do?
4. If you could be an inanimate object for a day, what would you be?
5. If you could be any age again for one month, what age would you choose?
6. If you could live in the world of a TV show for a week, what show would you choose?

B. Share some of your answers with the class.

A. Read each situation. Write a sentence using an *if* clause about what could, might, or would have happened if the situation were different.

1. Henry's e-mail crashed, so he didn't get the message in time.
   If his e-mail hadn't crashed, he would have gotten the message in time.
2. Ginger lost the race because she tripped just before the finish line.
3. Due to the heavy rain, the wedding was held indoors.
4. Since Paula answered the final question correctly, she won a new car.
5. She survived the accident because Cal knew CPR.
6. I became a veterinarian. I worked on a farm when I was a teenager.
7. They won three matches in a row, so the game ended quickly.
8. I lost money when I sold my house because my realtor gave me bad advice.

B. Work with a partner. Choose one of the situations below. Take turns telling about the event. Then say how the situation could have happened differently.

- a time when something embarrassing happened
- a time when you were disappointed
- a time when you did something that you now regret

   In high school, I played violin in the school orchestra. In our last concert of the year, I had a solo. I was very excited about it. As luck would have it, I got sick the day before the concert and couldn't play. It was so disappointing! If I hadn't gotten sick, I could have played my solo. I would have made my parents so proud of me. I may even have continued playing violin in college.

A. Complete the sentences. Use the ideas from the box. Use the past unreal in one clause, and the present unreal in the other.

I'm not good at math.	I lost my job. ✔	My car broke down.
I lost my wallet.	I'm living in Beverly Hills now.	I visited Angkor Wat last year.

1. If I weren't always late to work, *I wouldn't have lost my job*_____.
2. _____, I could have become an astronomer.
3. If I hadn't won the lottery, _____.
4. _____, I wouldn't be spending time buying a new one.
5. If I didn't like to photograph old temples, _____.
6. _____, I wouldn't need to take the bus to work every day.

B. Circle your answers to complete these sentences. How have these personal qualities affected your life <u>in the past</u>? Write four sentences with mixed time unreal conditionals.

1. I (know how to / don't know how to) budget carefully.

2. I (like / don't like) to study.

3. I (speak / don't speak) English well.

4. I (enjoy / don't enjoy) going to parties.

If I didn't know how to budget carefully, I could have had a lot of money troubles last year.

C. Complete these sentences. How do these events from the past affect you <u>now</u>? Write four sentences with mixed time unreal conditionals.

1. I grew up in _____.

2. I learned how to _____ at an early age.

3. I enjoyed studying _____ in high school.

4. I grew up listening to _____.

If I hadn't grown up in a small town in Australia, I wouldn't be such a friendly person today.

C6 Using *As if* and *As though*

A. Match the ideas in the first and second columns.

1. I could barely hear him. _g_

2. She completely ignored me. ____

3. Don't sleep through your life. ____

4. There were dark circles under his eyes. ____

5. It seems impossible that it happened twenty years ago. ____

6. It's so damp today. ____

7. I'm so happy today. ____

8. Was that someone at the door? ____

a. I remember it like it was yesterday.

b. You should live every day as if it were your last day.

c. It feels as though it's going to rain.

d. I feel like I'm on top of the world.

e. She pretended as if I hadn't walked into the room.

f. It sounds as though they've arrived.

g. He spoke as if it were very difficult.

h. It looked as though he hadn't slept all night.

B. Complete the sentences using *as if* or *as though*.

1. My older brother bosses me around _____.

2. I didn't recognize her, but she said "hello" _____.

3. While we were in France, she acted _____ even though she only speaks English.

4. I was so hungry that I felt _____.

5. He's so critical of other people. He behaves _____.

6. Due to the blizzard, our three-hour bus trip took seven hours. It seemed _____

   _____.

7. When I heard the news about the car accident I felt _____.

Read each sentence and the statements that follow it. Choose the statement that follows most logically from the meaning of the sentence.

1. How do languages evolve?
   a. If different cultures came together, they'd influence each other's language.
   b. If different cultures come together, they influence each other's language.

2. I keep trying to call Sue, but she's not picking up the phone.
   a. If you're not getting an answer, you may be dialing the wrong number.
   b. If you weren't getting an answer, you could dial the wrong number.

3. Judy Miller is running for office.
   a. She needs a strong message if she's going to succeed.
   b. She would have needed a strong message if she was going to succeed.

4. Unless scientists find a cure, the number of patients will increase.
   a. If scientists find a cure, the number of patients will increase.
   b. If scientists don't find a cure, the number of patients will increase.

5. Can you pick up some milk?
   a. Sure. And as long as I'm going out, I'll stop by the bank, too.
   b. Sure. And even if I'm going out, I'll stop by the bank, too.

6. When you lived in San Francisco, how long was your commute?
   a. If I'd caught the bus, it would have taken about 15 minutes.
   b. If I caught the bus, it would take about 15 minutes.

7. Is the store still opening on Friday?
   a. I don't know. If the stock didn't arrive yesterday, they won't be opening on time.
   b. I don't know. If the stock hadn't arrived already, they wouldn't be opening on time.

8. If you knew Russian, you'd be able to read the subtitles.
   a. You understand Russian.
   b. You don't understand Russian.

9. If Sam hadn't studied, he wouldn't feel so confident about taking the exam.
   a. Sam has already studied.
   b. Sam hasn't studied yet.

10. Even if she had known the consequences, she would have spoken out.
    a. She would have spoken out regardless of the consequences.
    b. She regrets speaking out because of the consequences.

11. I'm so disappointed that James didn't come to the party.
    a. Yeah. If James had come, he would be arriving by now.
    b. Yeah. If James were coming, he would have arrived by now.

12. She acts as if she's the head of the department.
    a. She's the head of the department.
    b. She isn't the head of the department.

A. Read the situation and answer the questions. What do you think Andrea should do?

> Last week, Andrea's supervisor informed her that she would be receiving a promotion and an increase in salary. He also told her that five of her colleagues, including her friend Mark, were going to be laid off sometime in the next month. She was instructed not to tell this news to anyone.
>
> Mark reports to Andrea. He is also her friend. She knows that he is seriously considering buying an expensive new home. He hasn't signed the papers yet, but he may do so in the next week or two. Obviously, he has no idea that he is about to lose his job.

1. Should Andrea ignore the situation? What could happen if she ignores it?
2. Should she complain about the situation? What could happen if she complains?
3. Should she tell Mark? What could happen if she tells him?
4. Is there something else she could do?

B. Join two or three other students and discuss your choices. Use conditional sentences to explain your answers.

> A: *She could complain to her supervisor, but if she complains to her supervisor, he probably won't listen.*
>
> B: *That's true, but I think she has to do something. Mark is her friend. If I were her, I'd . . .*

C. Now read what actually happened. Talk with your partners about what might have happened if Andrea had acted differently.

> Andrea couldn't decide what to do. After about 10 days, she finally decided to tell Mark about the layoffs. Unfortunately, it was too late. Mark had received his notice that very morning. He had also just bought his new home. Mark was very upset that Andrea hadn't told him the news sooner. Mark is now desperately looking for a new job, and he no longer speaks to Andrea. Meanwhile, Andrea feels terrible about the situation, yet she doesn't feel completely responsible.

> A: *Everything would've turned out better if Andrea had told Mark sooner.*
>
> B: *I don't know about that. There's no guarantee that . . .*

Writing

Editing: *Conditional Sentences*

Study the errors. Pay attention to the areas that you make mistakes in.

> **1. Fragments**
>
>   unless
> We practice every day. ~~Unless~~ the weather is bad.
>
> **2. Punctuation**
>
>   ,
> If I had a car ⌃ I would be able to get to work easier.
> I would be able to get to work easier~~,~~ if I had a car.
>
> **3. Placement of *if***
>
> If it is cloudy,
> ~~It is cloudy~~ if you cannot observe the stars.
>
> **4. Use of *would/will* in the *if* clause**
>
>   am
> If I ~~will be~~ elected mayor, I will create more jobs. *(real)*
>   found
> If she ~~would find~~ another apartment, she would move. *(unreal)*
>
> **5. Use of tenses in unreal sentences**
>
>   lost
> Imagine this, if he ~~loses~~ his job, he would go back to school. *(present unreal)*
>   have fired
> If I had been the boss, I would ~~fire~~ her last week. *(past unreal)*

D1 **Editing**

Correct the errors in these sentences. Be prepared to explain your answers.

1. You should read *The Worst-Case Scenario,* if you want to learn how to survive in different bad situations.

2. If you should back away slowly, you need to escape from a mountain lion.

3. The lion will pay more attention to you if you'll try to run from it.

4. You would suffer an internal injury if someone punches you hard in the stomach.

5. However, you can protect yourself from injury. If you tighten your stomach muscles.

6. If I'll get a raise, I'll definitely save more money.

7. You hear three shots if it means the race has begun.

8. If you need more money I can lend you some.

9. Whenever I had paid attention in class last semester, I would have passed the course.

10. I would take a trip abroad if I would have some vacation days left.

Beyond the Sentence: *Using Implied Conditionals*

In extended writing about conditional situations and results, good writers don't use sentences with *if* clauses repeatedly. Rather, they use a combination of sentences with *if* clauses as well as sentences that imply a conditional meaning.

Even though most people are more conscious about recycling these days, landfills and dumps across the nation continue to fill up. Some basic changes in our behavior could have a major effect in reversing this trend.

Large corporations could have the biggest impact. **If corporations used less packaging,** everyone <u>would save</u>. Less packaging <u>would mean</u> less garbage. In addition, consumers <u>would be attracted</u> by environmentally friendly packaging, and they <u>would be</u> more likely to buy the company's products.

Companies <u>would also save</u> money on waste disposal. On an individual level, everyone needs to start recycling consistently and, more importantly, properly. <u>Recyclables must be cleaned and sorted correctly</u>. **Otherwise,** <u>they become too costly to process.</u> For example, at one point several years ago, New York City stopped its recycling program entirely when it became too expensive. <u>The program could have worked,</u> **but** <u>people didn't follow the rules.</u> Since then, it has been reinstated with simpler rules, but the program's success still lies in individual participation and adherence to the rules. <u>**With** some small changes, we can all have a big impact.</u>

> *When a single condition has many results, the* if *condition is usually stated only once. The sentences that follow can just include the result clause. The condition is implied.*

> *Sometimes a condition can be implied by words such as* otherwise/or else, with/without, *and* but. *For example:* Recyclables must be cleaned and sorted correctly. Otherwise, they become too costly to process. = *If recyclables aren't cleaned and sorted correctly, they become too costly to process.*

A. Work with a partner. Write sentences using an *if* clause with the same meaning.

   1. With some small changes, we can have a big impact.

      If we *make some small changes, we can have a big impact.*

   2. The program could have worked, but people didn't follow the rules.

      The program _____

   3. People need to visit their doctor regularly, or else serious problems can go undetected.

      If people _____

   4. Without good eating habits, people risk serious health problems.

      If people _____

   5. People must recycle the garbage they create. Otherwise, there won't be enough places to dump it all.

      If people _____

   6. Her presentation would have been more impressive, but she didn't prepare thoroughly.

      Her presentation _____

   7. The fuel efficiency legislation would have helped clean the air, but it wasn't passed.

      If the legislation _____

B. **Think of a choice you made in the past that was a positive turning point in your life. What would have happened if you had not made the same choice? How would your life be different? Make a list of the consequences.**

   Learning to speak English
   If I hadn't learned to speak English, . . .

C. **Write one or two short paragraphs describing how your life would be different if you had not made the same choice. Omit *if* clauses where possible and use other implied conditional forms, too.**

   Learning to speak English was a big turning point for me. If I hadn't learned to speak English, I wouldn't have been able to come to school in the United States. I also wouldn't have met my girlfriend, who lives here. Coming to the United States gave me a lot of confidence, too. I used to be pretty shy, and I really came out of my shell when I started school in the U.S. I needed the experience of leaving home. Otherwise, I might still be quiet and insecure.

Conditionals are often used in persuasive writing because they help to relate problems with solutions, and causes with effects. Real conditionals can be used to argue about what will happen if a certain action is taken. Unreal conditionals can be used to discuss hypothetical problems and outcomes.

Choose one of the topics to write a short essay of two to three paragraphs. Decide if you agree or disagree with the initial statement. Say why you agree or disagree and persuade your reader to agree with you. Then, use the Writing Checklist to check your work.

- A mandatory garbage recycling law should be passed. Think about the following: What will happen if we don't control the amount of garbage being produced? How would such a law benefit people? How would different people and organizations react to it? What would have to happen to make it practical?

- Everyone should have access to free healthcare and prescriptions. Think about the following: Why is free health care necessary? How would this service help people? What about the drawbacks? Who would provide this service? Who should pay for it? What could happen to the quality of health care?

- Art museums should not be permitted to charge high admission fees. Think about the following: Is art important? If so, why? Why do museums feel the need to charge high fees? Who would lower admission fees benefit or harm?

Writing Checklist

Reflect on your ability to use conditionals by answering the questions.

- ☐ **1.** Did you use real conditionals to talk about possible situations and their results?
- ☐ **2.** Did you unreal conditional sentences to consider imaginary events and situations?
- ☐ **3.** Did you use alternatives to *if*?
- ☐ **4.** Did you omit *if* clauses where possible?
- ☐ **5.** Did you use any other implied conditional forms?
- ☐ **6.** Did you check your sentences for correct form?

▶ Beyond the Classroom

Writing

Write an essay using one of these topics.

1. Some people say that children are not getting the social experiences or exercise that they did in the past because they spend so many hours watching TV and sitting in front of computers. They argue that these activities are essentially passive and have a "dumbing" effect on today's children. Others argue that television and computers have expanded students' access to knowledge and made learning a much more dynamic process. What is your opinion? First explain whether you believe television and computers have had a positive or negative effect on today's children. Then explain the reasons why you feel this way. In your conclusion, summarize your opinion.

2. The 20th century was a period of rapid change and technological advancements. In your opinion, what was the most important invention of the 20th century? Why? Describe the invention. Then give specific reasons why it has changed peoples' lives in an important way. In your conclusion, summarize your opinion.

Searching for Authentic Examples

Find examples of English grammar in everyday life by completing the task below. Bring your examples to class, and be prepared to discuss them.

Look at editorials in a newspaper or on the Internet. Find two examples of real and two examples of unreal conditional sentences. Why do you think they were used? In what way do they help to convey the writers' opinions?

Noun Clauses

A | E-waste

A1 | Before You Read

Complete the task and discuss the questions.

Check (✓) the items that you own or have in your home.

☐ cell phone   ☐ television   ☐ DVD player   ☐ MP3 player   ☐ computer

Do you have more than one of each of these items?

How frequently do you replace these items? For example, do you get a new cell phone every year?

What do you think happens to old cell phones and computers when they are no longer needed?

A2 | Read

 Read this article to find out about recycling and e-waste.

E-WASTE *Do you ever wonder* **what happens to your old cell phones and computers?**

Vanessa is getting a new cell phone today, and she's not sure **if she should get a new flip phone or one with a digital camera.** She's had her old phone for two years now and it works fine, but her cell phone provider offers a replacement phone every 24 months—free of charge, no questions asked. "It's one of the perks[1] of signing the contract with this company," she says. "Besides, I want to get the newest model—it's really cool."

Whether Vanessa needs a new cell phone or not is beside the point. She, like most consumers, will take advantage of the company's offer simply because she can. Ten years ago, if someone had suggested **that you throw away your home telephone every other year**, you would have thought they were insane.[2] Now we do that very thing—with cell phones—without a second thought. And the fact is

that most people don't think twice[3] about tossing even large electronic items.

All these cell phones, computers, monitors, VCRs, and other electronic gadgets end up in our garbage dumps, clogging[4] our landfills. However, the story doesn't end once they are taken to the dump. The biggest problem is **that many electronic parts are extremely toxic.** For example, experts estimate **that 20 million computers a year are discarded in the United States alone.** While these old models make up only 1 percent of the content in landfills, they represent 70 percent of the toxins released in those landfills. That's because a typical computer monitor contains at least 4 pounds of lead. While these devices are safe to handle, when they are crushed in garbage trucks, their toxins are released. These toxins can then leach[5] into the soil and the groundwater.

We can't just blame the consumer for contributing to this pollution of the environment, however. It is troubling **that many of today's electronic devices are "made to break."** This means **that they are built less sturdily than they were a generation ago,** and often stop working after only a few years. That, coupled with the message of advertisers promoting everything new as "better," makes it all too easy for consumers to toss their electronic toys without considering **where they are going.**

Many people don't know the first thing about **how to recycle their hardware** or, in some cases, **if recycling is even possible.** That is changing, though, as more nonprofit organizations are getting the word out. Environmental activists are developing websites and holding special events where you can drive to a central location to donate your computer or television. They will recycle your donation responsibly, with the promise **that it won't harm the environment.** This kind of action may be only a drop in the bucket,[6] but the tide[7] is slowly changing as people become more aware of the problem of e-waste and its effect on the environment.

---

1 **perk:** an extra benefit
2 **insane:** mad; foolish
3 **think twice:** to consider (a decision) carefully
4 **clog:** to block

5 **leach:** to gradually soak into
6 **a drop in the bucket:** a very small amount (= having little effect)
7 **tide:** tendency (of public opinion)

A3 After You Read

Discuss these questions.

1. What is e-waste?

2. What happens to e-waste after it gets thrown out?

3. If e-waste is bad for the environment, why do so many consumers throw away their electronic devices?

4. What solutions to address this issue are suggested in the article? Can you come up with other solutions?

A. Work in pairs. Look at the highlighted clauses in the reading. Write them in the correct categories. Some items are already done.

that clauses

In a sentence beginning with *it* _____

_____

After *be* _____

_____

After a verb   *that you throw away your home telephone every other year*

_____

After a noun _____

_____

wh and *if/whether* clauses

As a subject _____

After a preposition _____

After a verb   *what happens to your old cell phones and computers*

_____

After an adjective _____

_____

B. Discuss your observations with the class. Refer to page A-24 and to the notes on pages 265–267 if you need to.

FORM, MEANING, AND USE

B Noun Clauses

Examining Meaning and Use

Read each sentence and the statements that follow it. Check (✓) the correct statement. Discuss your answers. Then read the notes to check them.

1. I suggest that he come before office hours begin.

   ____ **a.** This is a very informal suggestion.
   ____ **b.** This has a formal tone.

2. The fact is that the company is downsizing.

   ____ **a.** It's true that the company is downsizing.
   ____ **b.** Maybe the company is downsizing.

3. I'm not sure if the manager is coming.

   ____ **a.** The speaker is asking a question.
   ____ **b.** The speaker is making a statement.

4. She didn't realize how serious the situation was.

   ____ **a.** She didn't know if it was serious.
   ____ **b.** She knew that it was serious.

That *Clauses*

We were going to win. + We knew it. → We knew **that we were going to win**.

If/Whether *Clauses*

Did he lock the door? + He doesn't remember that. → He doesn't remember **if he locked the door**.

Wh- *Clauses*

Why would he lie? + It still confuses me. → **Why he would lie** still confuses me.

- Noun clauses usually function in the same way as nouns. (In a sentence, they can occur in the same place as a noun.) Noun clauses are dependent clauses; they cannot stand alone.
- Sentences with noun clauses can be thought of as a combination of two independent sentences.
- *That* **clauses** are a combination of two statements.
- *If/whether* **clauses** are a combination of a statement and a *yes/no* question.
- *Wh-* **clauses** are a combination of a statement and a *wh-* question.
- Noun clauses usually begin with *that, if/whether,* or a *wh-* word (*who, what, why, where, when, how, which,* or *whose*). These words are usually followed by a subject + a verb.
- Like all noun clauses, noun clauses that begin with question words use statement word order. (Do not use the auxiliaries *do* or *did.*) Use a question mark only if the main clause is a question.

    I don't know **what he did last night.**   * I don't know what did he do last night. (INCORRECT)

Time in Sentences with Noun Clauses

When the main verb is in the present, the noun clause event may happen . . .

Before the Main Clause:	We still <u>don't know</u> **what <u>happened</u>**.
At the Same Time as the Main Clause:	I <u>think</u> **that someone <u>is</u> at the door.**
After the Main Clause:	I <u>wonder</u> **if we<u>'re going to hear</u>** from Dave.

When the main verb is in the past, the noun clause event may have happened . . .

Before the Main Clause:	We <u>didn't know</u> **what <u>had happened</u>**.
At the Same Time as the Main Clause:	We <u>thought</u> **that someone <u>was</u> at the door.**
After the Main Clause:	I <u>wondered</u> **if we <u>were going to hear</u>** from you.

- The information in a noun clause usually uses the same tense it would in an independent sentence. The choice depends on whether the event in the noun clause happened before, at the same time, or after the event in the main clause.
- **Main verb is in the present:** The verb in the noun clause uses a past, present, or future form.
- **Main verb is in the past:** The verb in the noun clause uses a past perfect form, a simple past form, *was/were going to,* or *would* (the past of *be going to* and *will*).

Objects of Verbs
We <u>knew</u> **(that) we were going to win**.

Subjects
<u>It</u> amazes me **that you don't like jazz.**   (Less common: ***That you don't like jazz** amazes me.)*
<u>It</u> was clear **(that) he worked very hard.**   (Less common: ***That he worked very hard** was clear.)*

Subject Complements
The problem <u>was</u> **(that) I didn't have time to help him.**

Adjective and Noun Complements
Everyone was <u>worried</u> **(that) the computers might go down.** *(adjective + clause)*
<u>The belief</u> **(that) she would recover** kept her spirits up. *(noun + clause)*

- ***That* clauses can follow some verbs:** These verbs are often related to mental activities, such as *believe, feel, know, think, learn, mean,* and *realize.*
- ***That* clauses can be subjects:** These sentences usually sound more formal. Using *it* subjects is more common. These sentences often describe feelings or opinions about a fact. (The main clause usually contains *be* + adjective or verb + object.)
- *The fact that* may be used to sound less formal.
    The fact that <u>you don't like jazz</u> still amazes me.
- ***That* clauses can be subject complements (after *be*):** The subject is usually a noun related to thoughts or facts (e.g., *belief, fact, hope, idea, problem, thought,* and *truth*).
- ***That* clauses can follow adjectives and nouns:** They are often used after adjectives to talk about people's feelings. *That* clauses often follow nouns related to thoughts and facts (e.g., *belief, fact, idea, possibility, rumor,* and *suggestion*). *That* clauses describe the content of the *belief, fact,* etc. (*belief* = that she would recover).
- **Other issues:** *That* can often be omitted from a sentence except if used as subject.

    For a list of verbs, adjectives, and nouns followed by noun clauses, see pages A-24–26.

After Verbs of Necessity and Advice
I <u>suggest</u> / <u>advise</u> / <u>ask</u> **(that) you <u>be</u> on time tomorrow.**

After It Subject + Adjective of Necessity and Advice
It is <u>important</u> / <u>essential</u> / <u>crucial</u> **(that) he <u>win</u> the match.**

- *That* clauses can follow certain verbs of necessity and advice or an *it* subject + an adjective of necessity and advice. The verb in the *that* clause uses the base form for all subjects. This is called the subjunctive. These sentences often sound more formal.
- Verbs that follow this pattern include: *advise, ask, demand, insist,* etc. Adjectives that follow this pattern include: *advisable, best, crucial,* etc.

    For a list of verbs and adjectives followed by the subjunctive, see page A-25.

Subjects

Why she would lie still confuses me.

Whether (or not) you like the decision doesn't matter.

Subject Complements

The <u>problem</u> is **who will take his place**.

The <u>question</u> is **whether or not** to proceed.

Objects of Verbs

I <u>wonder</u> **where he has been**.

I couldn't <u>decide</u> **if/whether I wanted to go to the concert**.

Objects of Prepositions

You should listen <u>to</u> **what the teacher is saying**.

I worried <u>about</u> **whether (or not) I would have enough money to pay my bills**.

Adjective Complements

I'm not <u>sure</u> **how it happened**.

We're not <u>certain</u> **if/whether he's going to call**.

- *Wh-* and *if/whether* clauses are sometimes called embedded questions. Because these clauses originate from questions, sentences with these clauses often refer to things that are uncertain or undecided.

- **Wh- and *whether* clauses can be subjects:** They are followed by third-person singular verbs. *It* subjects are often preferred.

- **Wh- and *whether* clauses can be subject complements (after *be*):** The subject may be a small set of words related to questions and uncertainty (e.g., *question, problem, issue, confusion, uncertainty*).

- **Wh- and *if/whether* clauses can follow some verbs:** This is a small set of verbs related to thoughts or learning facts (e.g., *consider, decide, forget, know, learn, see, understand,* and *wonder*).

- **Wh- and *whether* clauses can follow prepositions:** The prepositions may come after verbs, nouns, or adjectives. *Whether* clauses most often follow *about, as to,* and *of*.

- **Wh- and *if/whether* clauses can follow adjectives:** This is a small set of adjectives usually related to certainty (e.g., *certain, clear, convinced,* and *sure*).

- **Other issues:** *What* and *who* can be noun clause subjects followed directly by a verb.

    Everyone knows **<u>what happened</u> yesterday**.   I'm not sure **<u>who called</u> last night**.

- *If* can only be used after verbs or adjectives. *Whether* can begin any clause.

- *Or not* can immediately follow *whether*, but it can't follow *if. Or not* can also be added to the end of short *if* or *whether* clauses.

    I can't decide **if/whether <u>or not</u> I want to go**. I can't decide **if/whether I want to go <u>or not</u>**.

    For a list of verbs, adjectives, and nouns followed by noun clauses, see pages A-24–26.

A. 🎧 Each sentence in the passage is incomplete. Listen to the entire passage first. Then listen again and put a caret (∧) where you hear a missing word. Listen once more to fill in the missing words, and correct the punctuation.

Whether we
∧ ~~We~~ admit it, our reliance on electronic equipment is ruining the environment. That new equipment is better and faster means consumers are filling garbage dumps with an unprecedented amount of toxic waste from discarded electronics. As a consumer, it is essential that you aware of this problem. Here are some suggestions about do:

1. Find out your local electronic recycling center.

2. Decide you can repair or upgrade your old equipment.

3. Challenge newer is always better.

B. 🎧 Listen. Choose the best sentence to complete each conversation.

1. **a.** Yes, it was clear that we were going to win.
   b. Yes, it wasn't clear whether we were going to win.

2. **a.** He had an emergency.
   b. Did he leave early?

3. **a.** I appreciate your advice.
   b. I appreciate your promise.

4. **a.** What kind did you buy?
   b. What kind are you buying?

5. **a.** I wonder what.
   b. I wonder why.

6. **a.** That she took a leave of absence.
   b. That she take a leave of absence.

B2 **Identifying Noun Clauses**

Read the theater review. Underline all the *that, wh-,* and *if/whether* noun clauses.

It was with high hopes <u>that this reviewer attended the opening night production of *Henry* at Broadway's Limelight Theater</u>. Unfortunately, the show did not live up to my expectations. I found myself wondering aloud why I had bought a ticket to see it. In a nutshell, I thought that *Henry* was terrible.

The play is supposed to be a comedy. However, one of the main problems was that the script simply wasn't funny. The person sitting next to me actually fell asleep—twice. In addition, the plot was difficult to follow because of the poor writing. For example, by intermission it wasn't clear if the leading couple knew each other, yet by the end of the play they were getting married!

Of course, I may not have been able to hear everything. The Limelight was renovated last year, but the acoustics remain a problem. It's often difficult to hear what's happening on stage. The actors need to speak up or they need better microphones!

One other problem was the costumes. Although the play is supposed to take place in the 19th century, the actors' costumes looked surprisingly modern. How the director didn't notice this is a mystery to me.

I think the producers should listen to how the audience responded at the end of the show—with lukewarm applause at best. I suggest that they go back to the drawing board on this one: the script needs a complete revision, and the two leading actors should be replaced.

So, when it comes to seeing *Henry* on Broadway, don't worry about whether you're missing a good production or not. Trust me: you're better off saving your money and using it for something else—like a good dinner with friends.

B3 Introducing Noun Clauses

Choose the best word to complete each sentence.

1. (Where / How) she lives is considered a very upscale neighborhood.
2. There's a rumor (that / whether) he's going to step down from his position.
3. I can't see (whether / where) I'm going in this snow!
4. I don't know (whether / if) or not their office is open today.
5. (That / Whether) an active jazz scene developed in New Orleans is not surprising.
6. You shouldn't ignore the question of (when / if) to invest your money.
7. My professor advised (that / when) I take the exam for graduate school.
8. An explosion occurred, but no one is sure (that / how) it happened.
9. It's not necessary (whether / that) he write a detailed report.
10. I'll be really happy (if / that) we meet our sales goal this year.
11. I'm uncertain about (that / what) happened.
12. The fact (that / if) he lost was surprising.
13. Nobody knows (who / whose) cat this is.
14. I wonder (that / why) we weren't informed of the delay.
15. (How / What) this means is we have to act now.
16. It's inconvenient (why / when) I miss the bus.

Combining Sentences

Combine each pair of sentences to form a noun clause with *that*, a *wh-* word, or *if/whether*. (More than one answer may be possible.)

1. She's still working at 90. It's inspiring.

   That she's still working at 90 is inspiring. / It's inspiring that she's still working at 90.

2. The ground was shaking. We realized it.

   _____

3. Can I tell you the answer? I don't know.

   _____

4. What does that sign say? I can't read it.

   _____

5. Who is going to win? It hasn't been determined yet.

   _____

6. We don't have enough money. It's a problem.

   _____

7. What did you see while you were on vacation? I want to hear about it.

   _____

8. Does he have the time to help me? I'm not certain.

   _____

B5 **Using *That* Clauses After Verbs**

A. Read the information about lottery winners and the statements that follow. Some of the statements are true and some are false. Use these verbs to give your opinion about the statements: *believe, doubt, guess, suppose,* or *think.*

> Researchers have been studying people who have suddenly won a large amount of money. After winning more than £1 million in a lottery, citizens of the United Kingdom were interviewed. Can you guess how they felt? Consider the following possibilities.

1. After receiving the money, the lottery winners were happier overall.

   I doubt that the lottery winners were happier overall. Having more money is convenient, but it doesn't make you happy.

2. After receiving the money, their lifestyles changed dramatically.
3. After receiving the money, they took more exotic vacations.
4. After receiving the money, they bought bigger houses.
5. After receiving the money, they moved to new areas.

B. Compare your ideas in small groups.

A. Read the sentence. Write a yes/no question about the sentence. Then complete the noun clause using the question.

1. I might have to work late.

   Question: *Do you have to work late?*

   Noun clause: It depends on *if you have to work late.*

2. We may or may not be meeting tomorrow.

   Question: Are _____

   Noun clause: I'm confused about _____

3. I might attend the party.

   Question: Are _____

   Noun clause: I'd like to know _____

4. I may have left my keys in the car.

   Question: Did _____

   Noun clause: I wonder _____

5. I may not have turned off the lights.

   Question: Did _____

   Noun clause: I can't remember _____

B. Read the sentence. Write a *Wh-* question about the underlined words. Then complete the noun clause using the question.

1. He's talking about <u>grammar</u>.

   Question: *What's he talking about?*

   Noun clause: I don't know *what he's talking about.*

2. She speaks <u>Spanish</u> but <u>not French</u>.

   Question: Which _____

   Noun clause: It depends on _____

3. Alexander Fleming discovered penicillin <u>by accident</u>.

   Question: How _____

   Noun clause: We learned about _____

4. They were absent <u>because they were sick</u>.

   Question: _____

   Noun clause: We need to find out _____

Read about the worldwide phenomenon. Complete the sentences. (Use your own ideas to complete item 5.) Then compare your ideas with a partner.

> In many industrialized nations the birthrate has fallen dramatically. This is called "sub-replacement fertility rate" in countries where the birthrate is not high enough to replace an area's population. There are several explanations for this phenomenon, including increasing urbanization worldwide and the increasing role of women in the workplace. (Women who live in cities and work outside the home tend to have fewer children). Areas with the lowest birthrate are Hong Kong, Singapore, Ukraine, and Lithuania.

1. What this article is about is *sub-replacement fertility rate or the declining birthrate.*

2. What this means is that _____

3. Why this has happened is because _____

4. Where this is the biggest problem is _____

5. How this issue could be solved is _____

Usage Note: *Using Infinitives in Place of Noun Clauses*

> Sometimes it is more concise and natural to use an infinitive instead of a noun clause.
>
> 1. **Objects of verbs and prepositions:** When talking about something uncertain or undecided, we often use an infinitive instead of a *wh-* clause. (The subject of the sentence and the noun clause must be the same.)
>
> | | | |
> |---|---|---|
> | I was unsure of **how I should answer the question.** | → | I was unsure of **how to answer the question.** |
> | He didn't know **what he could do.** | → | He didn't know **what to do.** |
>
> 2. **After expressions of necessity and advice:** After certain verbs (e.g., *advise*, *ask*, *require*, *order*, *tell*), infinitives are often used instead of a *that* clause with the subjunctive. The infinitive is often preferred because it sounds less formal.
>
> | | | |
> |---|---|---|
> | She advised **(that) the student take the test again.** | → | She advised the student **to take the test again.** |
> | I have to ask **that you be on time tomorrow.** | → | I have to ask you **to be on time tomorrow.** |
>
> 3. **After *it* subjects:** We often use *for* + object + infinitive to express the same meaning.
>
> | | | |
> |---|---|---|
> | It is important **(that) you not miss any classes.** | → | It is important **for you not to miss any classes.** |

Using Infinitives in Place of Noun Clauses

Read about an area of Italy called the Cinque Terre. John is planning a trip there. Read his concerns about his trip and the advice he received from a travel agent. Rewrite each sentence using an infinitive.

> The Cinque Terre is a rugged and beautiful area along the northern Italian coast. It is popular with tourists who enjoy hiking and swimming, as well as relaxing in the five villages in the area.

1. **John:** I'm not exactly sure what I should pack.
   I'm not exactly sure what to pack.
2. **Agent:** It's essential that you pack some sturdy walking shoes.
3. **John:** I have to ask that you tell the truth. Do I need to get in better shape for the trip?
4. **Agent:** The hills are very steep, so I advise that you exercise and get in shape.
5. **John:** I don't know how I should get there.
6. **Agent:** It's necessary that you travel by train. There are almost no cars in the villages.
7. **John:** I can't decide when I should go.
8. **Agent:** I advise that you avoid the high season in the summer. It's very crowded then.
9. **John:** I wonder how long I should stay there.
10. **Agent:** It's best that you stay a few nights. That way you can enjoy the area.

Completing Sentences

A. Complete the sentences with your own ideas. Use noun clauses.

1. I'm very careful about . . . how I look.
2. It's important that we talk about . . .
3. I truly believe . . . is important in a healthy society.
4. What frustrated me most when I first studied English was . . .
5. I'm concerned about whether or not I'll . . .
6. I find it annoying that . . .
7. The problem with cell phones is . . .
8. It's obvious that . . . is/are an important part of American culture.
9. There is a possibility . . .
10. Some people think . . . The truth is . . .

B. Work with a partner. Choose four of the sentences to share with your partner. Ask follow-up questions about your partner's sentences.

A: *I'm very careful about how I look.*

B: *Really? Do you spend a lot of money on clothes?*

Read the sentences. Check (✓) *Same* if the sentences have the same meaning. Check (✓) *Different* if their meanings are different.

		SAME	DIFFERENT
1.	I'm surprised that there are so many new stores downtown.	✓	☐
	It's surprising that there are so many new stores downtown.		
2.	It was upsetting that he didn't win.	☐	☐
	He was upset that he didn't win.		
3.	That there is still no answer to the problem is frustrating.	☐	☐
	The fact that there is still no answer to the problem is frustrating.		
4.	I had the idea that we should sell the video and the CD together.	☐	☐
	One idea is that we should sell the video and the CD together.		
5.	I was unsure of how she would answer the question.	☐	☐
	She was unsure of how to answer the question.		
6.	What has been discussed in the meeting will remain a secret.	☐	☐
	That it had been discussed in the meeting will remain a secret.		
7.	His reply to what I said surprised me.	☐	☐
	What I said to him surprised me.		
8.	I'm confused about whether we're meeting or not.	☐	☐
	I don't know if we're meeting or not.		
9.	Where the money will come from is an important issue.	☐	☐
	The issue of where the money will come from is important.		
10.	I wonder if I'm going to hear from my sister this week.	☐	☐
	I don't know whether or not I'm going to hear from my sister this week.		

A. Read the statements about changes in our lifestyles. Work with a partner and take turns making up sentences that describe your feelings about the facts. Use the expressions in the box or other similar expressions.

It's surprising that . . .	The problem is that . . .	I'm worried that . . .
The fact that . . .	It is significant that . . .	The fact is that . . .
I'm amazed that . . .	The idea that . . .	

1. Reality TV has become the most popular new television format.

   A: The idea that reality TV is so popular shocks me. The shows are so predictable.

   B: It's surprising that reality TV is so popular. I find it boring!

2. Because of a slow economy, people are giving less money to charity these days.

3. A large number of retirees—people in their 60s and 70s—are starting second careers.

4. Children are spending more time indoors on home computers and less time outside playing.

5. More and more new music is being purchased through downloads.

6. An increasing number of people say that they have at least one "virtual friend"—someone whom they correspond with regularly via e-mail but whom they have never actually met.

7. A "reverse migration" is happening as young parents are moving their families out of the city and back to their more rural childhood homes.

B. Now write an embedded question about each of the statements in part A. Use the expressions in the box or other similar expressions. Then compare your sentences with a partner.

I wonder . . .	I want to know . . .	I'm confused about . . .
I don't know . . .	I can't understand . . .	We need to find out . . .

I wonder why people like reality TV so much. Maybe it provides an escape for them.

_____

_____

_____

_____

_____

_____

C WRITING

Editing: *Noun Clauses*

Study the errors. Pay attention to the areas where you make mistakes.

> 1. **Use of subject or object pronoun**
>   He knew ~~it~~ what he wanted to buy.
>   That he lied ~~it~~ still makes me angry.
>
> 2. **Use of auxiliaries / word order**
>   he said
>   Many people still wonder what ~~did he say~~ to her.
>   uses
>   Do scientists know whether or not ~~does~~ a bird ~~use~~ language?
>
> 3. **Choice of *that*, *wh-* words, or *if / whether***
>   whether
>   They could not decide ~~that~~ they should continue or give up.
>   what
>   I couldn't remember ⌃ the first word of the song was.
>
> 4. **Use of subjunctive**
>   not invest
>   They advised that she ~~didn't invest~~ the money in real estate.

C1 Editing

Correct the errors in the passage. Be prepared to explain your answers.

                                                              that

    Are video games too violent? Do they provide any benefit? I believe ~~what~~ today's debate about video games is actually nothing new. During my childhood, radio was what my brother and I listened to it for entertainment. Even then, my grandmother was worried that we were being exposed to too much violence, so she suggested that my mother didn't allow radio in the house.

    However, I remember spending many wonderful afternoons sitting next to my brother listening to whatever show was on that day. It was not a problem we could not see the images. The sound effects were so well done. It was amazing that how perfectly we could picture everything. What did we do was use our imaginations. And when the show was over, we would go outside and pretend we were the characters.

Computer video games tap into imagination in a similar way. My nephew loves to play video games. What engages his mind is not whether or not can he see the picture. It's his imagination that he uses to direct the events of the game. After finishing a game, he often goes outside and plays with his friend—just like I did.

Beyond the Sentence: *Presenting Ideas Clearly and Concisely*

Noun clauses allow writers easily to condense facts and questions in order to present them quickly and concisely.

> When choosing a musical instrument, it is important to decide **what kind of music you want to play, where you want to play it, and how much work you want to put into perfecting your skills.** What is right for one potential musician may not be right for another, so it is recommended that people try out different instruments before investing money in one.
>
> **What makes a piano a good choice** is **that it sounds good almost from the first day.** A beginner can learn simple songs within a month. On the downside, a piano is expensive and heavy. **What this means** is **that once a family invests in a piano, they are likely to keep it in the family for generations . . .**

Wh- clauses and if/whether clauses often appear in topic sentences to introduce questions that the writer intends to answer.

Wh- clauses and that clauses are often linked together by be as a way to clarify and summarize ideas.

C2 Condensing Information and Clarifying Ideas

A. Write topic sentences. Combine the following sentences into single sentences that use noun clauses.

1. Human resource departments gather certain types of information about a prospective employee including the following: How well does someone get along with others? And how hard will someone work?

   Human resource departments gather certain types of information about a prospective employee including how well someone gets along with others and how hard someone will work.

2. At the end of the day, student travelers to foreign countries often have not planned the following: What will they eat? Where will they sleep? Or how will they pay for their next ticket?

3. Historians are still wondering about the following questions: Did the great Mayan culture decline because of environmental causes, or did social and political issues cause its decline?

4. In the United States, it is inappropriate to ask an acquaintance certain questions: How old are you? How much money do you make? Or how much do you weigh? These are all considered private.

5. Anthropologists disagree about many questions such as the following: Did early humans first appear in Africa or not? And was tool-making responsible for an increase in human brain capacity?

6. When choosing a career, it is important to identify certain characteristics: What tasks are you good at? What environment do you enjoy? And what sort of rewards do you expect?

B. **Work with a partner. Clarify these ideas by completing the sentences.**

1. People are getting married when they are older. What this means is . . .
   People are getting married when they are older. What this means is that fewer children are being born overall.

2. Honesty is not always the best policy. What this implies is . . .

3. Statistics show that people in Western countries are getting heavier and heavier. What this suggests is . . .

4. Temperatures are slowly increasing worldwide. What we can conclude is . . .

Vocabulary Notes: *Passive Verbs + Noun Clauses*

> *It* subjects are often used with passive verbs to express commonly held beliefs or to say that something is believed by a group of people. These sentences often sound more objective and impersonal.
>
> It **was once thought** that the earth was flat.
> It **is widely believed** that the impact of a large meteor caused massive extinction.
> It **was once assumed** that advances in technology would provide more leisure time.
> It **is well-known** that birds are descended from dinosaurs.

C3 Making Objective Comments

Rewrite the sayings and beliefs with an *it* subject and a passive verb. Then work in small groups. Choose one of sentences and discuss it.

1. Many people used to believe that tomatoes were poisonous.
   It was once believed that tomatoes were poisonous.

2. Having too much power corrupts people.

3. City people are unfriendly.

4. People used to think that smoking was perfectly safe.

5. Exercise improves one's energy.

6. Reading is a pathway to intelligence.

Noun clauses are common in academic writing. They allow writers to summarize information, clarify ideas, and arrive at concise conclusions. In using noun clauses, writers reduce the number of words needed to state a point, which makes for more focused and effective writing.

Choose one of the topics to write a short essay of two to three paragraphs. Be sure to clarify your questions and ideas. Then, use the Writing Checklist to check your work.

- Rock, pop, and hip-hop music have been the dominant musical forms of the past few decades. Choose one of the styles and explain its popularity. Why is it so appealing? What sorts of life experience does the music come from? What does it express that allows it to connect to its fans?

- Many people continue to smoke in spite of the serious health problems associated with smoking. Explain the attraction of smoking. Why do people decide to take up this habit? What do people claim they enjoy about smoking? Is there an image associated with smoking?

- People who are said to have been bitten by the "travel bug" often sacrifice security, home, and family to travel around the world—never staying in one place for very long. Explain the travel bug. What is appealing about this lifestyle? What advantages might it have over a more traditional lifestyle?

- Find out how e-waste is handled in your community. What exactly happens to old TVs, computers, cell phones, and so on? What different options are available to individuals and businesses for recycling e-waste? How effective are these programs? What problems are there? What solutions do you suggest?

Writing Checklist

Reflect on your ability to use noun clauses by answering the questions.

- [ ] **1.** Did you use *that* clauses to explain your thoughts and feelings about something?
- [ ] **2.** Did you use any *that* clauses after expressions of necessity or advice?
- [ ] **3.** Did you link *wh-* clauses with *that* clauses to clarify or summarize information?
- [ ] **4.** Did you use *wh-* clauses and *if/whether* clauses to talk about a question that you want to answer?
- [ ] **5.** Did you use *that* clauses with *it* subjects + passive verbs?
- [ ] **6.** Did you check your sentences for correct form?

Writing

Write an essay using one of these topics.

1. There are many non-profit organizations that do research or provide help to people in need. Some examples are OXFAM and The Red Cross. Choose an organization that you would support financially. Begin by describing the mission of the organization and the need that it fulfills. Then write a paragraph or two giving reasons why you think this organization is doing an effective job.

2. Filmmakers and writers have the ability to inspire people in different ways. Choose someone that you think has made a useful contribution through written or cinematic work and explain the artist's strengths and weaknesses. Begin by describing the artist, his or her background and genre (e.g., western, mystery, thriller, drama). Then select and describe specific examples of the artist's work that have influenced you.

3. Think of a historical event or person that you would like to memorialize with a monument. Write an essay describing the event or person, and why you think they deserve a memorial. Then state where you think it should be and how it might be designed.

Searching for Authentic Examples

Find examples of English grammar in everyday life by completing the task below. Bring your examples to class, and be prepared to discuss them.

Find a short article in a textbook (three or four paragraphs) about a topic that interests you. Look for different types of noun clauses: *that* clauses, *if/whether* clauses, and *wh-* clauses. Which type is the most common? Can you find any examples where *that* is omitted? Can you find any noun clauses used as subjects or as complements?

Reported Speech

A Pinocchio's Nose or The Art of Lying

A1 Before You Read

Discuss these questions.

Do you think most people are better at lying or at detecting lies?

What are some examples of typical lies people tell? Do you think some lies are OK to tell? If yes, which ones?

A2 Read

Read this excerpt from a magazine article to find out what current research says about lying.

PINOCCHIO'S NOSE OR THE ART OF LYING

Michel de Montaigne, the 16th-century French philosopher, said that lies came in all sorts of shapes and sizes, and he was right. Generally, we are raised to believe that all lies are bad and wrong, yet we know that a little lie is not as bad as a big lie. Take for example, the "white" lie: Imagine that you had a dinner party where, unfortunately, the meal turned out terribly. At the end of the party, however, your guests complimented you enthusiastically. **They told you how delicious your cooking was. They asked politely whether you could give them the recipe.** They lied to you because they wanted to spare[1] your feelings. Now set that against a criminal who killed someone. Even though he was guilty of this crime, **he informed the police that he did not do it.** He lied to save his own neck. Were these falsehoods of equal size and seriousness? The purist[2] might say that they are, because it is the act of lying that matters rather than the size of the crime.

However, it is clear to most people that there are degrees of lying.

Do we even know when someone is lying to us? In his children's tales, *The Adventures of Pinocchio*, published in 1883, **Carlo Collodi warned the young that lying could make their noses grow longer with each lie they told.**

That seems to be a strange assertion,[3] but now 200 years or so after Collodi, researchers say that there might well be a connection between lying and the nose on your face. A psychiatrist from Chicago, Dr. Alan Hirsch,* examined people when they were known to be lying. He came up with a list of signs that betray[4] a liar. Among these tell-tale[5] signs is one notable one: people often touch their noses when they are lying. **Hirsch told *USA Today* that when people were lying, the tissue[6] in the nose began to fill with blood, causing swelling.** The swelling in turn led people to scratch their noses. **Hirsch also said that people's stuttering rate and errors in speech increased when they weren't telling the truth**. Additionally, liars tended to cross their arms, laugh inappropriately, lean forward more often, use hesitations such as "umm," and "er," and lick their lips.

The fact is that we humans tell lies. **Researchers studying mendacity**—the psychologist and sociologist's word for lying—**explain that most of us try to fool[7] someone at least once a day. They also say that we frequently try to find out whether others are deceiving us.** Interestingly, while we are quite good at lying, we are not so good at detecting a liar. It was partly for this reason that the so-called lie-detector machine was invented. The machine, more correctly named a *polygraph*, is still regularly used by government agencies, employers, the police force, and others. **Some say it is an invaluable[8] tool**, but **others reply that nothing could be further from the truth. They warn that a polygraph cannot and never will tell us who's a liar**. It can only tell us that a person is stressed. That information is open to interpretation and may be caused by a variety of factors.

*Dr. Alan Hirsch, M.D. is neurological director of the Smell and Taste Treatment and Research Foundation in Chicago, IL.

1 **spare:** to not hurt or harm
2 **purist:** a person who tries to be absolutely correct; an overly precise person
3 **assertion:** a claim
4 **betray:** to show the truth, usually without meaning to
5 **tell-tale:** revealing
6 **tissue:** a group of organic cells
7 **fool:** to lie to
8 **invaluable:** very useful

 ## After You Read

Discuss these questions.

1. Does the writer feel that all lies are equally bad? What examples does the writer give?
2. What are some outward signs that someone is lying?
3. Why was the polygraph invented? What can it tell us?
4. Do you think that lying is a necessary part of everyday social interaction? Why or why not?

A. Work in pairs. Look at the highlighted examples of reported speech in the reading. Write them in the correct categories.

Present in the reporting clause

_____

_____

_____

Past in the reporting clause

_____

_____

_____

B. Discuss your observations with the class. Refer to the notes on pages 286–288 if you need to.

FORM, MEANING, AND USE

 Reported Speech

Examining Meaning and Use

Read each sentence and the statements that follow it. Check (✓) the correct statement. Discuss your answers. Then read the notes to check them.

1. We inquired whether Maria needed a ride.
   ____ We asked Maria to do something.
   ____ We asked Maria a question.

2. She told me that her computer will be repaired.
   ____ The computer hasn't been repaired yet.
   ____ The computer was repaired already.

3. Luis said he was going home that day.
   ____ Luis went home yesterday.
   ____ Luis went home the day he said this.

4. Jim told me I had to call his boss for him.
   ____ Jim needs to call my boss.
   ____ I need to call Jim's boss.

Statements	*That Clauses*
He said, "It's a problem."	→ <u>He said</u> **(that) it was a problem.**
	<u>He told me</u> **(that) it was a problem.**

Yes/No Questions	*If/Whether Clauses*
"Is it OK to leave?" he asked.	→ <u>He asked (me)</u> **if it was OK to leave.**

Wh- Questions	*Wh- Clauses*
He asked, "What do people lie about most?"	→ <u>He asked (me)</u> **what people lied about most.**

Imperatives	*Infinitives*
"Stop the car," he said.	→ He said **to stop the car.**
"Don't worry," he said.	→ He told me **not to worry.**
"Could you hand me the drill?" he asked.	→ He asked me **to hand him the drill.**

- Quoted (or direct) speech gives someone's exact words. It usually occurs in written material.

- Reported (or indirect) speech uses a noun clause to restate what someone has said or written. It expresses the same meaning, but doesn't usually use the exact words. It occurs frequently both in writing and conversation.

- Reported speech uses a reporting verb (e.g., *say, ask*) in the main clause + a noun clause or infinitive.

- *That* clauses report statements. *If/Whether* and *wh-* clauses report questions. Infinitives report imperatives.

- *Say, tell,* and *ask* are the most common reporting verbs:

  - *Say* is used to report statements and imperatives.

  - *Tell* + an object is also used to report statements and imperatives. The object tells who heard the sentence.

  - *Ask* (+ an object) is used to report questions and imperatives, especially requests. The object is optional in reported questions but necessary with reported imperatives.

- All noun clauses use statement word order, including *if/whether* and *wh-* clauses. (Do not use the auxiliaries *do* or *did*.) Reported speech uses no quotation marks or question marks.

For punctuation rules for quoted speech, see pages A-26 and A-27.
For reporting verbs + noun clauses, see page A-25.
For reporting verbs + infinitives, see page A-26.

Quoted Speech		*Reported Speech*
"I <u>don't know</u> the answer."	He **said** (that) . . .	he **didn't know** the answer.
"I'<u>m working</u> hard."		he **was working** hard.
"I'<u>ve found</u> a solution."		he **had found** a solution.
"I <u>finished</u> the report."		he **had finished** the report.
"I <u>hadn't heard about</u> it."		he **hadn't heard about** it. *
"I <u>used to/would leave</u> class early."		he **used to/would leave** class early. *
"I'<u>ll discuss</u> it later."		he **would discuss** it later.
"I'<u>m going to look</u> it up."		he **was going to look** it **up**.
"I <u>can/may pick</u> you <u>up</u> after school."		he **could/might pick** me **up** after school.
"I <u>have to/must find</u> a solution."		he **had to find** a solution.
"I <u>might/could/should/ought to win</u>."		he **might/could/should/ought to win**. *

- We use reported speech to talk about things said in the past. We use a past reporting verb. The verb in the reported language usually changes from its original form. (The forms marked with * don't change.)

- As with other noun clauses, since the main clause verb is in the past, the verb in the noun clause usually uses a simple past form, a past perfect form, *was/were going to*, or *would*.

- *Can, may, have to*, and *must* typically change forms. *Might, could, should*, and *ought to* typically don't change forms.

Quoted Speech	*Reported Speech*
"I can't answer <u>your</u> question."	He said **he** couldn't answer **my** question.
"<u>You</u> need to talk to <u>our</u> manager."	She told me **I** needed to talk to **their** manager.
"We're expecting it <u>today</u>."	She said **they** were expecting it **that day**.
"I'll e-mail you <u>tomorrow</u>."	He said **he**'d e-mail me **the next day**.
"Did you work <u>yesterday</u>?"	She asked if **I** had worked **the day before**.
"I called two weeks <u>ago</u>."	He said **he**'d called two weeks **earlier**.

- The subject pronouns *I, you*, and *we* and their object and possessive forms (e.g., *me, my, mine*) change when you report what someone else has said or written. (They change from the original speaker's perspective to the reporter's perspective.)

- Adverbs of time (e.g., *today*) change to relate to the time when the speech is being reported.

- When you report your own words, the pronouns won't change. When you report something at the same time or place, the adverbs won't change.

    "I don't know the date." → <u>I said</u> I didn't know the date. *(I'm reporting my own words.)*

    "We're sending it <u>today</u>." → He said they're sending it **today**. *(It's still the same day.)*

Timeless Statement

"Crime is a very serious problem." → The speaker <u>said</u> that crime **is** a very serious problem.
(This is a general truth. It is still true.)

Habitual/Current Situation

"The board meets on Tuesdays." → The receptionist <u>said</u> that the board **meets** on Tuesdays.
(This is a habitual activity. It is still true.)

"My son is away at college." → She <u>said</u> her son **is** away at college.
(This is the current situation. It is still true.)

Future Event

"I'm going on a date next week." → He <u>said</u> he**'s going on a date** next week.
(The date still hasn't occurred yet.)

Immediate Reporting

"Flight 103 is now boarding." → The announcer <u>just said</u> that our flight **is** boarding.
(This sentence was spoken right after the announcement.)

Past in Informal Speech

"I finished the report." → She <u>said</u> (that) she **finished** the report.
(Speakers often do not change the past to the past perfect.)

- Sometimes we choose not to change the verb in the reported language to keep the meaning clear.

Quoted Speech	*Reported Speech*
"We'd love to come. Unfortunately, we're busy."	She said **they wanted to come but they were busy**.
"What do you think of this idea?"	He asked **what I thought of an idea he had**.
"Can I leave work early on Friday? I have a doctor's appointment."	He asked **if he could leave work early on Friday to go to the doctor**.
"Are you coming here first?"	He asked **if I was going to the office first**.

- Reported speech often requires that you change more than a few words or grammatical forms. Reported language is often combined to make it more concise, or language is added to clarify the meaning.

Present Tense Reporting

Quoted Speech	*Present Tense Reporting*
"You <u>were</u> late again this morning."	My boss **says** I **was** late again, but I wasn't. Now I have to talk to human resources.
"The situation <u>is</u> serious."	The President **says** the situation **is** serious.
"It<u>'s going to snow</u> tomorrow."	They **say** it**'s going to snow** tomorrow. We'll need to leave early.
"Lying <u>is</u> a part of everyday life."	Researchers **say** that lying **is** a part of everyday life.

- Sometimes we use a present tense reporting verb. In this case, the verb in the reported speech does not change from its original tense.
- Present tense reporting is often used to report things that affect the present. These are often things that are said regularly, or they involve current opinions, or ongoing situations. Present tense reporting can convey a sense of immediacy or urgency.
- Present tense reporting is also very common in explaining research in academic writing.

B1 Listening

A. Each sentence in the passage is incomplete. Listen to the entire passage first. Then listen again and put a caret (^) where you hear a missing word. Listen once more to fill in the missing words.

said
A man ^ he his birthday gifts. In fact, he was really disappointed with them. A child watching TV that she her homework. She really hadn't. A woman she had to get off the phone because the doorbell ringing. It wasn't! Psychologists that these all lies. They that if a person intends to be misleading, then he or she lying. Indeed, psychologists these are small lies, often called "white lies," but since they all attempts to deceive, they still fall under the category of lying.

B. Listen to the reported speech. Then choose the quoted speech that best expresses the meaning of the reported speech.

1. a. "I guess I can help you just this one time."
   b. "Don't worry. I can help you. No problem."

2. a. "I might come over the next day."
   b. "I'll come over tomorrow."

3. a. "Do you need any tools?"
   b. "Do I need any tools?"

4. a. "Don't forget to fill up the car."
   b. "I need to fill up the car."

5. a. "I found out the truth."
   b. "I must find out the truth."

6. a. "This discovery has implications at the present time."
   b. "This discovery had implications at one time."

Identifying Reported Speech

Check (✓) the sentences that contain reported speech.

____ 1. I could tell you the truth, but you wouldn't like it!

____ 2. John told me he'd already read my report.

____ 3. My grandmother said she used to swim in the Pacific every morning.

____ 4. We think we'll have to find another solution to the problem.

____ 5. Andrew said he'd leave by six, but he's not here yet.

____ 6. Ask Matt where he put the TV remote.

____ 7. My friend asked why I hadn't called her yesterday.

____ 8. Why didn't James tell us about the prize he won?

____ 9. It's OK for him to go because he asked me if he could leave early today.

____ 10. Aren't you going to see a doctor about the pain in your stomach?

B3 **Choosing Reporting Verbs and Introducing Reporting Clauses**

Choose the best word to complete each sentence.

1. He (said / told / asked) me he worked for a fast-food chain.
2. She (told / said / asked) Bill was having his 42nd birthday.
3. Guess what? He (said / told / asked) me he loved me!
4. The little boy (said / told / asked) he felt sick.
5. I (said / told / asked) if you'd like to go out tonight.
6. She asked me (that / if / who) I'd like a second helping of cake.
7. Help! I'm going to fall! I told you (that / if / where) I couldn't ride a bike, didn't I?
8. They asked her (that / does / when) she planned to arrive.
9. See? It's easy! I promised you (that / if / who) it wasn't going to be difficult.
10. Someone asked me (that / if / what) my last name meant.

B4 Choosing Verb Forms in Past Tense Reporting

These statements were made in the past. Choose the best answer to complete each report.

1. "Did you see Mark?"
   She asked me if . . .
   a. I was seeing Mark.
   b. I'd seen Mark.

2. "Do you think he may be angry?"
   She asked if . . .
   a. I thought he might be angry.
   b. I thought he may be angry.

3. "Harry hadn't met Susan before."
   You said . . .
   a. Harry didn't meet Susan before.
   b. Harry hadn't met Susan before.

4. "I might get a promotion."
   She told us . . .
   a. she might have gotten a promotion.
   b. she might get a promotion.

5. "I would often work late."
   He said . . .
   a. he would have often worked late.
   b. he would often work late.

6. "How many times have you been to China?"
   He asked how many times . . .
   a. they had been to China.
   b. they have been to China.

7. "Are you having some trouble?"
   He asked us if . . .
   a. we were having some trouble.
   b. we had some trouble.

8. "Did you have to leave early?"
   They asked if . . .
   a. I have to leave early.
   b. I had to leave early.

9. "We're going to have dinner with friends."
   I told them . . .
   a. we would have had dinner with friends.
   b. we were going to have dinner with friends.

10. "I think your answer is correct."
    He said . . .
    a. he thought my answer was correct.
    b. he had thought my answer was correct.

B5 Making Other Changes in Reported Speech

Complete the past tense reports with the correct pronoun, possessive, or adverb. Each past tense report was made one week after the quoted speech.

1. "I speak Spanish."
   She said that _____ spoke Spanish.

2. "We used to live in Rome."
   They said that _____ used to live in Rome.

3. "Why don't you believe me?"
   She asked me why I didn't
   believe _____.

4. "Would you give this book to him?"
   She asked me to give this book
   to _____.

5. "I don't understand your question."
   He told us that he didn't
   understand _____ question.

6. "Have you seen my shoes?"
   He asked me if I had seen _____ shoes.

7. "I e-mailed you two days ago."
   She said she had e-mailed me two
   days _____.

8. "I'll take Joe to school tomorrow."
   He said he would take Joe to school
   _____, but he didn't.

9. "I'll never forget what happened today."
   He said he'd never forget what
   happened _____.

10. "Did you call your mother yesterday?"
    She asked me if I had called my mother
    _____.

B6 Writing Quoted Speech

Rewrite what the people said in quoted speech. Change tenses, pronouns, and adverbs where appropriate. Check pages A-26–27 if you need help with punctuation.

1. He asked if I was sleeping better these days.
   "Are you sleeping better these days?"
2. They asked what we had learned about life.
3. She said she had been dancing when she lost her necklace.
4. Steve told me he would call me that day.
5. She said that I had to talk to her if I had any problems.
6. He said I could use his phone anytime I needed it.

B7 Keeping the Same Verb Form

Read the sentences and complete the reported speech. If possible, keep the same verb form in the reported speech. Be prepared to explain your answers.

1. "Air pollution in the city is getting worse."

   A recent news report said *that air pollution is getting worse.*

2. "I'll take the purple sweater."

   I said _____, but they gave me the red one!

3. "What was your grandfather like?"

   He asked me _____.

4. "Global warming is a serious matter."

   The experts have all told us that _____.

5. "You need to hurry! The train's coming into the station!"

   A: What did he say?

   B: He said _____.

6. "If you really want to go, you can use my car."

   I didn't think I would be able to go on vacation last summer. But my sister said

   _____.

7. "I don't have the time to talk."

   I wanted to ask Jill a question earlier, but she said _____.

8. "Are you going to see Angelo soon?"

   She asked me _____. Honestly, I really don't know.

Vocabulary Notes: *Other Reporting Verbs*

Many verbs, including *say*, *ask*, *tell*, *reply*, and *respond*, are neutral reporting verbs. Some reporting verbs (e.g., *agree*, *assure*, *complain*, *promise*) add an opinion or state an intention.

Other verbs used to report statements: *add, admit, agree, answer, claim, complain, confess continue, emphasize, explain, promise, reply, respond,* and *warn.*

"The **economy** is improving." → He **claimed** that the economy was improving.

Like *tell*, some verbs require objects to say who heard the statement: *assure, convince, inform, notify,* and *remind.* For other verbs (e.g., *promise*, *warn*) the object is optional.

"Everything is being ordered." → She **assured me** that everything was being ordered.

With *say, admit, complain,* and *explain,* we add *to* + object to say who heard the statement.

"I won't be able to help." → He **explained to me** that he wouldn't be able to help.

Other verbs used to report questions: *inquire, question, want to know,* and *wonder.*

"How are you going to get home?" → She **wanted to know** how I was going to get home.

Verbs of necessity and advice to report statements: *advise, ask, demand, insist, propose, recommend, request,* and *suggest.* We normally use the base form of the verb in the *that* clause. This is called the subjunctive. These sentences often sound more formal. (See Chapter 14, page 266: *That* Clauses After Expressions of Necessity and Advice.)

"Everyone must be quiet!" → She **demanded** that everyone **be** quiet.

For reporting verbs + noun clause, see page A-25.
For reporting verbs + base form (subjunctive), see page A-25.

B8 Using Other Reporting Verbs

Report each sentence using an appropriate reporting verb (other than *say, tell,* or *ask*) from the Vocabulary Notes. (More than one answer is often possible.)

1. "So, when are you thinking of moving? I'm curious."

   She *wondered when I was thinking of moving.* _____.

2. "Are you really committed to your job? You don't seem interested."

   He _____.

3. "OK, watch. You have to log on first, like this, then enter a password."

   She _____.

4. I really think you should see a dentist about your tooth."

   She _____.

5. "Sure, I'd love to take on the project for you."

   He _____.

6. "No, please, you must accept my gift. I bought it especially for you."

   He _____.

Usage Note: *Changing Demonstrative Adjectives and Pronouns*

When we report speech, we often change a demonstrative adjective to an article or other determiner (e.g., a possessive).

"I can tell I'm not going to enjoy <u>this</u> meeting." → He said he could tell that he wasn't going to enjoy **the** meeting.

"What do you think of <u>these</u> designs?" → He asked what I thought of **his** designs.

When the demonstrative is a pronoun, we usually change it to *it/they*, or we use the word itself.

"<u>This</u> is delicious!" → He said **it/the cake** was delicious.

"<u>These</u> are beautiful!" → She said **they/the flowers** were beautiful.

We can also make the reported speech more explicit by adding more detail than the speaker actually gave.

"I don't like <u>those</u> shoes." → He said he didn't like **the** shoes **in the window.**

"Look at <u>this</u> job ad!" → He asked me to look at **an** ad **that he found online.**

B9 ## Changing Demonstrative Adjectives and Pronouns

Complete the reported sentences in two different ways using an article, a pronoun, and/or more details.

1. "I know I'm not going to like this idea."

   She said she knew she wasn't going to like my idea.

   She said she knew she wasn't going to like the idea I'd come up with.

2. "Those are the funniest cartoons I've ever seen."

   _____

   _____

3. "Do these jeans look big on me?"

   _____

   _____

4. "That's gorgeous!"

   _____

   _____

5. "Could you read this application? I'm about to send it in."

   _____

   _____

Paraphrasing in Reported Speech

Read each conversation and paraphrase it in at least two different ways.

1. **Jill:** Can you come to dinner on Friday?
    Joe: I'd love to but I'm afraid not. My mother is coming to stay with me.

    Jill asked Joe to come to dinner on Friday, but he said he couldn't. His mom was coming to visit.

    Jill asked Joe to have dinner with them that Friday, but he wasn't able to because his mom was

    staying with him.

2. **Joe:** Would it be OK for me to start that new project on February 1? I have a vacation booked.
    Jill: Sure, that's no problem.

    _____

    _____

    _____

3. **Jill:** What do you think I should do? Marry José or not?
    Joe: Marry him. He's great.

    _____

    _____

    _____

4. **Jill:** What do you think of this new suit? I'm not sure.
    Joe: Well, I think you look better in the blue one, actually.

    _____

    _____

    _____

5. **Joe:** Did you get the job?
    Jill: I did! My experience was perfect so they offered it to me there and then.

    _____

    _____

    _____

Read each sentence and complete the reported speech with the reporting verb in parentheses. If possible, use a present tense report. Be prepared to explain your answers.

1. "You won't pass the course unless you get an A on the test." (say)

   I need a tutor. My professor _says I won't pass the course unless I get an A on the test._

2. "People use only 10 percent of their brains." (claim)

   Some experts _____, but I think this statement is false.

3. "You have to look for a new apartment?" (say)

   Liz _____, and I think she's right.

4. "I didn't go to your ball game last night." (admit)

   My brother _____. It really hurt my feelings!

5. "Lisa is doing very well at her job." (tell me)

   Lisa, your boss _____. Keep up the good work!

6. "I used to ski but I don't anymore." (explain)

   My mother _____. She broke her leg once while skiing.

7. "I lost your CD." (admit)

   My sister _____, but she still won't replace it!

8. "Fatty foods are bad for you." (tell us)

   Doctors _____, but who knows really? I'm not changing my diet!

Read each sentence and the sentence that follows it. Write *T* if the second sentence is true, *F* if it is false, and *?* if there isn't enough information to decide. Then discuss your answers in small groups.

1. Tina informed me that I had lost my job.

   ____ Tina lost her job.

2. She said she used to buy candy bars for a nickel.

   ____ She would buy candy bars for a nickel.

3. Manuel admitted that he had plagiarized the essay.

   ____ It is uncertain if Manuel cheated.

4. I said I'd meet him later.

   ____ I met him.

5. I want to know when the movie ends.

   ____ I know when the movie ends.

6. He says he'll clean his room.

   ____ He's finished cleaning his room.

7. My advisor suggested that I invest in real estate.

   ____ I've invested in real estate.

8. James asked Tai if he would water his plants.

   ____ The plants belong to James.

B13 **Speaking**

A. Think about an interesting issue or piece of news. Write a short summary of it. Think about "the journalist's five *Ws*:" What happened or is happening? Where? When? To whom and by whom? and Why?

B. In small groups, take turns sharing the details about your news story or issue. The group takes notes. When you finish, the group works together to report back what you said. Use past or present reporting as appropriate.

A: I read a story about two people who are getting a divorce. They are still living in the same house. To keep them from fighting, a judge had a wall built down the middle of the house . . .

B: Tetsu told us about a story he had read. He said it was about two people who were getting a divorce. The article he read said that they are still living in the same house. It explained that a judge made them build a wall down the middle of the house to stop their fighting . . .

C Writing

Editing: *Reported Speech*

Study the errors. Pay attention to the areas that you make mistakes in.

---

1. **Punctuation**

   whether
   The lawyer asked the judge , "Whether the trial could be postponed a few weeks ∧ ? "
                              (comma struck out; period and ? added)

2. **Word order and use of auxiliaries**

   if I thought
   My brother asked did I think I should go to the hospital.

   we needed
   She wanted to know when did we need to leave.

3. **Use of object pronouns**

   me
   My supervisor told ∧ to cover up for the mistake he had made.

   The professor agreed us that we could turn in our papers late.

4. **Use of modals**

   would
   She asked me yesterday if I ∧ meet her today.

   had to
   She told me last spring that she must move immediately.

C1 Editing

Correct the errors in the passage. Be prepared to explain your answers.

I recently saw a program on TV about a new exhibit on traditional textiles and fabrics. The

interviewer, a young man, was talking with the exhibit curator and asked what did the exhibit

included
include besides things like blankets and clothing. The curator explained, "That because

traditional textiles are rich in symbolism and color, they had had a significant effect on certain

artists." She told that because of this influence, the exhibit also included works by painters

who had been influenced by woven designs. I remember thinking at the time, "That's very

thought-provoking. I'd love to see this exhibit." Then, the interviewer added that admission to the exhibition was included with the regular museum admission fee, and asked the curator did she think more people visit it for that reason? The curator responded him that the museum never charges additional fees for special exhibitions because they want as many people as possible to enjoy them. I can't wait to see it.

Beyond the Sentence: *Combining Quoted and Reported Speech*

Good writers use a variety of language forms to keep the reader's attention. Using a combination of quoted speech, reported speech, and alternatives to reporting verbs will help you maintain the audience's interest by making what you say sound more credible.

"Everyone stretches the truth sometimes," a friend of mine says. "Bankers use tricks to help clients save on their taxes; and people who write ads say that you can lose 50 pounds if you drink a diet drink. That's not lying." **In her opinion,** these are honest people trying to make a living. However, **in other people's view,** the behavior is wrong.

Certain phrases, such as according to X, in X's opinion, and in X's view, are used instead of reporting verbs to restate what someone has said or written.

According to Dr. Peter Fritzell, the head of the Psychology Department at Lawrence University, there are many reasons why people are dishonest. **While studying honesty in adults,** Fritzell found that cheating may excite some people. For other people, it is a way of getting back at someone—an employer or friend. Still others cheat simply because they can.

In sentences reporting what someone has said or written, a (reduced) relative clause or adverb phrase is sometimes used to give background information about the speaker. This information increases the credibility of the statements.

Sebastian Rosero, **who is director of the Center for Ethical Development and Behavior,** claims people are amazingly proficient at justifying their actions. He comments, "Most people cheat because others do. They feel this excuses their behavior." He also **makes the observation that** people don't usually judge themselves in the same way that they judge others. "One teenager admitted that he had cheated on a test, but he also said he would be embarrassed if his parent lied to a cop to get out of a speeding ticket."

Another alternative to reporting verbs is the use of expressions that include nouns related to reporting verbs. For example: make the observation / recommendation / statement / suggestion / claim / assertion / point + that.

C2 **Using Alternatives to Reporting Verbs**

A. Work with a partner. Write reports of the statements. Use alternatives to reporting verbs, such as *according to X* or *make a statement*. Change the time in the reported statement where necessary.

1. My mother always said, "People should think for themselves and not pay attention to rumors."
In my mother's opinion, people should think for themselves and not pay attention to rumors.

2. My brother told me, "The movie is awful."

3. Sociologists once claimed, "Women are less intelligent than men."

4. My parents have often asserted "Honesty is the best policy."

5. My teacher assured me, "Any dream can come true if you have the courage to pursue it."

6. Andy Warhol, the notable artist, once observed, "Everyone will be famous for 15 minutes."

B. Choose one sentence from part A and develop it into a short paragraph. Use a combination of quoted and reported speech.

In my mother's opinion, people should think for themselves and not pay attention to rumors. As a child, she used to tell me, "People will say all sorts of things, but you need to find out the truth."

C3 **Writing Tip:** *Explaining Different Viewpoints*

One important use of reported speech is to explain different viewpoints or give more than one example of what people think about a specific issue or event.

Choose one of the topics to write a short essay of two to three paragraphs. Explain your own and other people's viewpoints about the topic using quoted speech, reported speech, and alternatives to reporting verbs. Give reasons why your viewpoint is correct. Then, use the Writing Checklist to check your work.

• Often what one person considers to be cheating or lying is considered acceptable behavior by someone else. What do you and people you know think about cheating? Provide specific examples of statements you have heard these people say.

• We all have people who give us advice: family members, friends, neighbors, and co-workers. It may be good advice or bad advice. Think of a problem you had that you asked people advice about. What was the problem? What different advice did you receive? Whose advice did you follow? In the end, was it good advice?

• With increasing use of the Internet, some have expressed concern that we are becoming more isolated. Others support the opposite view: that people are more connected than they were in the past because communication is much easier. Provide specific examples of the arguments you have heard expressed on each side of the issue.

Beyond the Classroom

Writing

Write an essay using one of these topics.

1. Reviewers have an enormous influence over how well a movie does at the box office. Often direct quotations of reviewers' comments are the most prominent feature in movie advertisements. Choose a movie that you have seen. What were some of the things reviewers said about the film? What did you and your friends or family think of the film? Choose your favorite (or least favorite) scene from the movie. What happened in the scene? What did the characters say to each other?

2. When we watch the news or read the newspaper, a controversial story will often catch our attention. Think of a controversial issue that you recently read about or heard about. What did people on each side of the issue have to say about the topic? Which side do you agree with?

Searching for Authentic Examples

Find examples of English grammar in everyday life by completing the task below. Bring your examples to class, and be prepared to discuss them.

Listen to a news report for three examples of present tense reporting and three examples of past tense reporting. Which is more common? Try to find some examples with verbs other than *say*, *tell*, and *ask*. Why do you think the present tense reports were used?

Appendices

1 Verb Forms

Long Forms	Contractions

Simple Present of *Be*

I **am (not)**
he/she/it **is (not)**
we/you/they **are (not)**
Am I?   **Is** he/she/it?   **Are** we/you/they?

I**'m (not)**
he/she/it**'s**   he/she/it**'s not/isn't**
we/you/they**'re (not)**   we/you/they **aren't**

Simple Present

I/we/you/they **work/do not work**
he/she/it **works/ does not work**
Do I/we/you/they **work**?   **Does** he/she/it **work**?

I/we/you/they **don't work**
he/she/it **doesn't work**

Present Continuous

I **am (not) working**
he/she/it **is (not) working**
we/you/they **are (not) working**
Am I **working**?   **Is** he/she/it **working**?
Are we/you/they **working**?

I**'m (not) working**
he/she/it**'s (not)/isn't working**
we/you/they**'re (not)/aren't working**

Simple Past of *Be*

I/he/she/it **was (not)**
we/you/they **were (not)**
Was I/he/she/it?   **Were** we/you/they?

I/he/she/it **wasn't**
we/you/they **weren't**

Simple Past of Regular Verbs

I/he/she/it/we/you/they **worked/did not work**
Did I/he/she/it/we/you/they **work**?

I/he/she/it/we/you/they **didn't work**

Simple Past of Irregular Verbs

I/he/she/it/we/you/they **went**
I/he/she/it/we/you/they **did not go**
Did I/he/she/it/we/you/they **go**?

I/he/she/it/we/you/they **didn't go**

Past Continuous

I/he/she/it **was (not) working**
we/you/they **were (not) working**
Was I/he/she/it **working**?
Were we/you/they **working**?

I/he/she/it **wasn't working**
we/you/they **weren't working**

Present Perfect

I/we/you/they **have (not) worked**
he/she/it **has (not) worked**
Have I/we/you/they **worked**?
Has he/she/it **worked**?

I/we/you/they**'ve/haven't worked**
he/she/it**'s worked**   he/she/it **hasn't worked**

Present Perfect Continuous

I/we/you/they **have (not) been working**
he/she/it **has (not) been working**
Have I/we/you/they **been working**?
Has he/she/it **been working**?

I/we/you/they**'ve/haven't been working**
he/she/it**'s/hasn't been working**

Past Perfect

I/he/she/it/we/you/they **had (not) worked**
Had I/he/she/it/we/you/they **worked?**

I/he/she/it/we/you/they**'d worked/hadn't worked**

Past Perfect Continuous

I/he/she/it/we/you/they **had (not) been working**
Had I/he/she/it/we/you/they **been working?**

I/he/she/it/we/you/they**'d/hadn't been working**

Simple Future

I/he/she/it/we/you/they **will (not) work**
Will I/he/she/it/we/you/they **work?**

I/he/she/it/we/you/they**'ll work/won't work**

Be going to Future

I **am (not) going to work**
he/she/it **is (not) going to work**
we/you/they **are (not) going to work**
Am I **going to work?** **Is** he/she/it **going to work?**
Are we/you/they **going to work?**

I**'m (not) going to work**
he/she/it**'s (not)/isn't going to work**
we/you/they**'re (not)/aren't going to work**

Future Continuous

I/he/she/it/we/you/they **will (not) be working**
Will I/he/she/it/we/you/they **be working?**

I/he/she/it/we/you/they**'ll/won't be working**

Future Perfect

I/he/she/it/we/you/they **will (not) have worked**
Will I/he/she/it/we/you/they **have worked?**

I/he/she/it/we/you/they**'ll/won't have worked**

Future Perfect Continuous

I/he/she/it/we/you/they **will (not) have been
    working**
Will I/he/she/it/we/you/they **have been working?**

I/he/she/it/we/you/they**'ll/won't have been
    working**

Modals

I/he/she/it/we/you/they **can(not)/could (not)
    work**
I/he/she/it/we/you/they **should (not) work**
I/he/she/it/we/you/they **may/might/must (not)
    work**
I/he/she/it/we/you/they **ought (not) to work**
Can/could... I/he/she/it/we/you/they **work?**

I/he/she/it/we/you/they **can't/couldn't work**

I/he/she/it/we/you/they **shouldn't work**

Past Modals

I/he/she/it/we/you/they **cannot have worked**
I/he/she/it/we/you/they **could (not) have worked**
I/he/she/it/we/you/they **should (not) have
    worked**
I/he/she/it/we/you/they **may/might (not) have
    worked**
I/he/she/it/we/you/they **must (not) have worked**
I/he/she/it/we/you/they **ought (not) to have
    worked**
Could/should... I/he/she/it/we/you/they **have
    worked?**

I/he/she/it/we/you/they **can't have worked**
I/he/she/it/we/you/they **couldn't have worked**
I/he/she/it/we/you/they **shouldn't have worked**

Present Real Conditional

If I **have** the time, I **will work** more.
If I **do not have** the time, I **will not work** more.

If I **have** the time, I**'ll work** more.
If I **don't have** the time, I **won't work** more.

Present Unreal Conditional

If I **had** the time, I **would work** more.
If I **did not have** the time, I **would not work** more.

If I **had** the time, I**'d work** more.
If I **didn't have** the time, I **wouldn't work** more.

Past Real Conditional

If I **had** the chance, I **worked** abroad.

Past Unreal Conditional

If I **had had** the time, I **would have worked** more.
If I **had not had**..., I **would not have worked**...

If I**'d had** the time, I**'d have worked** more.
If I **hadn't had**..., I **wouldn't have worked**...

Simple Present Passive

I **am (not) allowed**
he/she/it **is (not) allowed**
we/you/they **are (not) allowed**
Am I **allowed**?   **Is** he/she/it **allowed**?
Are we/you/they **allowed**?

I**'m (not) allowed**
he/she/it**'s not/isn't allowed**
we/you/they**'re (not)/aren't allowed**

Present Continuous Passive

I **am (not) being allowed**
he/she/it **is (not) being allowed**
we/you/they **are (not) being allowed**
Am I **being allowed**?   **Is** he/she/it **being allowed**?
Are we/you/they **being allowed**?

I**'m (not) being allowed**
he/she/it**'s (not)/isn't being allowed**
we/you/they**'re (not)/aren't being allowed**

Simple Past Passive

I/he/she/it **was (not) allowed**
we/you/they **were (not) allowed**
Was I/he/she/it **allowed**?
Were we/you/they **allowed**?

I/he/she/it **wasn't allowed**
we/you/they **weren't allowed**

Past Continuous

I/he/she/it **was (not) being allowed**
we/you/they **were (not) being allowed**
Was I/he/she/it **being allowed**?
Were we/you/they **being allowed**?

I/he/she/it **wasn't being allowed**
we/you/they **weren't being allowed**

Present Perfect

I/we/you/they **have (not) been allowed**
he/she/it **has (not) been allowed**
Have I/we/you/they **been allowed**?
Has he/she/it **been allowed**?

I/we/you/they**'ve been/haven't been allowed**
he/she/it**'s been/hasn't been allowed**

Past Perfect

I/he/she/it/we/you/they **had (not) been allowed**
Had I/he/she/it/we/you/they **been allowed**?

I/he/she/it/we/you/they**'d/hadn't been allowed**

Simple Future Passive

I/he/she/it/we/you/they **will (not) be allowed**
Will I/he/she/it/we/you/they **be allowed**?

I/he/she/it/we/you/they**'ll/won't be allowed**

Future Perfect Passive

I/he/she/it/we/you/they **will (not) have been allowed**

Will I/he/she/it/we/you/they **have been allowed**?

I/he/she/it/we/you/they**'ll/won't have been allowed**

Modal Passive

I/he/she/it/we/you/they **cannot be allowed**

Should I/he/she/it/we/you/they **be allowed**?

I/he/she/it/we/you/they **can't be allowed**

Past Modal Passive

I/he/she/it/we/you/they **should (not) have been allowed**

Could I/he/she/it/we/you/they **have been allowed**?

I/he/she/it/we/you/they **shouldn't have been allowed**

---

❷ Verbs Ending in *-s* and *-es*

Spelling Rules

1. For most third-person singular verbs, add *-s* to the base form.

   swim — swims

2. If the base form ends with the letters *s, z, sh, ch,* or *x,* add *-es.*

   miss — misses

3. If the base form ends with a consonant + *y,* change *y* to *i* and add *-es.* (Compare vowel + *y:* obey — obeys.)

   try — tries

4. If the base form ends with a consonant + *o,* add *-es.*

   do — does
   echo — echoes
   go — goes

5. *Have* and *be* are irregular:

   have — has
   be — is

Pronunciation Rules

1. If the base form ends with the /s/, /z/, /ʃ/, /ʒ/, /tʃ/, /dʒ/, or /ks/, then pronounce *-es* as an extra syllable /ɪz/.

slice — slices	watch — watches
lose — loses	judge — judges
wash — washes	relax — relaxes

2. If the base form ends with the voiceless sounds /p/, /t/, /k/, /f/, or /θ/, then pronounce *-s* and *-es* as /s/.

sleep — sleeps	work — works	hit — hits	laugh — laughs

3. If the base form ends with any other consonant or with a vowel sound, then pronounce *-s* and *-es* as /z/.

learn — learns	go — goes

③ Verbs Ending in *-ing*

1. For most verbs, add *-ing* to the base form.

   sleep — sleeping   talk — talking

2. If the base form ends in a single *e*, drop the *e* and add *-ing*.

   live — living   write — writing

3. If the base form ends in *ie*, change *ie* to *y* and add *-ing* (exception: be — being).

   die — dying   lie — lying

4. If the base form of a one-syllable verb ends with a single vowel + consonant, double the final consonant and add *-ing*.(Compare two vowels + consonant: eat — eating.)

   hit — hitting   stop — stopping

5. If the base form of a verb with two or more syllables ends in a single vowel + consonant, double the final consonant only if the stress is on the final syllable. Do not double the final consonant if the stress is not on the final syllable.

   ad<u>mit</u> — admitting   be<u>gin</u> — beginning   de<u>ve</u>lop — developing   <u>lis</u>ten — listening

6. Do not double the final consonants *x*, *w*, and *y*.

   fix — fixing   plow — plowing   obey — obeying

④ Stative Verbs

Descriptions and Measurements

appear	fit	represent	suit
be	indicate	resemble	weigh
cost	look (like)	seem	
equal	mean	signify	
exist	measure	sound (like)	

Possession and Relationships

belong	depend on	involve	pertain to
concern	entail	lack	possess
consist of	have	owe	
contain	include	own	

Knowledge and Beliefs

agree	find	know	recollect
believe	forget	mean	remember
disagree	guess	notice	suppose
doubt	hope	realize	think
feel (=think)	imagine	recognize	understand

Attitudes and Desires

admire	dislike	matter	respect
appreciate	fear	mind	want
care	hate	need	
desire	like	prefer	
despise	love	regret	

Senses and Sensations

ache	hurt	see	sting
burn	itch	sense	taste
feel	notice	smell	
hear	recognize	sound	

5 Adverbs of Frequency

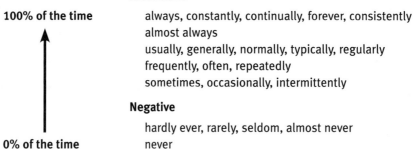

Affirmative

100% of the time

always, constantly, continually, forever, consistently
almost always
usually, generally, normally, typically, regularly
frequently, often, repeatedly
sometimes, occasionally, intermittently

Negative

hardly ever, rarely, seldom, almost never

0% of the time   never

6 Regular Verbs: Simple Past and Past Participle Forms

Spelling Rules

1. To form the simple past and past participle of most regular verbs, add *-ed* to the base form.

   brush — brushed   play — played

2. If the base form ends with *e*, just add *-d*.

   close — closed   live — lived

3. If the base form ends with a consonant + *y*, change the *y* to *i* and add *-ed*.
   (Compare vowel + *y*: play — played; enjoy — enjoyed.)

   study — studied   dry — dried

4. If the base form of a one-syllable verb ends with a single vowel + consonant, double the final consonant and add *-ed*.

   plan — planned   shop — shopped

5. If the base form of a verb with two or more syllables ends in a single vowel + consonant, double the final consonant and add *-ed* only when the stress is on the final syllable. Do not double the final consonant if the stress is not on the final syllable.

   pre<u>fer</u> — preferred   <u>en</u>ter — entered

6. Do not double the final consonants *x*, *w*, and *y*.

   coax — coaxed   snow — snowed   stay — stayed

Pronunciation Rules

1. If the base form of the verb ends with the sounds /t/ or /d/, then pronounce *-ed* as an extra syllable /ɪd/.

/t/	/d/
start — started	need — needed
wait — waited	decide — decided

2. If the base form ends with the voiceless sounds /f/, /k/, /p/, /s/, /ʃ/, /tʃ/, or /ks/, then pronounce *-ed* as /t/.

laugh — laughed	jump — jumped	wish — wished	fax — faxed
look — looked	slice — sliced	watch — watched	

3. If the base form ends with the voiced sounds /b/, /g/, /dʒ/, /m/, /n/, /~/, /l/, /r/, /ð/, /v/, /z/, or with a vowel, then pronounce *-ed* as /d/.

rob — robbed	hum — hummed	call — called	wave — waved
brag — bragged	rain — rained	order — ordered	close — closed
judge — judged	bang — banged	bathe — bathed	play — played

7 Irregular Verbs: Simple Past and Past Participle Forms

Base Form	Simple Past	Past Participle	Base Form	Simple Past	Past Participle
arise	arose	arisen	draw	drew	drawn
be	was/were	been	drink	drank	drunk
beat	beat	beaten	drive	drove	driven
become	became	become	eat	ate	eaten
begin	began	begun	fall	fell	fallen
bend	bent	bent	feed	fed	fed
bet	bet	bet	feel	felt	felt
bind	bound	bound	fight	fought	fought
bite	bit	bitten	find	found	found
bleed	bled	bled	fit	fit	fit
blow	blew	blown	flee	fled	fled
break	broke	broken	fly	flew	flown
bring	brought	brought	forbid	forbade	forbidden
build	built	built	forget	forgot	forgotten
burst	burst	burst	forgive	forgave	forgiven
buy	bought	bought	freeze	froze	frozen
catch	caught	caught	get	got	gotten
choose	chose	chosen	give	gave	given
cling	clung	clung	go	went	gone
come	came	come	grind	ground	ground
cost	cost	cost	grow	grew	grown
creep	crept	crept	hang	hung	hung
cut	cut	cut	have	had	had
deal	dealt	dealt	hear	heard	heard
dig	dug	dug	hide	hid	hidden
dive	dove (or dived)	dived	hit	hit	hit
do	did	done	hold	held	held

Base Form	Simple Past	Past Participle	Base Form	Simple Past	Past Participle
hurt	hurt	hurt	sit	sat	sat
keep	kept	kept	sleep	slept	slept
know	knew	known	slide	slid	slid
lay (= put)	laid	laid	speak	spoke	spoken
lead	led	led	speed	sped	sped
leave	left	left	spend	spent	spent
lend	lent	lent	spin	spun	spun
let	let	let	split	split	split
lie (= recline)	lay	lain	spread	spread	spread
light	lit	lit	spring	sprang	sprung
lose	lost	lost	stand	stood	stood
make	made	made	steal	stole	stolen
mean	meant	meant	stick	stuck	stuck
meet	met	met	sting	stung	stung
pay	paid	paid	stink	stank	stunk
prove	proved	proven (or proved)	strike	struck	struck
put	put	put	string	strung	strung
quit	quit	quit	swear	swore	sworn
read	read	read	sweep	swept	swept
ride	rode	ridden	swim	swam	swum
ring	rang	rung	swing	swung	swung
rise	rose	risen	take	took	taken
run	ran	run	teach	taught	taught
say	said	said	tear	tore	torn
see	saw	seen	tell	told	told
seek	sought	sought	think	thought	thought
sell	sold	sold	throw	threw	thrown
send	sent	sent	understand	understood	understood
set	set	set	undertake	undertook	undertaken
sew	sewed	sewn	upset	upset	upset
shake	shook	shaken	wake	woke	woken
shine	shone	shone	wear	wore	worn
shoot	shot	shot	weave	wove	woven
show	showed	shown	weep	wept	wept
shrink	shrank	shrunk	wet	wet	wet
shut	shut	shut	win	won	won
sing	sang	sung	wind	wound	wound
sink	sank	sunk	write	wrote	written

8 Common Intransitive Verbs

These verbs can only be used intransitively. (They cannot be followed by an object.)

ache	emerge	itch	sit
appear	erupt	laugh	sleep
arrive	faint	live	smile
be	fall	look	snow
come	frown	matter	stand
cry	go	occur	stay
depart	grin	rain	talk
die	happen	remain	weep
disappear	hesitate	seem	

9 Regular Plural Nouns

Spelling Rules

1. For most plural nouns, add -s to the base form.

   lake — lakes   computer — computers

2. If the noun ends with the letters s, z, sh, ch, or x, add -es.

   kiss — kisses   box — boxes
   bush — bushes   fax — faxes

3. If the noun ends with a consonant + y, change y to i and add -es.
   (Compare vowel + y: toy — toys.)

   baby — babies   country — countries

4. If the noun ends with a consonant + o, add -s or -es. Some words take -s, -es, or both -s and -es. (Compare vowel + o: radio — radios; zoo — zoos.)

   -s
   auto — autos
   photo — photos
   piano — pianos
   solo — solos

   -es
   echo — echoes
   hero — heroes
   potato — potatoes
   tomato — tomatoes

   Both **-s** and **-es**
   tornado — tornados/tornadoes
   volcano — volcanos/volcanoes
   zero — zeros/zeroes

5. If the noun ends in a single *f* (*e*), change *f* (*e*) to *v* and add *-es*.

calf — calves
shelf — shelves
knife — knives

Exceptions
belief — beliefs
chief — chiefs
roof — roofs
scarf — scarfs/scarves

6. Certain plural nouns have no singular forms:

belongings	groceries	scissors	tropics
clothes	jeans	shorts	trousers
congratulations	pajamas	(sun)glasses	
goods	pants	tongs	

Pronunciation Rules

1. If the noun ends with the sounds /s/, /z/, /ʃ/, /ʒ/, /tʃ/, /dʒ/, or /ks/, then pronounce *-es* as an extra syllable /ɪz/.

watch — watches   price — prices   language languages
loss — losses   judge — judges   size — sizes
bush — bushes   tax — taxes   garage — garages

2. If the noun ends with the voiceless sounds /p/, /t/, /k/, /f/, or /θ/, then pronounce *-s* and *-es* as /s/.

grape — grapes   cuff — cuffs   book — books
laugh — laughs   cat — cats   fifth — fifths

3. If the noun ends with any other consonant or with a vowel sound, then pronounce *-s* and *-es* as /z/.

fern — ferns   name — names
toe — toes   boy — boys

---

⑩ Irregular Plural Nouns

Singular	Plural	Singular	Plural
appendix	appendices	moose	moose
---	cattle	mouse	mice
child	children	ox	oxen
deer	deer	person	people
fish	fish	people (= ethnic group)	peoples
foot	feet	---	police
goose	geese	sheep	sheep
index	indices/indexes	tooth	teeth
man	men	woman	women

Note the following plural forms of Greek and Latin words:

-is → *-es*

analysis	analyses
axis	axes
basis	bases
crisis	crises
diagnosis	diagnoses
hypothesis	hypotheses
oasis	oases
parenthesis	parentheses

-us → *-i*

alumnus	alumni
cactus	cacti
fungus	fungi
nucleus	nuclei
radius	radii
stimulus	stimuli
syllabus	syllabi (syllabuses)

-um/-on → *-a*

bacterium	bacteria
criterion	criteria
curriculum	curricula (curriculums)
datum	data
memorandum	memoranda (memorandums)
phenomenon	phenomena

11 Collective Nouns

These collective nouns usually take singular verbs but may be referred to with singular or plural pronouns:

audience	congregation	firm	mob
band	council	flock	orchestra
choir	couple	gang	public
class	crew	government	school
club	crowd	group	staff
committee	faculty	herd	team
company	family	jury	union

12 Noncount Nouns

Abstract Nouns

adolescence	fun	love	safety
advice	hate	luck	security
beauty	health	mercy	sex
birth	help	news	speech
childhood	honesty	pain	strength
courage	importance	patience	time
crime	independence	peace	truth
death	information	pollution	violence
evidence	intelligence	power	wealth
existence	justice	poverty	wisdom
experience	labor	progress	work
force	leisure	research	youth
freedom	life	respect	

Liquids

blood	juice	shampoo	wine
coffee	lotion	soup	
cream	milk	tea	
honey	oil	water	

Food

beef	cheese	fruit	yogurt
bread	chicken	garlic	
butter	chocolate	meat	
cake	fish	pasta	

Materials & Elements

coal	hair	plastic	steel
copper	iron	plutonium	wood
cotton	glass	silver	wool
gold	metal	skin	

Gases

air	hydrogen	oxygen	steam
carbon dioxide	nitrogen	smoke	

Grains & Powders

barley	dirt	pepper	sand
cereal	dust	rice	sugar
detergent	flour	salt	wheat

Natural Phenomena

dew	gravity	lightning	snow
electricity	hail	mist	weather
energy	heat	nature	wind
fog	humidity	rain	
frost	ice	sleet	

Areas of Study & Professions

accounting	economics	linguistics	physics
art	education	literature	plumbing
architecture	engineering	management	psychology
biology	English	manufacturing	religion
botany	finance	mathematics	science
business	healthcare	medicine	sociology
carpentry	history	music	teaching
chemistry	journalism	nursing	technology
dentistry	law	philosophy	

Activities

acting	chess	hockey	sleeping
archery	cooking	jogging	soccer
baseball	dining	lacrosse	speaking
basketball	eating	reading	swimming
bowling	football	rugby	tennis
camping	gardening	shopping	typing
checkers	hiking	skating	

General Categories

apparel	education	homework	make-up
candy	equipment	jewelry	money
cash	food	luggage	recreation
clothing	furniture	machinery	sports
communication	grammar	mail	transportation

---

⑬ Expressions for Measuring and Counting Nouns

These expressions can be used with noncount nouns to make them countable, as follows:

General Terms

a bit of luck / water	a piece of news / cake
a form of relaxation / carbon	a type of game / cooking
a kind of equipment / paint	

Food

a bar of chocolate	a loaf of bread
a cut of beef	a serving of chicken
a grain of rice	a slice of pie
a head of lettuce	a stick of butter
a portion of fish	a wedge of cheese

Measurements

a cup of flour	an ounce of perfume
a foot of snow	a quart of oil
a gallon of gas	a tablespoon of sugar
a liter of milk	a teaspoon of salt

Containers

a bag of candy
a bottle of lotion
a bowl of soup
a box of cereal
a can of paint
a container of milk
a cup of tea

a glass of juice
a mug of coffee
a pack of gum
a sack of rice
a thermos of soup
a tube of toothpaste

Nature

a blade of grass
a block of ice
a bolt of electricity
a clap of thunder
a cloud of smoke
a drop of rain

a flash of lightning
a grain of sand
a gust of wind
a lump of coal
a speck of dust
a unit of energy

Miscellaneous

a branch of mathematics /
   history, etc.

a game of football / tennis, etc.
a period of time

Materials & Objects

an article of clothing
a piece of equipment / furniture
a sheet of paper / steel

a stick of chalk
a strip of cloth

14 Possessive Adjectives and Pronouns: Form

Possessive Adjective	Possessive Pronoun	Examples
my	mine	my key /my keys → mine
your	yours	your order / your orders → yours.
his	his	his book / his books → his
her	hers	her uncle /her uncles → hers
its	---	its collar / its collars
our	ours	our office / our offices → ours
your	yours	your car /your cars → yours
their	theirs	their child / their children → theirs

15 Demonstrative Adjectives and Pronouns: Form

Demonstrative Adjective and Pronoun		Examples	
singular	**plural**	**singular**	**plural**
this	these	this decision → this	these decisions → these
that	those	that report → that	those reports → those

16 The Definite Article with Proper Nouns

In general, *the* is not used with proper nouns. The following are exceptions to this rule:

1. *The* is used with plural proper nouns:

the Alps	the Netherlands
the Andes	the Philippines
the Bahamas	the United States
the Great Lakes	the West Indies
the United Arab Emirates	the Smiths (=the Smith family)

2. *The* is frequently used with singular proper nouns referring to oceans, seas, rivers, canals, and deserts. It is *not* used with singular lakes (e.g., *Lake Erie*):

the Atlantic (Ocean)	the Mississippi (River)
the Pacific (Ocean)	the Nile (River)
the Mediterranean (Sea)	the Panama (Canal)
the Caribbean (Sea)	the Sahara (Desert)

3. *The* is also used with certain singular proper nouns, especially place names of two or more words:

the Dominican Republic	the Middle East	the South Pole
the United Kingdom	the Empire State Building	the Taj Mahal
the Brooklyn Bridge	the Hilton Hotel	the White House

4. *The* is generally used with nouns that are followed by *of* phrases:

the Emperor of Japan	the Museum of Natural History
the President of the United States	the University of Vermont
the Statue of Liberty	the Tropic of Capricorn

16 The Definite Article with Familiar and Unique Nouns

the airport	the environment	the newspaper	the store
the atmosphere	the government	the ocean	the supermarket
the bank	the gym	the office	the sun
the beach	the library	the pharmacy	the television
the dentist	the mall	the police	the universe
the doctor	the moon	the radio	the world
the earth	the movies	the sky	

18 Gerunds: Form

1. Types of Gerunds

Simple Gerund	We recommend	**(not) calling.**
Perfect Gerund	He admits	**(not) having called.**
Passive Gerund	She resents	**(not) being called.**
		(not) getting called.

2. Grammatical Functions of Gerunds

As Subjects	**Teaching yoga** was rewarding.
As Subject Complements	<u>Her first job</u> was **teaching yoga**.
As Objects of Verbs	<u>Consider</u> **teaching yoga**.
As Object Complements	I spend a lot of <u>time</u> **teaching yoga**.
As Objects of:	
Prepositions	<u>By</u> **teaching yoga**, she earned money.
Verb + Preposition	They <u>talked about</u> **teaching yoga**.
Verb + Particle	He <u>gave up</u> **teaching yoga**.
Adjective + Preposition	We were <u>interested in</u> **teaching yoga**.
Noun + Preposition	I have a <u>manual for</u> **teaching yoga**.

---

⑲ Gerunds

Verb + Gerund

These verbs may be followed by gerunds, but not by infinitives:

acknowledge	deny	keep (= continue)	recall
admit	detest	loathe	recollect
anticipate	discuss	mean (= involve)	recommend
appreciate	dislike	mention	report
avoid	enjoy	mind (= object to)	resent
(can't) help	escape	miss	resist
(can't) stand	excuse	omit	resume
celebrate	feel like	postpone	risk
consider	finish	practice	suggest
defend	go	prevent	tolerate
defer	imagine	prohibit	understand
delay	involve	quit	

Verb with Object + Gerund

This list contains (1) verbs followed by gerunds that may also occur with an object before the gerund (e.g., *dislike him*), and (2) phrases consisting of verbs with objects (e.g., *spend time*) that are followed by gerunds:

can't help	have a problem	mind	stop
dislike	have trouble	miss	tolerate
dread	imagine	prevent	understand
enjoy	involve	remember	waste time/money/
hate	justify	resent	an hour, etc.
have fun	keep	risk	
have a good/bad/	like	spend time/money/	
difficult time	love	an hour, etc.	

Verb with Preposition + Gerund

These verbs or verb phrases with prepositions may be followed by gerunds, but not by infinitives:

adapt to	believe in	depend on
adjust to	blame someone for	disapprove of
agree (with someone) on	care about	discourage (someone) from
apologize (to someone) for	complain (to someone) about	engage in
approve of	concentrate on	forgive (someone) for
argue (with someone) about	consist of	help (someone) with
ask about	decide on	

Adjective with Preposition + Gerund

These adjectives with prepositions may be followed by gerunds, but not by infinitives:

accustomed to	enthusiastic about	jealous of	tired of
afraid of	familiar with	known for	tolerant of
angry (at someone) about	famous for	nervous about	upset about
ashamed of	fond of	perfect for	useful for
capable of	glad about	proud of	worried about
certain of/about	good at	responsible for	
concerned with	happy about	sad about	
critical of	incapable of	successful in	
discouraged from	interested in	suitable for	

Noun with Preposition + Gerund

These nouns with prepositions may be followed by gerunds, but not by infinitives:

an alternative to	a criticism of	a mistake in	success in
an approach to	a delay in	opposition to	a talent for
an argument for/against	enthusiasm about	a reaction to/against	a thought of
a belief in	a fear of	a reason for	a tolerance for
a book about	an introduction to	research in	
a chance of	an interest in	responsibility for	

---

20 Infinitives: Form

1. Types of Infinitives

Simple Infinitive	I decided	**(not) to call.**
Continuous Infinitive	We expect	**(not) to be calling.**
Perfect Infinitive	He pretends	**(not) to have called.**
Passive Infinitive	They ask	**(not) to be called.**

2. Grammatical Functions of Infinitives

As Subjects	**To teach yoga** would be hard → It would be hard to teach yoga. (more common)
As Subject Complements	<u>My goal</u> is **to teach yoga.**

(Continued on page A-20)

As Objects of Verbs:
Verb + Infinitive	He <u>plans</u> **to teach yoga.**
Verb + Object + Infinitive	He <u>invited me</u> **to teach yoga.**
Verb + (Object) + Infinitive	He <u>wanted (me)</u> **to teach yoga.**
As Adjective Complements	She is <u>pleased</u> **to teach yoga.**
As Noun Complements	He made <u>a decision</u> **to teach yoga.**

21 Infinitives

Verb + Infinitive

These verbs may be followed by infinitives, but not by gerunds:

agree	decide	manage	struggle
aim	decline	plan	swear
appear	demand	pledge	tend
arrange	fail	pretend	volunteer
care	guarantee	refuse	wait
claim	hope	resolve	
consent	intend	seem	

Verb with Object + Infinitive

These verbs with objects may be followed by infinitives, but not by gerunds:

advise	get	persuade	tell
command	hire	remind	trust
convince	invite	require	urge
force	order	teach	warn

Verb (with Object) + Infinitive

These verbs with or without objects may be followed by infinitives, but not by gerunds:

ask	desire	need	promise
beg	expect	offer	want
choose	help	pay	wish
dare	know	prepare	would like

Adjective + Infinitive

These adjectives may be followed by infinitives. Many of them may also be followed by prepositions and gerunds. See page A-19.

afraid	disturbed	impossible	right
alarmed	eager	interested	sad
amazed	easy	likely	scared
anxious	embarrassed	lucky	shocked
astonished	excited	necessary	sorry
careful	fascinated	pleased	surprised
curious	fortunate	possible	unlikely
delighted	frightened	prepared	unnecessary
determined	glad	proud	willing
difficult	happy	ready	wrong
disappointed	hard	relieved	
distressed	hesitant	reluctant	

Noun + Infinitive

These nouns may be followed by infinitives:

ability	failure	plan	request
advice	hope	pledge	requirement
appeal	inability	power	right
attempt	instruction	preparation	tendency
capacity	motivation	promise	suggestion
chance	need	proposal	time
command	necessity	recommendation	willingness
decision	opportunity	refusal	wish
desire	order	reluctance	
effort	permission	reminder	

22 Verb + Infinitive or Gerund

These verbs may be followed by infinitives or gerunds, often with a change in meaning:

attempt	continue	neglect	start
begin	forget	prefer	stop
can/could bear	hate	propose	try
can/could stand	like	regret	
cease	love	remember	

23 Coordinating Conjunctions: Form

Compound Sentence

Sentence 1	Conjunction	Sentence 2
Humans don't always get along,	**and**	they often have difficulty making up.
Many animals fight with each other,	**but**	they make up almost immediately.
Some people try making up,	**or**	they seek outside help.
Human beings don't get along well,	**nor**	**do they** settle their disputes easily.
Making up is important among animals,	**for**	they don't thrive in stressful situations.
Dolphins are sociable animals,	**so**	it makes sense that they make up easily.
Our behavior can be very destructive,	**yet**	it's hard to break the cycle of violence.

24 Transition Words and Phrases

These words and phrases are used as transitions to connect ideas between separate sentences or between larger blocks of text such as paragraphs.

Additional Ideas

actually	as well	in addition	namely
additionally	besides	indeed	plus
also	for example	in fact	specifically
as a matter of fact	for instance	in particular	to illustrate
as an example	furthermore	moreover	what is more (what's more)

Similar Ideas

in the same way	like + noun	similarly	similar to + noun
in the same way as + noun	likewise		

Contrast Between Ideas

actually	even so	instead (of this/	rather
alternatively	however	that + noun)	still
anyway	in any case	nevertheless	though
at any rate	in contrast	nonetheless	
despite this/	in spite of this/	on the contrary	
that (+ noun)	that (+ noun)	on the other hand	

Results

accordingly	consequently	on account of	thus
as a result (of this/	for this/that	this/that	to this end
that + noun)	reason	then	
because of this/	hence	therefore	
that (+ noun)			

Time

after (this/that)	before (this/that)	hitherto	previously
afterwards	for now	in the meantime	soon
at last	from now on	later	until then
at the same time	henceforth	meanwhile	up to now
at this moment			

Sequence & Organization

after (this/that)	in conclusion	most importantly	to return to this point
finally	in short	next	to summarize
first, second, third, etc.	in sum	then	
first of all, second	in summary	to begin	
of all, etc.	last	to conclude	

Point of View

amazingly	frankly	mercifully	thankfully
certainly	happily	sadly	truthfully
clearly	honestly	significantly	understandably
coincidentally	incredibly	strangely	unexpectedly
evidently	ironically	surely	unfortunately
fortunately	luckily	surprisingly	

25 Placement of Transition Words and Phrases

1. **Beginning of a sentence:** Transition words usually occur in sentence-initial position.

   It's raining hard. **However,** we won't cancel the event yet.

2. **Middle of a sentence:** Most transition words may also occur in various positions within a sentence. These positions typically include:

   After the first word:

   The decision has been made. <u>If</u>, **however,** you don't agree, call me.

   After the subject:

   John was fired. <u>His manager</u>, **therefore,** took over his clients.

   After the auxiliary or main verb be:

   The company is growing fast. We <u>have</u>, **in fact,** just expanded our staff.

   The weather is awful. They <u>are</u>, **nevertheless,** unlikely to cancel the event.

3. **End of a sentence:** Final position is most common in conversation with the transitions *though*, *then*, and *anyway*. Final position is used in writing with some transitions, but since it suggests that the transition is an afterthought, the transition is not as strong as in other positions.

   The weather is awful. They're unlikely to cancel the event, **though.**   (conversational)

   There is a budget deficit. We need to spend wisely, **therefore.**

26 Subordinators Introducing Adverb Clauses

These words and phrases are used as subordinators introducing adverb clauses. In most cases, the adverb clause may come before or after the main clause.

Contrast & Concession

although	despite the fact that	in spite of the fact that	whereas
as much as	even though	though	while

Time

after	before	once	until
as	by the time (that)	since	when
as long as	every time (that)	the first /next/last time (that)	whenever
as soon as	now that	till	while

Place

anywhere	everywhere	where	wherever

Reason

as	because of the fact that	inasmuch as	since
because	due to the fact that	now that	

Purpose or Result

in order that	so	so that

Condition

as if	if	only if	unless
as though	if only	provided that	when
as long as	in case	providing that	whether (or not)
even if	in the event that	so long as	

---

27 Noun Clauses: Form

1. Types of Noun Clauses

	Main Clause	Noun Clause
Wh- Clauses	They don't know	**what this means.**
		where the concert is.
		why he left.
That Clauses	I thought	**(that) the team played well.**
If/Whether Clauses	It's not clear	**if she's coming later (or not).**
		whether she's coming later (or not).
		whether (or not) she's coming later.

2. Grammatical Functions of Noun Clauses

As Subjects	**That she called** surprised us all.
	What we need is better information.
	Whether (or not) you stay is unimportant.
As Objects	We <u>know</u> **(that) e-waste contains lead.**
	how the items are recycled.
	if the item contains lead.
As Subject Complements	The problem <u>is</u> **how much we should spend.**
	whether we really need a new phone.
	It <u>seems/appears</u> **(that) the computer is not working.**
As Adjective Complements	It's <u>clear</u> **(that) the show won't be cancelled.**
	It's <u>interesting</u> **how jazz developed in New Orleans.**
	It's <u>unclear</u> **whether she's coming (or not).**
As Noun Complements	We heard <u>a rumor</u> **that the show was cancelled.**
After Prepositions	Let's talk <u>about</u> **what you saw.**
	That depends <u>on</u> **whether (or not) they called.**

---

28 Noun Clauses

Mental Activity Verb + Noun Clause

agree	doubt	hope	recall
assume	dream	imagine	recognize
believe	expect	know	regret
bet	feel	learn	remember
calculate	figure out	mean	suppose
conclude	find (out)	notice	think
consider	forget	pretend	understand
decide	guess	prove	wonder
discover	hear	realize	

Reporting Verb + Noun Clause

acknowledge	conclude	maintain	respond
add	confess	mention	roar
admit	confirm	murmur	say
advise (someone)	convince (someone)	mutter	scream
affirm	cry	note	shout
agree	declare	notify (someone)	shriek
announce	deny	observe	sneer
answer	emphasize	persuade (someone)	stammer
argue	estimate	point out	state
ask	exclaim	promise	suggest
assert	explain	propose	swear
assure (someone)	grumble	protest	tell (someone)
boast	guess	recommend	threaten
brag	imply	remark	warn
caution	indicate	remind (someone)	whisper
claim	inform (someone)	repeat	write
comment	insist	reply	yell
complain	instruct (someone)	report	

Reporting Verb + Base Form (Subjunctive)

These reporting verbs of advice and necessity may be followed by *that* + the base form of the verb, also called the subjunctive form:

advise that	demand that	propose that	suggest that
ask that	insist that	recommend that	urge that
beg that	order that	request that	
command that	prefer that	require that	

Adjective + Noun Clause

*advisable	*crucial	(im)possible	sorry
afraid	*desirable	lucky	strange
angry	*essential	*mandatory	sure
apparent	evident	*necessary	surprised
astonished	excited	nice	thankful
aware	fortunate	*obligatory	(un)likely
awful	funny	obvious	upset
*best	glad	odd	*urgent
certain	grateful	pleased	*vital
clear	happy	relieved	worried
confident	hopeful	right	wrong
content	*important	sad	

*Adjectives of advice and necessity marked with an asterisk (*) may be followed by
that + the base form of the verb, also called the subjunctive form.

Noun + Noun Clause

acknowledgment	conclusion	idea	*recommendation
admission	*demand	*insistence	report
*advice	determination	memory	*request
assumption	doubt	notion	*requirement
belief	dream	*order	response
claim	expectation	possibility	rumor
*command	explanation	promise	*suggestion
comment	fact	realization	thought
complaint	hope	recognition	wish

*Nouns of advice and necessity marked with an asterisk (*) may be followed by *that* + the base form of the verb, also called the subjunctive form.

29 Reporting Verb + Infinitive

These reporting verbs are used with infinitives to report imperatives and requests:

advise (someone) to	forbid (someone) to	tell (someone) to
ask (someone) to	instruct (someone) to	urge (someone) to
beg (someone) to	oblige (someone) to	want (someone) to
command (someone) to	order (someone) to	
direct (someone) to	request (someone) to	

30 Punctuation Rules for Quoted Speech

1. If quoted speech comes after the reporting verb:
   - Place a comma after the reporting verb.
   - Place quotation marks at the beginning and end of reported speech. Put them near the top of the letter.
   - Begin quoted speech with a capital letter.
   - Use the correct punctuation (a period, an exclamation mark, or a question mark) and place the punctuation inside the quotation marks.

   Examples
   He said, "We are staying."
   He shouted, "We are staying!"
   He asked me, "Are we staying?"

2. If quoted speech comes before the reporting verb:
   - Place quotation marks at the beginning and end of reported speech. Put them near the top of the letter.
   - Begin quoted speech with a capital letter.
   - Use a comma if the quoted speech is a statement. Use an exclamation mark if the quoted speech is an exclamation. Use a question mark if the quoted speech is a question. Place the punctuation inside the quotation marks.
   - Begin the phrase that follows the quoted speech with a lowercase letter.
   - Use a period at the end of the main sentence.

Examples

"We are staying," he said.
"We are staying!" he shouted.
"Are we staying?" he asked me.

---

31 Phrasal Verbs

Separable Phrasal Verbs

Many two-word phrasal verbs are separable. This means that a noun object can separate the two words of the phrasal verb or follow the phrasal verb. If the object is a pronoun (*me, you, him, her, it, us, them*), the pronoun must separate the two words.

Noun Object	Pronoun Object
She **turned** the offer **down**.	She **turned** it **down**.
She **turned down** the offer.	*She turned down it. (INCORRECT)

These are some common separable phrasal verbs and their meanings:

Phrasal Verb	Meaning
ask (someone) out	invite someone to go out
ask (someone) over	invite someone to come to your house
blow (something) up	inflate, cause something to explode
boot (something) up	start or get a computer ready for use
bring (someone) up	raise a child
bring (something) up	introduce or call attention to a topic
burn (something) down	destroy by fire
call (someone) back	return a phone call to someone
call (something) off	cancel something
call (someone) up	telephone
call (something) up	retrieve from the memory of a computer
check (something) out	borrow a book, tape, video from the library; verify
clean (something) out	clean the inside of something thoroughly
clean (something) up	clean thoroughly and remove anything unwanted
clear (something) up	explain a problem
cross (something) out	draw a line through
cut (something) up	cut into little pieces
do (something) over	do something again
figure (something) out	solve a problem
fill (something) in	write in a blank or a space
fill (something) out	write information on a form
fill (something) up	fill completely with something
find (something) out	discover information
give (something) back	return something
give (something) up	quit something; get rid of something
hand (something) in	submit homework, a test, an application
hand (something) out	distribute something
hang (something) up	put on a clothes hanger; end a telephone call
keep (someone) up	prevent someone from going to sleep
kick (someone) out	force someone to leave
leave (something) out	omit

Phrasal Verb	Meaning
look (something) over	examine carefully
look (something) up	look for information in a book
make (something) up	create or invent something; do work that was missed
make (something) up to (someone)	return a favor to someone
pay (someone) back	return money owned to someone
pick (something) out	choose
pick (something/someone) up	lift something or someone; stop to get something or someone
point (something) out	mention, draw attention to something
put (something) away	put something in its usual place
put (something) back	return something to its original place
put (something) down	stop holding something
put (something) in	install
put (something) off	postpone
put (something) on	get dressed
put (something) out	extinguish a fire, cigarette, or cigar
put (something) over on (someone)	deceive someone
set (something) up	make something ready for use
shut (something) off	turn off a machine
start (something) over	start again
take (something) away	remove
take (a time period) off	have a break from work or school
take (something) off	remove
take (someone) out	accompany to the theater, a restaurant, a movie
take (something) out	remove something from something else
tear (something) down	destroy completely
tear (something) off	detach something
tear (something) up	tear into pieces
think (something) over	reflect upon something before making a decision
think (something) up	invent
throw (something) away	put something in the trash
throw (something) out	put something in the trash
try (something) on	put on clothing to see how it looks
turn (something) down	lower the volume; refuse an offer or invitation
turn (something) in	return; submit homework, a test, an application
turn (something) off	stop a machine or light
turn (something) on	start a machine or light
turn (something) up	increase the volume
use (something) up	use something until no more is left
wake (someone) up	cause someone to stop sleeping
wear (someone) out	cause someone to become exhausted
work (something) out	solve something
write (something) down	write something on a piece of paper

Nonseparable Phrasal Verbs

Some two-word verbs and most three-word verbs are nonseparable. This means that a noun or pronoun object cannot separate the two parts of the phrasal verb.

Noun Object

The teacher **went over** the lesson.

*The teacher went the lesson over.

(INCORRECT)

Pronoun Object

The teacher **went over** it.

*The teacher went it over.

(INCORRECT)

These are some common nonseparable phrasal verbs and their meanings:

Phrasal Verb	Meaning
blow up	explode
break down	stop functioning properly
break up with (someone)	end a relationship with someone
burn down	be destroyed by fire
call on (someone)	ask someone to answer or speak in class
catch up with (someone/something)	travel fast enough to overtake someone who is ahead
check out of (a hotel)	leave a hotel after paying the bill
clear up	become fair weather
come back	return
come over	visit
come up with (something)	think of a plan or reply
cut down on (something)	reduce
eat out	have a meal in a restaurant
face up to (something)	be brave enough to accept or deal with
fall down	leave a standing position; perform in a disappointing way
get away with (doing something)	not be punished for doing something wrong
get down to (something)	begin to give serious attention to
get off (something)	leave a plane, bus, train
get on (something)	enter a plane, bus, train
get over (something)	recover from an illness or serious life event
get up	arise from a bed or chair
give up	stop trying, lose hope
go back	return
go down	(of computers) stop functioning; (of prices or temperature) become lower; (of ships) sink; (of the sun or moon) set
go off	stop functioning; (of alarms) start functioning; explode or make a loud noise
go on	take place, happen
go out	leave one's house to go to a social event
go out with (someone)	spend time regularly with someone
go over (something)	review
grow up	become an adult
hold on	wait on the telephone
keep on (doing something)	continue doing something
keep up with	stay at the same level or position
look out for (something/someone)	be careful of something or someone
move out	stop occupying a residence, especially by removing one's possessions
pack up	prepare all of one's belongings for moving

Phrasal Verb	Meaning
put up with (something/someone)	tolerate
run out	come to an end, be completely used up
run out of (something)	have no more of something
show up	appear, be seen, arrive at a place
sit down	get into a seated position
stay out	remain out of the house, especially at night
stay up	remain awake, not go to bed
take off	leave (usually by plane)
turn up	appear
wake up	stop sleeping
work out	exercise vigorously

32 Phonetic Symbols

Vowels

i	see /si/	u	too /tu/	oʊ	go /goʊ/
ɪ	sit /sɪt/	ʌ	cup /kʌp/	ər	bird /bərd/
ɛ	ten /tɛn/	ə	about /əˈbaʊt/	ɪr	near /nɪr/
æ	cat /kæt/	eɪ	say /seɪ/	ɛr	hair /hɛr/
ɑ	hot /hɑt/	aɪ	five /faɪv/	ɑr	car /kɑr/
ɔ	saw /sɔ/	ɔɪ	boy /bɔɪ/	ɔr	north /nɔrθ/
ʊ	put /pʊt/	aʊ	now /naʊ/	ʊr	tour /tʊr/

Consonants

p	pen /pɛn/	f	fall /fɔl/	m	man /mæn/
b	bad /bæd/	v	voice /vɔɪs/	n	no /noʊ/
t	tea /ti/	θ	thin /θɪn/	ŋ	sing /sɪŋ/
t̬	butter /ˈbʌt̬ər/	ð	then /ðɛn/	l	leg /lɛg/
d	did /dɪd/	s	so /soʊ/	r	red /rɛd/
k	cat /kæt/	z	zoo /zu/	y	yes /yɛs/
g	got /gɑt/	ʃ	she /ʃi/	w	wet /wɛt/
tʃ	chin /tʃɪn/	ʒ	vision /ˈvɪʒn/	x	Chanukah /ˈxɑnəkə/
dʒ	June /dʒun/	h	how /haʊ/		

Glossary of Grammar Terms

ability modal *See* **modal of ability**.

active sentence In active sentences, the agent (the noun that is performing the action) is in subject position and the receiver (the noun that receives or is a result of the action) is in object position. In the following sentence, the subject **Alex** performed the action, and the object **letter** received the action.

    Alex mailed the letter.

adjective A word that describes or modifies the meaning of a noun.

    the **orange** car   a **strange** noise

adjective clause *See* **relative clause**.

adjective complement *See* **complement**.

adjective phrase A phrase that functions as an adjective. Adjective phrases are often in the form of reduced relative clauses.

    These shoes are **too tight.**

    I spoke to the man **in the room.**
      (reduced relative clause)

    I know the lady **driving the car.**
      (reduced relative clause)

adverb A word that describes or modifies the meaning of a verb, another adverb, an adjective, or a sentence. Adverbs answer such questions as *How? When? Where?* or *How often?* They often end in **-ly.**

    She ran **quickly.**   She ran **very** quickly.

    a **really** hot day   **Maybe** she'll leave.

adverb clause A dependent clause that functions as an adverb in a sentence. Adverb clauses modify main clauses and tell when, where, how, or why.

    I called the police **because I heard strange noises.**

    When it rains, the roof leaks.

adverb of frequency An adverb that tells how often a situation occurs. Adverbs of frequency range in meaning from *all of the time* to *none of the time*.

    She **always** eats breakfast.   He **never** eats meat.

adverb phrase A phrase that functions as an adverb. Adverb phrases are often in the form of reduced adverb clauses of time, concession, and reason. They modify main clauses.

    Amy spoke **very softly.**

    He was tired **though happy.** (reduced adverb clause)

    While walking home, she met her friend.
      (reduced adverb clause)

affirmative statement A positive sentence that does not have a negative verb.

    Linda went to the movies.

agent The noun that is performing the action in a sentence. *See* **active sentence, passive sentence**.

    The letter was mailed by **Alex.**

agentless passive A passive sentence that doesn't mention an agent.

    The letter was mailed.

agreement The subject and verb of a clause must agree in number. If the subject is singular, the verb form is also singular. If the subject is plural, the verb form is also plural. Also called *subject-verb agreement*.

    He comes home early.   **They come** home early.

article The words **a, an,** and **the** in English. Articles are used to introduce and identify nouns.

    a potato   **an** onion   **the** supermarket

antecedent A noun (phrase) in a sentence or longer text that a pronoun or other noun refers back to.

    I love **jogging.** <u>It</u> makes me feel good. I was surprised that <u>this form of exercise</u> . . .

auxiliary verb A verb that is used before main verbs (or other auxiliary verbs) in a sentence. Auxiliary verbs are usually used in questions and negative sentences. **Do, have,** and **be** can act as auxiliary verbs. Modals (**may, can, will,** and so on) are also auxiliary verbs.

    Do you have the time?   I **have** never been to Italy.

    The suitcase **was** taken.   I **may** be late.

base form The form of a verb without any verb endings; the infinitive form without *to*. Also called *simple form*.

> sleep   be   stop

clause A group of words that has a subject and a verb. *See also* **dependent clause** and **main clause**.

> If I leave, . . .   The rain stopped.
> . . . when he speaks.   . . . that I saw.

collective noun A noun that refers to a group of people (or animals). Singular collective nouns are used with singular verbs but may be referred to with either singular or plural pronouns.

> **The committee** is meeting soon.
>   (It is . . .   They are . . .)
> **The band** was terrific.
>   (It sounded . . .   They sounded . . .)

common noun A noun that refers to any of a class of people, animals, places, things, or ideas. Common nouns are not capitalized.

> man   cat   city   pencil   grammar

communication verb *See* **reporting verb**.

comparative A form of an adjective, adverb, or noun that is used to express differences between two items or situations.

> This book is **heavier than** that one.
> He runs **more quickly than** his brother.
> A CD costs **more money than** a cassette.

complement A word, phrase, or clause that completes the meaning of a subject, an object, adjective, or other noun in a sentence.

> subject complement: My goal is **to find a new job.**
> object complement: I can't imagine him **skydiving.**
> adjective complement: She is sorry **that she called.**
> noun complement: Did you hear about his decision **to leave?**

complex sentence A sentence that has a main clause and one or more dependent clauses.

> When the bell rang, we were finishing dinner.

compound modifier Two or more descriptive words combined to form an adjective. Before a noun, they are usually spelled with hyphens.

> a **four-mile** race   a **dark-haired** woman
> **sugar-coated** peanuts   **low-calorie** desserts

compound noun Two or more nouns put together to function as a single noun with a unique meaning. Some compound nouns are spelled as two words. Others are spelled as one word or with a hyphen.

> a credit card   the police station   a headache
> the bookstore   a nurse-practitioner
> kilowatt-hours

compound sentence A sentence that has two (or more) independent clauses joined by a coordinating conjunction.

> He is ill **but** he will recover.

concession An unexpected contrast often introduced by subordinators such as **although** and **even though**, coordinate conjunctions **but** and **yet**, and transitions such as **however**, **nevertheless**, and **on the other hand**.

> Business is booming around here, **even though prices are very high**
> Prices are very high, **yet business is booming around here.**
> Prices are very high. **Nevertheless, business is booming around here.**

coordinating conjunction A word joining together words, phrases, or clauses which are grammatically equivalent (e.g. two nouns, two sentences, two prepositional phrases, etc.) The words **and**, **but**, **or**, **nor**, **for**, **so** and **yet** are coordinating conjunctions. Also called *coordinators*.

> I watched TV **and** she read a magazine.
> It was on the table **or** on the floor.

conditional sentence A sentence that expresses a real or unreal situation in the *if* clause, and a (real or unreal) expected result in the main clause.

> If I have time, I will travel to Africa.
> If I had time, I would travel to Africa.

conjunction *See* **coordinating conjunction**.

contraction The combination of two words into one by omitting certain letters and replacing them with an apostrophe.

> I will = **I'll**   we are = **we're**   are not = **aren't**

count noun A common noun that can be counted. It usually has both a singular and a plural form.

> orange — oranges   woman — women

dangling participle A phrase or clause that does not modify anything in a sentence and which results in an illogical sentence. A dangling participle often results from mistakenly trying to reduce an adverb clause whose subject differs from the main clause subject.

>   *__Walking down the stairs,__ the phone rang. (INCORRECT) (This implies that the phone was walking down the stairs.)

defining relative clause *See* **restrictive relative clause.**

definite article The word **the** in English. It is used to identify nouns based on assumptions about what information the speaker and listener share about the noun. The definite article is also used for making general statements about a whole class or group of nouns.

>   Please give me **the** key.
>   **The** scorpion is dangerous.

demonstrative adjective The determiners **this, that, these,** and **those** that occur before nouns. They tell whether the noun is near or far from the speaker.

>   **This house** is affordable. **That house** isn't.
>   **These exams** are graded. **Those exams** aren't.

demonstrative pronoun The pronouns **this, that, these,** and **those** used to take the place of a demonstrative adjective + noun.

>   **This** is affordable. (This house is affordable.)
>   **That** isn't. (That house isn't.)
>   **These** are graded. (These exams are graded.)
>   **Those** aren't. (Those exams aren't.)

dependent clause A clause that cannot stand alone as a sentence because it depends on the main clause to complete the meaning of the sentence. Also called *subordinate clause.*

>   I'm going home **after he calls.**

determiner A word such as **a, an, the, this, that, these, those, my, some, a few,** and **three,** that is used before a noun to limit its meaning in some way.

>   **those** videos   **some** cookies   **three** cameras

direct speech *See* **quoted speech.**

embedded question *See* **wh- clause.**

fragment A group of words forming an incomplete sentence. A fragment cannot stand alone and is usually considered to be an error in more formal writing.

>   **If I need a ride.** (fragment) → I'll call if I need a ride. (completed sentence)
>   **Because it rained.** (fragment) → Because it rained, we left early. (completed sentence)

future A time that is to come. The future is expressed in English with **will, be going to,** the simple present, or the present continuous. These different forms of the future often have different meanings and uses. *See also* **future continuous, future perfect,** and **future perfect continuous.**

>   I **will** help you later.
>   David **is going to** call later.
>   The train **leaves** at 6:05 this evening.
>   I**'m driving** to Toronto tomorrow.

future continuous A verb form that expresses an activity in progress at a specific time in the future. It is formed with **will** + **be** + main verb + **-ing.**

>   I**'ll be leaving** for Hawaii at noon tomorrow.

future perfect A verb form that is used to show the time relationship between two future situations. The future perfect expresses the earlier (first) event or state. It is formed with **will / be going to** + **have** + past participle.

>   I'll **have read** most of the book by the time I see the play.

future perfect continuous A verb form that is used to show the time relationship between two future situations. The future perfect continuous expresses the earlier ongoing future situation that may or may not continue beyond the later event, state, or time. It is formed with **will / be going to** + **have been** + verb + **-ing.**

>   She**'ll have been working** there for a year by the time you join the firm.

general quantity expression A quantity expression that indicates whether a quantity or an amount is large or small. It does not give an exact amount.

>   **a lot of** cookies   **a little** flour

general statement A generalization about a whole class or group of nouns.

> Whales are mammals.
>
> A daffodil is a flower that grows from a bulb.

generic noun A noun that refers to a whole class or group of nouns.

> I like **rice**.
>
> **A bird** can fly.
>
> **The laser** is an important tool.

gerund An **-ing** form of a verb that is used in place of a noun or pronoun to name an activity or a situation.

> **Skiing** is fun.   He doesn't like **being sick**.

head noun The main or most important noun in a noun phrase. For example, in compound nouns, the head noun is the second word.

> A table **lamp** is a kind of lamp.
>
> A lamp **table** is a kind of table.

identifying relative clause *See* **restrictive relative clause.**

if clause A dependent clause that begins with **if** and expresses a real or unreal situation.

> **If I have the time,** I'll paint the kitchen.
>
> **If I had the time,** I'd paint the kitchen.

if/whether clause A noun clause that begins with either **if** or **whether.**

> I don't know **if they're here**.
>
> I don't know **whether or not they're here**.

imperative A type of sentence, usually without a subject, that tells someone to do something. The verb is in the base form.

> **Open** your books to page 36.
>
> **Be** ready at eight.

impersonal you The use of the pronoun **you** to refer to people in general rather than a particular person or group of people.

> Nowadays, **you** can buy anything on the Internet.

implied conditional Sentences in which a condition is suggested but not stated fully. Some implied conditional sentences omit the *if* clause when the condition is understood. Other implied conditional sentences use expressions such as *otherwise, with, without,* and *but.*

> What would you do if I didn't have a car? **I'd take a cab** or **I'd call Jim.**
>
> I need to leave early. **Otherwise I'll hit traffic.**
> (= If I don't leave early, I'll hit traffic.)

indefinite article The words **a** and **an** in English. Indefinite articles introduce a noun as a member of a class of nouns, or make generalizations about a whole class or group of nouns.

> Please hand me **a** pencil.
>
> **An** ocean is **a** large body of water.

independent clause *See* **main clause.**

indirect question *See* **wh- clause.**

indirect speech *See* **reported speech.**

infinitive A verb form that includes **to** + the base form of a verb. An infinitive is used in place of a noun or pronoun to name an activity or situation expressed by a verb.

> Do you like **to swim**?

information question A question that begins with a **wh-** word.

> Where does she live?   Who lives here?

intransitive verb A verb that cannot be followed by an object.

> We finally **arrived**.

irregular verb A verb that forms the simple past in a different way than regular verbs.

> put — put — put   buy — bought — bought

main clause A clause that can be used by itself as a sentence. Also called *independent clause.*

> I'm going home.

main verb A verb that can be used alone in a sentence. A main verb can also occur with an auxiliary verb.

> I **ate** lunch at 11:30.
>
> Kate can't **eat** lunch today.

mental activity verb A verb such as **decide, know,** and **understand,** that expresses an opinion, thought, or feeling.

> I don't **know** why she left.

mixed conditional A conditional sentence that does not follow the regular patterns. Instead, it mixes past time with present or future time.

> If you **hadn't gone to sleep** so late, you **wouldn't feel** so tired right now. (past + present)
>
> If he **didn't do** well in the course, he **won't be graduating.** (past + future)

modal The auxiliary verbs **can, could, may, might, must, should, will,** and **would.** They modify the meaning of a main verb by expressing ability, authority, formality, politeness, or various degrees of certainty. Also called *modal auxiliary.*

> You **should** take something for your headache.
>
> Applicants **must** have a high school diploma.

modal of ability **Can** and **could** are called modals of ability when they express knowledge, skill, opportunity, and capability.

> He **can** speak Arabic and English.
>
> **Can** you play the piano?
>
> Yesterday we **couldn't** leave during the storm.
>
> Seat belts **can** save lives.

modal of possibility **Could, might, may, should, must,** and **will** are called modals of possibility when they express various degrees of certainty ranging from slight possibility to strong certainty.

> It **could / might / may / will** rain later.

modal auxiliary *See* **modal.**

modifier A word, phrase, or clause used to add to or change the meaning of another word, phrase, or clause.

> The **red** coat is on sale.
>
> The car **in the parking lot** is running.
>
> The woman **who won the election** is an attorney.

modify To add to or change the meaning of a word, phrase, or clause.

> expensive cars (The adjective **expensive** modifies **cars.**)

noncount noun A common noun that cannot be counted. A noncount noun has no plural form and cannot occur with **a, an,** or a number.

> information   mathematics   weather

nondefining relative clause *See* **nonrestrictive relative clause.**

nonidentifying relative clause *See* **nonrestrictive relative clause.**

nonrestrictive relative clause A relative clause that adds extra information about the noun that it modifies. This information is not necessary to identify the noun, and it can be omitted. Also called *nondefining* or *nonidentifying relative clause.*

> Rick, **who is seven,** plays hockey.

nonseparable Refers to two- or three-word verbs that don't allow a noun or pronoun object to separate the two or three words in the verb phrase. Certain two-word verbs and almost all three-word verbs are nonseparable.

> Amy **got off** the bus.
>
> We **cut down on** fat in our diet.

nonspecific noun A noun that is not known by the speaker.

> I'd love to buy **a coat,** but I haven't found one yet.

noun A word that typically refers to a person, animal, place, thing, or idea.

> Tom   rabbit   store   computer   mathematics

noun clause A dependent clause that can occur in the same place as a noun, pronoun, or noun phrase in a sentence. Noun clauses begin with **wh-** words, **if, whether,** or **that.**

> I don't know **where he is.**   I wonder **if he's coming.**
>
> I don't know **whether it's true.**   I think **that it's a lie.**

noun complement *See* **complement.**

noun compound *See* **compound noun.**

noun phrase A phrase formed by a noun and its modifiers. A noun phrase can substitute for a noun in a sentence.

> She drank **milk.**
> She drank **chocolate milk.**
> She drank **the milk.**

object A noun, pronoun, or noun phrase that follows a transitive verb or a preposition.

> Steve threw **the ball.**   She likes **him.**
> Go with **her.**

object complement *See* **complement.**

object of a preposition The noun (phrase) that follows a preposition. These include gerunds and noun clauses. Also called a *prepositional complement.*

> He put the letter in **his pocket.**
> I look forward to **leaving.**
> Let's talk about **what to do.**

object relative clause A relative clause where the relative pronoun takes the place of the object of the relative clause. The relative pronoun is followed by a subject and a verb.

> The man **who I met** works for the electric company.

object relative pronoun A relative pronoun that is the object of a relative clause. It comes before the subject noun or pronoun of the relative clause.

> the letter **that / which** I wrote
> the man **who / whom** I saw

parallel structure A sentence containing a series of items (words, phrases, clauses) in the same grammatical form.

> They spent the day **mowing** the lawn, **trimming** the bushes, and **weeding** the garden.

passive gerund A gerund used to focus on the receiver of the action instead of on the performer (or agent). It is formed with **being / getting** + past participle.

> How did you avoid **being called** for jury duty?

passive infinitive An infinitive used to focus on the receiver of the action instead of on the performer (or agent). It is formed with **to** + **be / get** + past participle.

> This program needs **to be updated.**

passive sentence Passive sentences emphasize the receiver of an action by changing the usual order of the subject and object in a sentence. The subject (**The letter**) does not perform the action; it receives the action or is the result of an action. The passive is formed with a form of **be** + the past participle of a transitive verb.

> The letter was mailed yesterday.

past continuous A verb form that expresses an activity in progress at a specific time in the past. The past continuous is formed with **was** or **were** + verb + **-ing.** Also called *past progressive.*

> A: What **were** you **doing** last night at eight o'clock?
> B: I **was studying.**

past modal A modal that is used to express past certainty, past obligations, and past abilities or opportunities. It is formed with a modal + **have** + past participle of the main verb. Also called *perfect modal.*

> He **must have arrived** late.
> I **should have called,** but I forgot.
> We **could have come,** but no one told us.

past participle A past verb form that may differ from the simple past form of some irregular verbs. It is used to form perfect and passive verb forms.

> I have never **seen** that movie.
> By noon, we had already **taken** the exam.
> He claims **to have lost** his wallet.
> The letter was **sent** on Monday.

past perfect A verb form that expresses a relationship between two past times. The past perfect indicates the earlier event or situation. It is formed with **had** + the past participle of the main verb.

> I **had** already **left** when she called.

past perfect continuous A verb form that is like the past perfect, but it emphasizes the duration of the earlier event or situation. It is formed with **had** + **been** + main verb + **-ing.**

> When I was offered the position, I **had been looking** for a new job for several months.

past perfect progressive *See* **past perfect continuous.**

past progressive *See* **past continuous.**

past phrasal modal Examples of past phrasal modals are **ought to have, have to have,** and **have got to have.**

You **ought to have seen** that movie.

past unreal conditional sentence A **conditional** sentence that expresses an unreal condition about the past and its imaginary result. It has an **if** clause in the past perfect and a main clause with **would have** + the past participle of the main verb.

If I had been smarter, I would have complained to the manager.

past *wish* sentence A **wish** sentence that expresses a desire for something that didn't actually happen in the past. It is formed with a **wish** clause + a past perfect clause.

I wish I had moved to Colorado.

perfect gerund A gerund used to refer to a situation that happened before the time of the main verb. It is formed with **having** + past participle.

I don't mind **having cooked** all day.

perfect infinitive An infinitive used to refer to a situation that happened before the time of the main verb. It is formed with **to have** + past participle.

A witness claims **to have seen** the robber.

perfect modal *See* **past modal.**

phrasal modal A verb that is not a true modal, but has the same meaning as a modal verb. Examples of phrasal modals are **ought to, have to,** and **have got to.**

phrasal verb A two- or three-word verb such as **turn down** or **run out of.** The meaning of a phrasal verb is usually different from the meanings of its individual words.

She **turned down** the job offer.

Don't **run out of** gas on the freeway.

phrase A group of words that can form a grammatical unit. A phrase can take the form of a noun phrase, verb phrase, adjective phrase, adverbial phrase, or prepositional phrase. This means it can act as a noun, verb, adjective, adverb, or preposition.

The **tall man** left.   Lee **hit the ball.**

The child was **very quiet.**   She spoke **too fast.**

They ran **down the stairs.**

point of view adverb Adverbs such as **unfortunately, luckily,** and **ironically** that are often used as transitions to show the writer's opinions or reactions.

The team won in overtime last night. **Unfortunately,** they still haven't moved out of third place.

possessive adjective The determiners **my, your, his, her, its, our,** and **their** that occur before noun (phrases) to show possession.

They are under investigation for **their** spending practices.

possessive noun Determiners in the form of a singular noun + **'s** or a regular plural noun + **'**. They are used before noun (phrases) to show possession.

The **mayor's** report was not well received.

The **workers'** demands are being considered.

possessive pronoun The pronouns **mine, yours, his, hers, ours,** and **theirs** that are used to replace a possessive adjective or possessive noun + noun.

Don't use that suitcase. Take **mine** instead. (= my suitcase).

possibility modal *See* **modal of possibility.**

preposition A word such as **at, in, on,** or **to,** that links nouns, pronouns, and gerunds to other words.

prepositional phrase A phrase that consists of a preposition followed by a noun or noun phrase.

on Sunday   under the table

present continuous A verb form that indicates that an action is in progress, temporary, or changing. It is formed with **be** + verb + **-ing.** Also called *present progressive.*

I**'m watering** the garden.

Ruth **is working** for her uncle.

He**'s getting** better.

present perfect A verb form that expresses a connection between the past and the present. It indicates indefinite past time, recent past time, or continuing past time. The present perfect is formed with **have** + the past participle of the main verb.

I**'ve seen** that movie.

The manager **has** just **resigned.**

We**'ve been** here for three hours.

present perfect continuous A verb form that focuses on the duration of actions that began in the past and continue into the present or have just ended. It is formed with **have** + **been** + verb + **-ing.**

> They**'ve been waiting** for an hour.
> I**'ve been watering** the garden.

present perfect progressive *See* **present perfect continuous.**

present progressive *See* **present continuous.**

pronoun A word that can replace a noun or noun phrase. **I, you, he, she, it, mine,** and **yours** are some examples of pronouns.

proper noun A noun that is the name of a particular person, animal, place, thing, or idea. Proper nouns begin with capital letters and are usually not preceded by **the.**

> Peter   Rover   India   Apollo 13   Buddhism

purpose infinitive An infinitive that expresses the reason or purpose for doing something.

> **In order to operate this machine,** press the green button.

quantifier A word or phrase that occurs before a noun to express a quantity or amount of that noun.

> **a lot of** rain   **few** books   **four** trucks

quantity expression *See* **quantifier.**

quoted speech The form of a sentence that uses the exact words of a speaker or writer. Written quoted speech uses quotation marks. Also called *direct speech.*

> **"Where did you go?"** he asked.

real conditional sentence A sentence that expresses a real or possible situation in the **if** clause and the expected result in the main clause. It has an **if** clause in the simple present, and the **will** future in the main clause.

> If I **get** a raise, I **won't look** for a new job.

receiver The noun that receives or is the result of an action in a sentence. See **active sentence, passive sentence.**

> **The letter** was mailed by Alex.

reduced adverb clause *See* **adverb phrase.**

reduced relative clause *See* **adjective phrase.**

regular verb A verb that forms the simple past by adding **-ed, -d,** or changing **y** to **i** and then adding **-ed** to the simple form.

> hunt — hunted   love — loved   cry — cried

relative clause A clause that modifies a preceding noun. Relative clauses generally begin with **who, whom, that, which,** and **whose.**

> The man **who called** is my cousin.
> We saw the elephant **that was just born.**

relative pronoun A pronoun that begins a relative clause and refers to a noun in the main clause. The words **who, whom, that, which,** and **whose** are relative pronouns.

reported speech A form of a sentence that expresses the meaning of quoted speech or writing from the point of view of the reporter. **Wh-** clauses, **if/whether** clauses, **that** clauses, and infinitives are used to express reported speech after a reporting verb.

> He explained **why he was late.**
> He said **that he was tired.**
> We asked **if they could come early.**
> He told me **to sit down.**

reporting verb A verb such as **say, tell, ask, explain,** and **complain** that is used to express what has been said or written in both quoted speech and reported speech.

> Tony **complained,** "I'm tired."
> Tony **complained** that he was tired.

restrictive relative clause A relative clause that gives information that helps identify or define the noun that it modifies. In the following sentence, the speaker has more than one aunt. The relative clause **who speaks Russian** identifies which aunt the speaker is talking about. Also called *defining* or *identifying relative clause.*

> My aunt **who speaks Russian** is an interpreter.

separable Refers to certain two-word verbs that allow a noun or pronoun object to separate the two words in the verb phrase.

> She **gave** her job **up.**

short answer An answer to a *Yes/No* question that has *yes* or *no* plus the subject and an auxiliary verb.

> A: Do you speak Chinese?
> B: **Yes, I do. / No, I don't.**

simple past A verb form that expresses actions and situations that were completed at a definite time in the past.

Carol **ate** lunch.   She **was** hungry.

simple present A verb form that expresses general statements, especially about habitual or repeated activities and permanent situations.

Every morning I **catch** the 8:00 bus.
The earth **is** round.

social modals Modal auxiliaries that are used to express politeness, formality, and authority.

Would you please open the window?
May I help you?
Visitors **must** obey the rules.

specific noun A noun that is known by the speaker.

My neighbor has **an enormous dog**.
Can you read **that sign**?

stative verb A type of verb that is not usually used in the continuous form because it expresses a condition or state that is not changing. **Know, love, resemble, see,** and **smell** are some examples.

subject A noun, pronoun, or noun phrase that precedes the verb phrase in a sentence. The subject is closely related to the verb as the doer or experiencer of the action or state, or closely related to the noun that is being described in a sentence with *be*.

Erica kicked the ball.
He feels dizzy.
The park is huge.

subject complement *See* **complement.**

subject relative clause A relative clause where the relative pronoun is the subject of the relative clause. The relative pronoun is followed by a verb.

The man **who is speaking** works for the company.

subject relative pronoun A relative pronoun that is the subject of a relative clause. It comes before the verb in the relative clause.

the man **who** called

subordinate clause *See* **dependent clause.**

subordinator A connecting word such as **although, because, when, if,** and **that** used to begin a dependent clause. Also called *subordinating conjunction*.

Was your utility bill high **because** the weather was so cold?
Some people don't believe **that** we are experiencing global warming.

superlative A form of an adjective, adverb, or noun that is used to rank an item or situation first or last in a group of three or more.

This perfume has **the strongest** scent.
He speaks **the fastest** of all.
That machine makes **the most noise** of the three.

***that* clause** A noun clause beginning with **that.**

I think **that the bus is late**.

three-word verb A phrasal verb such as **break up with, cut down on,** and **look out for.** The meaning of a three-word verb is usually different from the individual meanings of the three words.

time clause A dependent clause that begins with a time word such as **while, when, before,** or **after.** It expresses the relationship in time between two different events in the same sentence.

Before Sandy left, she fixed the copy machine.

transition Words and phrases such as **however, nevertheless, moreover,** and **similarly** that are used to connect ideas between separate sentences.

A new building project would be time-consuming and expensive. **Moreover,** we would have to raise taxes.

transitive verb A verb that is followed by an object.

I **read** the book.

two-word verb A phrasal verb such as **blow up, cross out,** and **hand in.** The meaning of a two-word verb is usually different from the individual meanings of the two words.

unreal conditional sentence A sentence that expresses an unreal situation that is not true at the present time, and its imaginary result. It has an **if** clause in the simple past and a main clause with **would** + main verb.

If I **had** the time, **I'd walk** to work.

used to A special past tense verb. It expresses habitual past situations that no longer exist.

> We **used to** go skiing a lot. Now we go snowboarding.

verb A word that refers to an action or a state.

> Gina **closed** the window.
> Tim **loves** classical music.

verb phrase A phrase that has a main verb and any objects, adverbs, or dependent clauses that complete the meaning of the verb in the sentence.

> Who **called you?**
> He **walked slowly.**
> I **know what his name is.**

voiced Refers to speech sounds that are made by vibrating the vocal cords. Examples of voiced sounds are /b/, /d/, and /g/.

> **b**at   **d**ot   **g**et

voiceless Refers to speech sounds that are made without vibrating the vocal cords. Examples of voiceless sounds are /p/, /t/, and /f/.

> u**p**   i**t**   i**f**

wh- clause A noun clause that begins with a wh- word: **who, whom, what, where, when, why, how,** and **which.** Also called *indirect question* or *embedded question.*

> I would like to know **where he is.**
> Could you tell me **how long it takes**?

wh- word Who, whom, what, where, when, why, how, and which are wh- words. They are used to ask questions and to connect clauses.

wish sentence A sentence that has a **wish** clause in the simple present, and a simple past clause. A **wish** sentence expresses a desire to change a real situation into an unreal or impossible one.

> I wish I had more time.

Yes/No question A question that can be answered with the words **yes** or **no.**

> Can you drive a car?   Does he live here?

Index